Managing Evolving Risks

Thomas Tuke

Thomas Tuke

Managing Evolving Risks

Edited by

Michael W. Elliott, CPCU, ARM, AIAF, MBA

1st Edition • 2nd Printing

The Institutes
720 Providence Road, Suite 100
Malvern, Pennsylvania 19355-3433

1st Edition • 2nd Printing • October 2020

Library of Congress Control Number: 2020935627

ISBN: 978-0-89462-403-2

Welcome

To complement the online course, this course book is designed as a study aid. The online course provides the richest, and fullest, CPCU course experience and best allows students to master the material and prepare for the credentialing exam.

Introduction

Managing Evolving Risks gives learners a broad understanding of risk, with emphasis on managing risk data, modeling outcomes, and applying new risk technologies. It also provides learners with the communication and collaboration skills needed to build consensus around various risk-related decisions.

The Institutes are grateful to the risk professionals who provided their subject-matter expertise to this effort. Their assistance during the review and development stages helped ensure that the course reflects current industry practices. We are particularly grateful to Gerard Lancner; Christopher Mandel, RF, MBA, CPCU; Nicos Scordis, PhD; James Swanke, CPCU, ALCM, ARM; and Alan Walker for their insights on the content and selected risk topics.

In addition, The Institutes acknowledge content curator Michael W. Elliott, MBA, CPCU, ARM, as well as the following content contributors: Arthur L. Flitner, CPCU, ARM, AIC; Doug Froggatt, CPCU, AINS; Beth Illian, CPCU, AINS, AIS; Kevin Kibelstis, CPCU, AINS, AIS; and Christian Schappel.

About The Institutes

The Institutes are the trusted leading provider of risk management and property-casualty insurance education—and have been for more than 100 years. We are committed to developing innovative professional development and knowledge solutions that empower individuals worldwide to help those in need.

The Institutes' proven knowledge helps individuals and organizations achieve powerful results with a variety of flexible, customer-focused options:

Recognized Credentials—The Institutes offer an unmatched range of widely recognized and industry-respected specialty credentials, such as our flagship CPCU® designation.

Ethics—Ethical behavior is crucial to preserving not only the trust on which insurance transactions are based, but also the public's trust in the risk and insurance industry as a whole. Accordingly, all Institutes designations have an ethics requirement, which is delivered online and free of charge.

Flexible Online Learning—The Institutes have an unmatched variety of technical insurance content covering topics from accounting to underwriting, which we deliver through hundreds of online courses.

Continuing Education—A majority of The Institutes' courses are filed for CE credit in most states. Via CEU.com, we also deliver quality, affordable, online CE courses quickly and conveniently.

College Credits—Most Institutes courses carry college credit recommendations from the American Council on Education. A variety of courses also qualify for credits toward certain associate's, bachelor's, and master's degrees at several prestigious colleges and universities.

Custom Applications—The Institutes collaborate with corporate customers to develop customized solutions that help these customers achieve their unique organizational goals.

Insightful Analysis—Our Insurance Research Council (IRC) division conducts public policy research on important contemporary issues in property-casualty insurance and risk management. Visit www.Insurance-Research.org to learn more or purchase its most recent studies.

For more information about The Institutes' programs, please call our Customer Success Department at (800) 644-2101, email us at CustomerSuccess@TheInstitutes.org, or visit our website at TheInstitutes.org.

Peter L. Miller, CPCU
President and Chief Executive Officer
The Institutes

The Institutes·
RISK & INSURANCE
KNOWLEDGE GROUP

CPCU 500

Features videos by

Kelly Cusick
Managing Director, Deloitte Consulting

Kelly Cusick is a managing director with Deloitte Consulting LLP and a leader in Deloitte's Underwriting Excellence practice. She advises insurers on transformational initiatives related to underwriting, product management, and actuarial functions. Cusick is an associate of the Casualty Actuarial Society and a member of the American Academy of Actuaries.

Dante Disparte, MS
Chairman, Risk Cooperative

Dante Disparte is an entrepreneur, business leader, and global risk expert. He is the founder of Risk Cooperative, a strategic risk advisory and insurance brokerage based in Washington, D.C. Disparte serves on the Federal Emergency Management Agency's National Advisory Council and on the board of the American Security Project. He is also a member of the Bretton Woods II Council and a senior fellow at New America. He frequently speaks on risk, economic competitiveness, security issues and entrepreneurship, about which he spoke on behalf of the White House at the Global Entrepreneurship Summit in Kenya. His work is also regularly featured in Harvard Business Review, BBC, Forbes and International Policy Digest, among others. A graduate of Harvard Business School, where he chaired the D.C. alumni association and is a former member of the global alumni board, Disparte holds an MSc. in risk management from the NYU Stern School of Business and a bachelor's degree in international and intercultural studies from Goucher College. Additionally, he is fluent in six languages, co-authored Global Risk Agility and Decision Making (Macmillan, 2016), and was one of Washington Business Journal's "Forty Leaders Under Forty".

Karen Furtado
Partner, Strategy Meets Action

Karen Furtado, a partner at Strategy Meets Action, has expertise in insurance technology and how it fuels transformation within insurance companies. Her focus is on helping insurers prepare for the future of the industry through the decisions they make today. Furtado's knowledge stretches across policy, billing, claims, the implications of transformational technologies, and ways to enhance adaptability and flexibility in a changing market.

Jim Gkonos
Attorney, Saul Ewing Arnstein & Lehr

Jim Gkonos focuses his practice on insurance and reinsurance regulatory matters, financial guarantees, surety, and capital markets. He is a member of the Federation of Regulatory Counsel, which includes attorneys with at least 15 years of regulatory experience. Additionally, Gkonos is an ARIAS-certified reinsurance arbitrator who advises clients on reinsurance interpretation and disputes. He is a frequent speaker and author on numerous insurance topics.

David Hampson, CPCU, ARM
Managing Partner, Schrager Hampson Aviation Insurance Agency

David. B. Hampson is managing partner of Schrager Hampson Aviation Insurance Agency, a brokerage firm specializing in aviation insurance. He is a Federal Aviation Administration Safety Team representative with the Boston Flight Standards District Office and a volunteer pilot for the not-for-profit organization Above the Clouds. Hampson also serves on the boards of the Maine Aviation Business Association, the Corporate Pilots Association, and the Aero Club of New England.

Kimberly Holmes, MS, ACAS, CSPA
Executive Vice President, Chief Actuary and Strategic Analytics Officer, Kemper

Kimberly Holmes is the executive vice president, chief actuary and strategic analytics officer at Kemper. Previously, she led the global strategic analytics team at XL Catlin. Before that, Holmes served as chief actuary for both Endurance Risk Solutions and Enterprise Reinsurance Ltd., in various actuarial and underwriting roles for General Reinsurance, and as an actuarial consultant. She is a member of the American Academy of Actuaries.

Vickram Kooblall
President, Social Media Investigations

Vickram Kooblall is the founder and president of Social Media Investigations, Inc., a company born out of a critical void in the litigation process. From his work as operations and technology director of Picciano & Scahill—an insurance defense law firm—for more than 17 years, Kooblall is well versed in all sides of the litigation process, from management and internal operations to implementing workflow procedure and compliance. His responsibilities involved securing critical data and creating technical infrastructure to deal with network attacks. Kooblall's expertise in legal management and strong IT background led to his forming a new alternative to conventional investigations. Social Media Investigations has developed the in-depth analytical techniques and technology that allow social media to play a major role in determining a plaintiff's credibility.

Chris Mandel, MBA, CPCU, RIMS-CRMP
Senior Vice President, Strategic Solutions, Sedgwick

Chris Mandel is senior vice president of strategic solutions for Sedgwick and director of the Sedgwick Institute. He also founded two firms that specialize in risk management and insurance services and pioneered the development of integrated risk management at USAA. Mandel previously held leadership roles at Liberty Mutual, Marsh, Verizon, the American National Red Cross, PepsiCo, and USAA, as well as in the Risk and Insurance Management Society. He was elected to Risk Who's Who in 2008 and holds the CPCU, RIMS-CRMP, ARM, AIC, and CCSA designations.

William "Billy" Mauro
Senior Director—Commercial Casualty, ISO

Billy Mauro is senior director of commercial casualty product development at Insurance Services Office, Inc. (ISO). In this role, he leads teams that develop ISO casualty coverage initiatives, including those related to emerging issues, general liability, commercial auto, commercial umbrella/excess, medical professional liability and businessowners. Specifically, he has supported ISO's work related to construction defects, liquor liability, data breach exposures, marijuana, home healthcare, additional insureds and many more. Mauro has also contributed emerging issues articles to several insurance publications and is a frequent presenter at industry events.

Kevin Quinley, MA, CPCU, ARM, AIC, AIM, ARe
President, Quinley Risk Associates

Kevin Quinley has over forty years of experience in the insurance and risk management field, concentrated in insurance claims handling and managing claims-related risks. Quinley is president and principal of Quinley Risk Associates, LLC. He serves as an expert witness and consultant on claims issues for clients nationwide. Quinley is the author of 10 books and over 700 articles on various aspects of claims, litigation and risk management. He holds the CPCU, ARM, AIC, ARe, AIM and RPA designations.

Jim Swanke, MBA
Senior Director, Willis Towers Watson

Jim Swanke, senior director, Willis Towers Watson, concentrates on alternative risk financing design, including captive feasibility studies. In his 38 years with Willis Towers Watson, he has implemented or reengineered more than 250 captives. Swanke also serves as president for Willis Towers Watson's two captives in Vermont. Swanke holds degrees in risk management and insurance and corporate finance from the University of Wisconsin–Madison. In addition, he lectures at the University of Wisconsin–Madison on sustainability and environmental and social risk management and is a frequent speaker at industry meetings and author of numerous articles.

Hank Watkins
President, Lloyd's North America

As president of Lloyd's, North America, Hank Watkins is responsible for Lloyd's operations and market development activities in the United States and Canada. He has held a range of underwriting, client management, and leadership positions in the U.S. and Europe at Chubb, Johnson & Higgins, Marsh, and HRH. Watkins is a member of several industry boards, including that of the Insurance Information Institute.

Les Williams, CRM
Co-Founder and Chief Revenue Officer, Risk Cooperative

Les Williams, a Certified Risk Manager (CRM), is co-founder and chief revenue officer of Risk Cooperative, an innovative strategy and risk advisory firm based in Washington, D.C., that specializes in creating solutions for emerging risks, such as cyber liability, political risk, and other complex domestic and global challenges, as well as common risk needs, such as employee benefits and business insurance. Les is a featured Risk Insider with Risk & Insurance, which publishes his monthly columns and recognized him as a 2020 Power Broker for Specialty Lines.

Rita Williams-Bogar, MBA, CPCU, ChFC
Founder, Personal Development Solutions

Rita Williams-Bogar is the founder of Personal Development Solutions, LLC, and PDS Institute, LLC. She provides consultative services in leadership development, ethics, diversity, and insurance education in the United States and abroad. Rita is a platinum-level instructor for The Institutes, serves on the CPCU Society's Leadership Council and is executive director of the New Jersey CPCU Society Chapter. She is also a member of the Leadership and Managerial Excellence Interest Group. Rita holds the CPCU, ChFC, AU, AINS and ARM designations.

Contents

Embracing RiskTech

1

Educational Objectives	Outline

▶ Assess the current state of the risk management environment.

▶ Explain how risktech can be viewed as an ecosystem of technologies and objects that is transforming the way in which risks are assessed and controlled.

▶ Explain how the following emerging technologies are transforming risk management:

- Artificial intelligence

- Sensors/sensor networks

- Computer vision

▶ Illustrate how the following smart products employ emerging technologies and provide risk management data:

- Wearables

- Drones

- Robots

The Risk Management Environment

The Risktech Ecosystem

Emerging Technologies

Smart Products and Operations

Summary

Embracing RiskTech

THE RISK MANAGEMENT ENVIRONMENT

"What if?" is the simple question responsible for igniting invention, ingenuity, and even revolution throughout the history of business. And for every "What if?" that captured an aspiration (What if cars could be mass-produced? What if phones could fit in our pockets?), traditional risk management strategies helped bring it to life with "What ifs?" of their own that accounted for what might go wrong. (What if our factory burned down? What if our trade secrets are stolen?)

Today, however, businesses at the bleeding edge of innovation understand that risk management is more than an invisible safety net: It is essential to the DNA of every decision—the balance of opportunity and threat.

And as risk technology continues to increase the certainty with which the upside and downside of decisions can be predicted, we move toward a future in which at nearly every level of an organization, from the loading docks of a faraway link on the supply chain to the senior management boardroom, there are two kinds of people—those who formally manage risk and those who manage risk without necessarily realizing it. This is the future in which the fundamental tenets of risk management realize their destiny as the crucial ingredients of sound business strategy. And it's closer than you think.

How did we get here? And, more importantly, whether "risk manager" is in your title or you want to optimize your risk-based decision-making acumen, what does the transformed risk management landscape mean for you and your role in the industry?

To understand your role in today's environment, you must first understand how the latest strategies and technologies affect your industry. You cannot make this determination on your own, because simply learning about concepts does not necessarily prepare you to take appropriate action. Communicating and collaborating with experts are key to forming a complete perspective on risk management.

The transformation of the risk management environment has simultaneously occurred with the evolution of risk and risk management itself. Related to insurance, risk was traditionally considered a hazard posed to an individual or organization. Today, it is also known for its potential positive consequences—the idea that taking risks is necessary for growth. This holistic view reveals the full universe of threats and opportunities an organization faces. And the emergence of holistic risk management strategies, also known as enterprise risk management, or ERM, has enhanced the tools with which risk managers and other decision makers minimize threats and exploit opportunities.

These two ideas—the intersection of different types of risk and a method for identifying, assessing, and treating all of them—underlie nearly every important risk management concept. They are also essential to applying workplace skills, whether you're a risk manager or simply in a role that requires risk-informed decision making.

So before we discuss the specifics of today's risk management environment, let's take a quick look at how those building blocks work.

Traditional risk assessment techniques focus on root cause analysis (RCA), which identifies a loss's predominant cause. This approach's inherent weakness is obvious—RCA can only look backward. Plus, it might not identify all root causes and the related events that contribute to a loss and can be performed only periodically.

Big data

Sets of data that are too large to be gathered and analyzed by traditional methods.

Today, however, a universe of data about past events and previously imperceptible risk factors can empower decision making. Think of a worker's dangerous package-lifting technique, the presence of a hazardous chemical in the air at a factory, or the catastrophic intersection of seemingly disconnected financial transactions as they unfold in real time. The ways that technology and risk management intersect to achieve this can seem complex, but the basics are simple: The **big data** revolution is fueled by the capture, storage, and analysis of data. To learn more, see "How Big Data Has Transformed the Risk Management Environment."

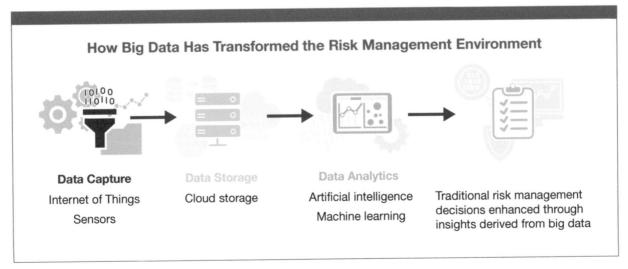

How Big Data Has Transformed the Risk Management Environment

Data Capture
Internet of Things
Sensors

Data Storage
Cloud storage

Data Analytics
Artificial intelligence
Machine learning

Traditional risk management decisions enhanced through insights derived from big data

[DA12739]

Data Capture

Data capture is enabled primarily by **smart products** that sense their environment, process data, and communicate with other smart products and smart operations through the **Internet of Things (IoT)**. These interactions generate the data to which advanced analytics can be applied.

The availability and sophistication of smart products and the IoT's continued growth have led to an explosion of risk management innovation.

Data Storage

The decision-making value of data produced by smart products, the IoT, and other data-capturing technology can be undermined by its volume, velocity, and veracity—more and faster is not necessarily better. **Cloud computing** enables vast amounts of data to be stored and shared.

But what if we could ensure that the data used for risk management analysis was from a trusted source and independently verified? That is the premise underlying the data storage and sharing medium known as **blockchain**.

The blockchain's roots lie in database technology. Picture a database as a collection of structured information stored in discrete units for ease of retrieval, manipulation, combination, or other basic applications—sort of a virtual filing cabinet organized like a spreadsheet. To learn more, see "Tabular Database Example: Auto Bodily Injury Claims File."

Smart product

An innovative item that uses sensors; wireless sensor networks; and data collection, transmission, and analysis to further enable the item to be faster, more useful, or otherwise improved.

Internet of Things (IoT)

A network of objects that transmit data to and from each other without human interaction.

Cloud computing

Information, technology, and storage services contractually provided from remote locations, through the internet or another network, without a direct server connection.

Tabular Database Example: Auto Bodily Injury Claims File

Case Number	Attorney	Claimant Sex	Marital Status	Claimant Insured	Seat Belt	Claimant Age	Loss
5	1	1	0	1	1	35	33.20
13	2	2	1	2	1	50	10.88
60	2	2	2	1	1	19	0.25
75	1	1	2	1	2	28	9.63
94	1	1	4	2	1	43	0.152

[DA12301]

Although its primary purpose is to store information, the blockchain isn't simply a database. Rather, it's a distributed database that serves as a collectively shared ledger. A ledger (whether physical or digital) is a document in which transactions are recorded. Basic examples of ledgers include those used to keep track of cash, inventory, accounts receivable, and fixed assets. Their common denominator is that they all track the chronology of a particular value's change over time—that is, the results of each recorded transaction.

Blockchain

A distributed digital ledger that facilitates secure transactions without the need for a third party.

Implicit in a ledger's accounting is that it is accurate, comprehensive, and independently verifiable. If a centralized database were used as a virtual ledger, though, it could be altered by anyone with access to the database's single location, so its reliability would depend on the authority controlling its access (such as a financial institution). If the value being tracked is connected to something tangible—cash, inventory, and so forth—it could theoretically be verified by measuring it independently of the ledger (by, for example, manually counting inventory). But what if the ledger is recording transactions involving intangible items whose value can't be independently verified?

This was the obstacle facing the innovators of cryptocurrency (the most prominent of which is Bitcoin), which you can imagine as electronic money. Cryptocurrency pioneers wanted to create a virtual currency that didn't derive its value from a governmental entity like traditional forms of money do and that could be used in online transactions. How do you keep track of virtual currency, though, if it doesn't exist in physical form and isn't monitored by a central authority? Further, in an unsupervised and decentralized environment, how could people be prevented from spending the same virtual coin in more than one transaction (this was known as the double-spending problem) other than by simply trusting everyone to be honest about the contents of their digital wallets?

The answer was to create what would ultimately become the system of verification and confirmation that makes the blockchain a reliable ledger and database. So, a blockchain is a distributed database and decentralized ledger that maintains a continuously growing list of records, called blocks, in chronological order. Each time a transaction occurs, a new block is created.

In most blockchains, new blocks and the data within (transactions, smart contracts, and so forth) are confirmed and verified through a consensus process called mining. This verification process removes intermediary validation and establishes trust without a centralized authority. After a block is confirmed and the data within it is verified through the decentralized consensus process, the block is time-stamped and added to the preexisting blocks in the chain, hence the term "blockchain."

Data Analytics

The collection, storage, and sharing of data empowers real-time risk management for organizations that use data gleaned from sensors to react immediately to hazardous situations. For instance, sensors affixed to the clothing of an assembly line laborer might sense that worker's hydration level dropping to a dangerous level.

Apply Your Knowledge

Learn more from an expert in the online video.

How are the investments that businesses are making in their big data infra-structures laying the groundwork for the continued evolution of the risk management landscape?

Feedback: Businesses' investments in big data infrastructure are laying the groundwork for the continued evolution of the risk management landscape in ways that include empowering organizations and their risk management professionals to better access and analyze data and to more efficiently and quickly conceive, develop, and distribute products.

Collected and stored data can also be used to develop forward-thinking risk management strategies when that data is organized and analyzed through methods that use artificial intelligence, including machine learning and neural network technologies. In short, insurers and risk managers can improve their business results through data-driven decision making in an ever-increasing variety of ways, such as these:

- Organizing large volumes of new data—A risk manager could organize data according to multiple characteristics, such as the information pro-vided by vehicle **telematics**, which can include speed, braking patterns, left turns, and distance traveled.

- Discovering new relationships in data—A risk manager could identify the characteristics of workers who have never had a workplace acci-dent and use that information to identify how to improve safety for all workers.

- Exploring new sources of data— **Text mining** can be used to compare documents and analyze notes for various purposes.

- Developing new products—The increasingly accurate predictive model-ing of hazards, particularly catastrophe modeling, enabled by sources of shared, comprehensive data about the complex interactions of contrib-uting factors, has led to product innovation. One notable example is parametric insurance, coverage that pays a predetermined amount to the insured if a particular set of parameters occur, such as a hurricane's wind speed.

Telematics

The use of technological devices in vehicles with wireless communication and GPS tracking that transmit data to businesses or government agencies; some return information for the driver.

Text mining

Obtaining information through language recognition.

THE RISKTECH ECOSYSTEM

Technology is ever increasing, and its effect on risk management is significant. Through technology, risk managers are better able to effectively assess and control risk by allowing people and objects to measure conditions in their environment and communicate those results to decision makers.

Insurtech

The use of emerging technologies in the insurance industry.

Risk monitoring and mitigation technology is known as risktech. It is similar to **insurtech**, and many of the technologies used in both realms are identical. However, risktech goes one step beyond insurtech by expanding its focus on how to make risk financing more efficient to include how to prevent and mitigate risk in a variety of industries. To learn more, see "Risktech Ecosystem."

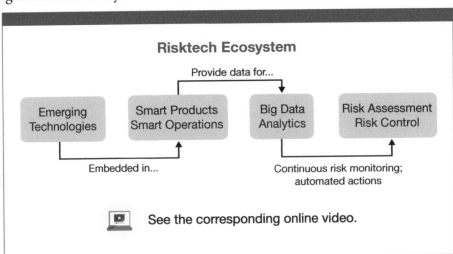

[DA13013]

Risktech

Risktech is largely the result of emerging technologies coupled with smart products. Their interactions generate big data, to which advanced analytics can be applied, ultimately reducing the uncertainty associated with predicting future events.

Learn more from an expert in the online video.

Sensor

A device that detects and measures stimuli in its environment.

The application of emerging technologies to risk assessment and control is largely being driven by the Internet of Things (IoT), which consists of IoT objects that collect and transmit data through the internet, primarily through the use of **sensors**. For example, sensor data can inform a supply chain manager that weather conditions have interrupted the production of parts or that cargo has been stolen.

Other technologies are also informing risk assessment and control. For example, virtual reality can be used to train workers in an artificial environment without the bodily injury and property damage risks present in a real-world setting. Artificial intelligence allows machines to simulate human intelligence and perform tasks that require critical thinking, such as making a risk assessment decision.

As technology evolves, the availability and sophistication of smart products that can help refine risk management techniques continue to grow. Smart products sense their environment, process data, and communicate with other smart products and smart operations.

Apply Your Knowledge

Learn more from an expert in the online video.

Can you think of some smart products being used in risk management today?

Feedback: A variety of smart products are being used in various industries to assess and control risk. Some of the most common include wearables, drones, robots, and smartphones.

Let's take a look at how these smart products are being used:

- Wearables such as helmets that monitor fatigue or wristwatches that measure vital signs can sense, monitor, report, and analyze workers' health or well-being and their surrounding environments. Data generated by wearables may be specific to one employee or aggregated for a project, a team, or an organization.
- Drones can be used in surveillance and aerial photography; being unmanned and highly versatile makes them ideal for assessing conditions or risks in dangerous or unfamiliar areas. The data generated by drones relies heavily on other technologies, such as computer vision, image recognition, and artificial intelligence, to mine the data collected and form conclusions about detected objects.

- Robots can measure, respond to, and produce data for monitored hazards or changing environmental conditions. And by performing certain activities, they can reduce the frequency of human error.
- Smartphones can measure acceleration, light, temperature, humidity, pressure, proximity, and location—all particularly relevant in transportation and workplace safety.

Preventive analytics

Statistical and analytical techniques used to influence or prevent future events or behaviors.

Using the data provided by technologies and smart objects, businesses can practice **preventive analytics**. Preventive analytics leverages modern technology, big data, and advanced analytics to identify root causes and their interactions. It is particularly effective because it can continuously monitor activity—whether arising from humans or machines. By learning patterns, a machine can identify situations or behaviors that are unexpected or will likely produce an unexpected result. Therefore, preventive analytics is forward looking. Consider how computer-vision technology in an auto identifies and analyzes risks, which can then lead to preventive actions. For example, a truck's brakes may automatically be applied because a front-facing camera determines that a vehicle has stopped directly in front of the truck.

Connected Ecosystems

A useful way to think about emerging technologies and their application to risk assessment and control is to view them as part of a connected ecosystem. An ecosystem is a system of interconnected parts, and, as we've discussed, the risktech ecosystem includes emerging technologies, smart products and smart operations, and big data analytics.

However, emerging technologies and smart products also connect the physical and virtual domains, resulting in connected ecosystems for a variety of risk management specialties, including property, supply chain, transportation, catastrophe, and workplace safety.

Overall, these connections enhance risk management decision making, as they allow property managers to detect leaks and malfunctions, transportation managers to respond to drivers' issues in real time, more people to be evacuated before an impending catastrophe, and prevention of countless other injuries and damages. To learn more, see "Connected Ecosystems."

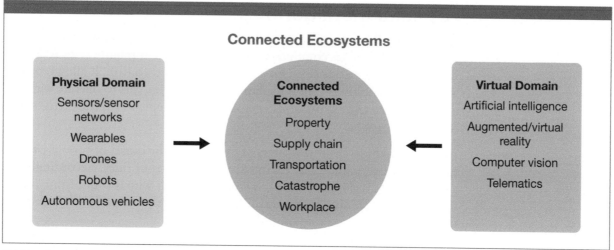

[DA13014]

EMERGING TECHNOLOGIES

Emerging technologies that can help organizations assess and control risks are continuously evolving. Using data provided by these technologies, businesses can practice preventive analytics.

As an example, consider an insurer's sending a text alert to its commercial auto policyholders when a hail storm is approaching and encouraging businesses to move vulnerable vehicles in their fleets to covered areas. A business that follows this guidance will effectively manage its risk by avoiding hail-related damage to its autos and injury to its drivers. Each auto hail claim that is prevented saves the insurer large sums of money, in turn saving its customers in premium cost. Both the organization and the insurer benefit from this risk management solution.

While many technologies apply to risk management, we are going to examine a few in detail: artificial intelligence, sensors, and computer vision.

What Do You Know?

Consider the example of a business being able to move its commercial autos based on a text alert about an impending storm. How do you think this prediction and the resulting risk management decision are enabled?

Feedback: The way in which weather can be accurately predicted for a specific location relies, in part, on the technology of sensors, located on satellites and deployed as part of a fleet management program.

Artificial Intelligence

Artificial intelligence (AI) refers to the ability of machines to simulate human intelligence. It enables computers to perform tasks that require critical thinking, such as making decisions for risk assessment and control. It allows robots to work collaboratively alongside humans in factories, cars to operate without human drivers, and claims adjusters to be quickly deployed in the event of a natural catastrophe.

AI trains machines on the nuances of sources and the causes of various risks, then it establishes automatic responses based on a set of rules. Accordingly, a financial institution can use AI to identify a trader who is committing the institution to excessive financial risk and immediately respond with built-in financial circuit breakers to limit the risk.

Deep learning, an extension of AI, attempts to understand and mimic neural networks in the brain through software that simulates image and speech recognition. One example of deep learning is IBM's Watson computer, which can be trained in many different areas—such as understanding medical information and its implications to assist medical personnel in crucial decision making. A more common example is improved voice-search capabilities on smartphones.

Learn more from an expert in the online video.

Sensors/Sensor Network

Sensors assess risk by detecting and measuring objects or conditions on a continuous basis; this provides early warnings of impending problems or malfunctions and determines whether expected results have occurred. Smart sensors may even trigger remedial actions, thereby controlling risk and helping reduce losses. With the expanding number, type, and specificity of sensors offered—and their ability to work together in networks—sensors will continue to play an important role in assessing and controlling risk.

Many different types of sensors are available—and they continually improve. A sensor may simply be a tool that takes input (such as heat, light, temperature, or touch) and communicates that input to a display or other location for processing.

For example, a thermometer senses temperature and provides a reading on a scale that is meaningful to the user. A smart sensor takes this procedure one step further and triggers the necessary change or adaptation in response to the stimulus. So if a machine's ambient temperature rises above a certain threshold, a smart sensor could automatically shut the machine down and/or trigger an alarm.

Specialized sensors include **transducers**, **actuators**, and **accelerometers**. These and other types of sensors are widely used in factories and many industries (such as construction, medicine, retail, and transportation).

Sensors can be categorized by their functions and applications for risk assessment and control. These classifications include mechanical, thermal, radiant, and biochemical sensors. To learn more, see "Sensor Categories and Examples for Risk Assessment and Control."

Transducer

A device that converts one form of energy into another.

Actuator

A mechanical device that turns energy into motion or otherwise effectuates a change in position or rotation using a signal and an energy source.

Accelerometer

A device that measures acceleration, motion, and tilt.

Sensor Categories and Examples for Risk Assessment and Control

Mechanical	Biochemical
• Pressure sensors	• Home diagnostic tests
• Flow sensors	• Wearable fitness monitors
• Motion detectors	• Diabetes test strips/meters/patches

Thermal	Radiant
• Smoke detectors	• Optical sensors
• Heat sensors	• Radar
• Computer hardware sensors	• Radio frequency identification (RFID) tags

[DA12615]

Sensors also enable the digital twin, which is a separate digital profile of a physical object that helps identify risks arising from the object. Sensors on the physical object generate data that is used by the digital twin to analyze risk and provide alerts or take automated actions, when necessary, such as triggering actuators on the physical object to prevent loss.

A digital twin allows data taken from the physical object to be analyzed. This analysis can lead to improvements in processes and mechanisms, such as in the manufacturing realm. It also provides orientation and training opportunities without the risk of employee injury or object damage. To learn more, see "Digital Twin."

Computer Vision

Computer vision is a technology that simulates human vision. It gains an understanding of images and then tries to help a machine not only recognize an object but also give that object context and respond to it as a human would. Computer vision is used in automobiles that are able to read traffic signs or detect pedestrians and other objects.

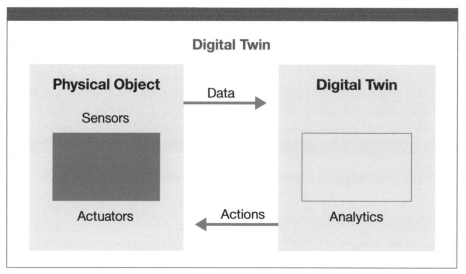

[DA13021]

Computer vision involves detecting, extracting, and analyzing images to better understand them. It does this by developing and using algorithms that can automatically provide visual understanding.

The technology was originally intended to mimic the human eye in making calculated, reason-based decisions about an image. But although computer vision has not managed to fully duplicate these actions, it has mastered some of them. For example, computer vision can help recognize a worker who is fatigued.

Although not a perfect science, computer vision is used in retail operations for automated checkout lanes; medical imaging; automotive safety, particularly related to automated vehicles; surveillance; and traffic control. As opposed to a single human with one pair of eyes, many different cameras (stationary or video), looking at one fixed point or panning a certain area, can provide a more comprehensive and integrated view over time. This technology is a blend of data science, engineering, statistics, and algorithms. It has become more specialized, accurate, and reliable over time as related computer technologies have also advanced.

One of the early tenets of computer vision was segmentation, or how images are seen and mapped. When combined with deep learning, this mapping of features through an algorithm relates to a commensurate action.

Computer vision has been used in this way with self-driving vehicles for both risk assessment and risk control. The many cameras and angles from which images are continuously received are matched with actions to recognize or assess risks (such as a car drifting into another driver's lane) and actions to control or mitigate the risk (by, for example, applying the brake or easing into another lane, whichever is more appropriate in the situation).

Computer vision and AI can be used in facial recognition software. Cameras capture images of faces, which are matched with file photos or information from other databases. The software then segments the person's face so that it can be easily compared with others. It can even assess a person's emotions from his or her facial expressions. This technology has potential uses in identifying criminals in a crowd or quickly and accurately confirming identities of people boarding an aircraft or entering a secure area. These examples give a glimpse of the many risk assessment and control opportunities offered by this emerging technology.

Apply Your Knowledge

We've talked about the ways emerging technologies can benefit risk management. Can you think of risks created by these same emerging technologies?

Feedback: As emerging technologies are used, emerging risks arise as well, particularly related to privacy and data protection, cybersecurity, and liability (for example, driverless autos). Organizations must monitor and address these new risks as they implement emerging technologies in their risk management programs.

SMART PRODUCTS AND OPERATIONS

The ability of devices connected to the Internet of Things (IoT) to collect data about their surroundings and then immediately transmit it to other devices or people lies at the heart of the ongoing shift from risk transfer to risk prevention. This shift is fundamentally changing the industry and the roles of those who work in it.

Smart products and operations, enabled by emerging technology, are part of the risktech ecosystem. This discussion will focus on how a number of industries use three common smart products: wearables, drones, and robots. As the number of connected objects and people increases, the IoT's risk management potential expands.

Smart Products

Before exploring how smart products are used in smart operations, let's first understand how they function.

Wearables are designed with **ergonomics** in mind; they sense, monitor, report, and analyze workers' health or well-being and their surrounding environments.

To be labeled a wearable technology, the product needs to be a type of clothing or accessory that is worn on the body, not carried. To be considered a

Ergonomics

The science of designing work space and equipment based on the needs of the people who use the work space and equipment.

smart wearable, the device must contain sensors that detect and measure impulses and convert them to useable data, microprocessors that change this data into a transmittable form, and transmitters that wirelessly relay the data for appropriate processing or further use.

Drones began as a hobby, but their range of applications now also includes use as a military tool and in various commercial services, many involving risk assessment and control. They are smart products, with unique capabilities in areas such as surveillance and aerial photography. That they are unmanned and highly versatile makes them ideal for going to dangerous or unknown areas and then assessing conditions or risks. And by entering such areas on humans' behalf, drones indirectly promote humans' health and safety.

Drones generally contain one or more cameras, batteries, and sensors, as well as a remote controller for the user and a communication source (usually Wi-Fi) that can accommodate smartphones or other devices. Infrared and thermal sensors in cameras can detect high temperatures, which can reveal overheating equipment and warn employees to move away from an area. Chemical sensors attached to drones can monitor the concentration of certain gases or other particles—and if dangerous amounts are detected, the sensors can report this through a connected transducer.

Apply Your Knowledge

Learn more from an expert in the online video.

Drones can be used in many industries. Can you think of specific risk management examples of how your industry could benefit, or is benefiting, from their use?

Feedback: Many industries—from farming to the military—are using drones for risk management. We'll go over some examples of how key industries have become smart operations by incorporating drones and other smart products.

Robots are another type of smart product. They may be either fixed (containing moveable parts but unable to travel) or mobile—equipped to travel to immediate, adjacent, or even distant environments.

Robots have evolved from simple machines built to resemble humans to valuable tools of various design that can collaborate with human workers. Robots also assist humans by performing dangerous tasks and monitoring environmental conditions.

Smart Operations

Smart products are increasing the information risk managers have on hand—information about dangerous chemicals in the air, shipping malfunctions, exhausted workers, or almost any other facet of an organization's operations. This information is already improving risk mitigation in many industries, and their success will lead to more operations becoming connected ecosystems. Here are some examples:

- Property management—Property managers use drones for surveillance and monitoring. This is a cost-efficient way to proactively identify damage or security risks at separate locations. Consider the cost difference in scaffolding a building to inspect it versus using a drone. As another example, robots are taking on the role of leasing agent by processing documents and payments and answering property-related questions.

- Supply chain management—Smart glasses can be used to provide inventory details to order pickers. They can also convey instructions and even training aids to wearers. Organizations are also exploring deliveries by drone. Robotics increase productivity and reduce risk on the warehouse floor. For example, Amazon has reduced order-fulfillment costs by using robots to bring items to human pickers.

- Transportation management—Wearables have many benefits for the transportation industry. They can analyze an operator's driving habits or physical condition in real time. Accelerometers can detect excessive vibration in a vehicle and warn transportation managers of vehicle conditions. Drones can take detailed photos of routes. But the most significant change to transportation management may come from autonomous, or robotic, vehicles.

- Catastrophe management—With the increased use of sensors in smart objects, the effects of catastrophes can be mitigated more effectively. Drones increase awareness of potentially dangerous situations as well. The more prepared a business is for an earthquake, tsunami, or fire, the better it can protect its workers and property. The American Red Cross promotes the use of wearables and smartphones in search-and-rescue missions, and robots can be used in unsafe environments.

- Workplace safety management—Many smart products can improve workplace safety and productivity. Thanks to wearables, sensors can be incorporated into safety vests or other gear, leaving workers' hands free to do their jobs. Drones provide information and help assess and control risks by going into unknown and potentially dangerous areas—on the ground, in the air, or underwater—without putting humans at risk. Robots operate in close proximity to workers but do more of the repetitive and heavy-lifting jobs. This allows workers to better use their skills and protects them from injury.

All these elements lead to truly smart operations, which protect both workers and products.

SUMMARY

Grounded in traditional risk management techniques, today's risk management environment is animated by increasingly potent combinations of inexpensive data-gathering and data-storage technology and predictive analytic techniques that can transform data into more certainty about risk management decisions than ever before.

Risktech incorporates emerging technologies into smart products and operations. In turn, this generates data for analytics, leading to improved risk assessment and control.

Emerging technologies, such as AI, sensors, and computer vision, greatly improve an organization's ability to handle risk. Understanding these technologies' functions and value is key to implementing them successfully.

Smart products, such as wearables, drones, and robots, can be used to enhance risk assessment and control in a variety of contexts, including property, supply chain, transportation, catastrophe, and workplace safety management.

Creating a Stronger RM Foundation

2

Educational Objectives	Outline

▶ Apply a process for managing an organization's risks.

▶ Explain how the following classifications of risk apply to and help in risk management:

- Pure and speculative risk

- Subjective and objective risk

- Diversifiable and nondiversifiable risk

- Quadrants of risk (hazard, operational, financial, and strategic)

▶ Summarize objectives for and benefits from managing risk.

▶ Explain how basic risk measures apply to the management of risk.

Outline

Process for Managing Risk

Classifications and Categories

Objectives and Benefits

Basic Risk Measures

Summary

Creating a Stronger RM Foundation

2

PROCESS FOR MANAGING RISK

Risk does not present itself in discrete units or on a predetermined timetable. Instead, it's an ever-present, ever-changing constellation of threats and opportunities that emerge from the intersection of an organization's ambitions and its overall environment. Risk professionals impose structure on the fundamental disorder of this circumstance by applying a process for managing risk to their organizations' activities.

Learn more from an expert in the online video.

This process is one of the most important tools you'll use on the job because, like a powerful telescope trained on distant stars, its proper implementation can give you the clearest picture of what lies in the distance. It can also shed light on the best methods to optimize risks' upside while minimizing their downside through assessment and treatment techniques.

The first thing you should know about the risk management process is that it isn't actually a process—at least not in its application.

Rather, it's a set of interconnected simultaneously and sequentially occurring activities that define an organization's holistic approach to managing risks. It also differs from organization to organization. This is because each organization's **risk management framework** is refined based on how well it's working and on significant changes in the organization's external and internal environments. Despite differences in its implementation, however, the process's success always relies on effective communication and collaboration among key stakeholders. Your ability to facilitate and maximize the value of those interactions brings the process to life.

Risk management framework

A foundation for applying the risk management process throughout the organization.

Let's take a look at the five essential activities of the risk management process and how they connect to what risk managers and other decision makers do every day. To learn more, see "Process for Managing Risk."

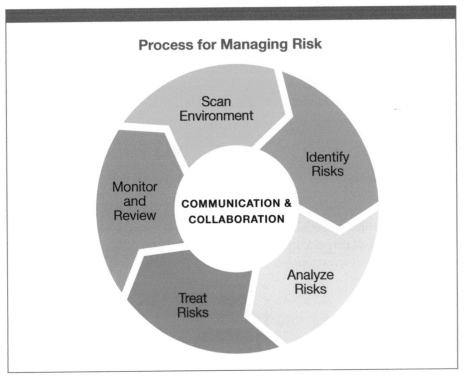

[DA13040_1]

What Do You Know?

True or false: The key to implementing a process for managing risk is to organize all of the risks an organization faces and move sequentially through the steps of the process by applying each one.

Feedback: False. The risk management process is really more of a set of interconnected activities that are occurring at the same time than a step-by-step process.

Scan the Environment

Risk management professionals should conduct specific, detailed reviews of both the internal and external environments of an organization. For example, risk management processes around employee safety in the United States include the legal and regulatory requirements of the Occupational Safety and Health Administration (OSHA) and state or federal workers compensation statutes, as well as external stakeholders' procedures (such as insurers') and the organization's internal procedures.

Scanning the environment includes evaluating how each of an organization's risk management processes aligns with its overall objectives.

For example, the organization's objectives may be to achieve profitable growth and promote the health, safety, and well-being of its employees. The risk management process related to employee safety should therefore be aligned with the goals of both these objectives. A risk management objective to reduce the number of employee injuries would align with organizational objectives. Reducing injuries would improve employee safety and reduce the expenses associated with employee injuries (and thereby increase profits).

Additionally, risk management professionals should collaborate with the organization's internal stakeholders to define its risk criteria. These criteria should be aligned with the organization's objectives, resources, and risk management policy and should consider these factors:

Risk criteria

Information used as a basis for measuring the significance of a risk.

- Causes of risk — i.e. *employees lifting improperly*
- Effects of risk — *employee injury*
- Metrics used to measure effects of risk — *disability payout, less productivity, less work output due to injured employee, profit loss, turnover, etc*
- Timeframe of potential effects — *how many months employees off work*
- Methods to determine level of risk
- Approach to combinations of risk

Identify Risks

The purpose of risk identification is to develop a comprehensive list of risks that could affect the organization's objectives. Identifying all risks is not feasible or practical, but identifying key and emerging risks is essential. This process relies on the risk professional's ability to perform or facilitate several key tasks involving communication, including these:

- Asking the right questions of departmental stakeholders to understand their perspectives on the most pressing risks they face
- Finding external experts who can shed light on emerging risks that the organization may not have anticipated previously and knowing how to speak their language to get the most from interactions with them
- Collaborating with senior management and the board to ensure that risk associated with the organization's strategy are identified

Identifying risk interactions is also important. For example, the risk of a customer being injured by an organization's product may traditionally have been viewed as a hazard risk. However, in an enterprise-wide process, related risks in other quadrants can be identified—such as reputational risk from publicity about the injury, which could have both strategic and financial effects. If a product recall becomes necessary, operational and financial risks would result. → *hazard risk; overlap w/ reputational risk; overlap w/ ops & financial risk*

Analyze Risks

Risk analysis involves applying the defined risk criteria to determine the source, cause, likelihood, and potential consequences of each of the identified risks. Depending on the circumstances, this analysis can be quantitative, qualitative, or both. Quantitative analysis, in particular, may entail interacting with experts.

For example, if the risk of customer injuries caused by an organization's product is identified, a specialist can quantify the potential cost of litigation based on the organization's prior experience or by benchmarking with other cases. The effect on the organization's reputation, however, would be more difficult to quantify and would probably be expressed qualitatively.

Treat Risks

After risk analysis, decisions are made regarding risk treatment. When no regulatory requirements are present, an organization should compare the total level of risk determined during the risk analysis with the established risk criteria. This comparison will guide decisions regarding risk treatment.

For example, say the organization's total level of risk exceeds past levels. In this instance, the organization may decide to employ risk treatment to reduce the level of risk to a range in line with its risk tolerance that would not unduly threaten profit objectives.

Learn more from an expert in the online video.

After completing this comparison, risk management professionals—in collaboration with appropriate organizational stakeholders—decide where and how to apply risk treatment. These are the major options available for risks:

- Avoid the risk
- Modify the likelihood and/or impact of the risk
- Transfer the risk
- Retain the risk
- Exploit the risk

Risk
Risk treatment

Monitor and Review

Effective risk management processes include ongoing monitoring with periodic review of results. These are the key purposes of monitoring:

- Determine the effectiveness of controls
- Obtain information to improve risk assessment
- Analyze events and their consequences to understand trends, successes, and failures
- Observe changes in internal and external environments
- Identify emerging risks

The data produced at this step about a risk management strategy's effectiveness is only as valuable as a risk professional's ability to transform it into action by other stakeholders. How can a set of information be used as a persuasive tool? Although conversations with decision-makers are just as vital here as they are at every step in the process for managing risk, dynamically updated documents can breathe life into seemingly inert data and be used to create narratives and arguments that help make the risk professional's case for the importance of vigilance at every level of an organization. Prominent examples of such documents include risk registers, heat maps, risk maps, and targeted communications to the board and c-suite that focus on the ramifications of strategic risks.

[handwritten note: → your monitoring & review should cause buy-in from stakeholders]

CLASSIFICATIONS AND CATEGORIES

Risk professionals' most recognizable contributions to an organization often are the strategies they help implement to minimize threats and maximize opportunities. Those accomplishments, however, don't come easily. They're the by-product of experience, skill, intuition, and rigorous methodology that elevate risk management to an art. So where do you start?

[handwritten note: ↓ threats ↑ opportunities]

One essential attribute of anyone who manages risk is the ability to classify it. Classification can help with assessing risks because many risks in the same class have similar attributes. It also can help with managing risk, because many risks can be managed with similar techniques. Finally, classification helps with the administrative function of risk management by helping to ensure that risks in the same class are less likely to be overlooked.

[handwritten note: classification help by: ① many risks in same class have similar attributes ② many risks in same class can be managed/treated w/ similar techniques ③ can help administrating so helping to ensure risks in same class are not overlooked]

These classifications of risk are some of the most commonly used:

- Pure and speculative risk
- Subjective and objective risk
- Diversifiable and nondiversifiable risk
- Quadrants of risk (hazard, operational, financial, and strategic)

What Do You Know?

True or false: The most experienced risk professionals understand how to exploit pure risk for upside.

Feedback: False. Although risk professionals ultimately try to manage threats and opportunities holistically, not all individual risks have upsides. In fact, the defining feature of pure risk, which constitutes a significant portion of the risks that organizations confront, is that there is no associated chance of gain—only loss or no loss.

Pure and Speculative Risk

Pure risk
A chance of loss or no loss, but no chance of gain.

either 0 or −1 but no +

A **pure risk** is a chance of loss or no loss, but no chance of gain. For example, the owner of a commercial building faces the risk associated with a possible fire loss. The building will either burn or not burn. If the building burns, the owner suffers a financial loss. If the building does not burn, the owner's financial condition is unchanged. Neither of the possible outcomes would produce a gain. Because there is no opportunity for financial gain, pure risks are always undesirable. To learn more, see "Classifications of Risk."

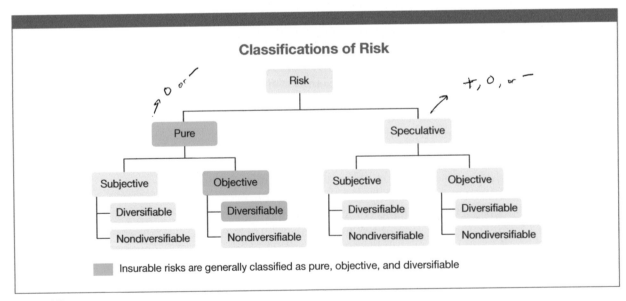

Classifications of Risk

0 or −1   Risk   *+, 0, or −*

Pure   Speculative

Subjective   Objective   Subjective   Objective

Diversifiable   Diversifiable   Diversifiable   Diversifiable

Nondiversifiable   Nondiversifiable   Nondiversifiable   Nondiversifiable

Insurable risks are generally classified as pure, objective, and diversifiable

[DA02396]

Speculative risk
A chance of loss, no loss, or gain.

But **speculative risk** involves a chance of gain. As a result, it can be desirable, as evidenced by the fact that every business venture involves speculative risks. For example, an investor who purchases an apartment building to rent to tenants expects to profit from this investment; however, rental price controls could render the endeavor unprofitable. So the venture is a speculative risk.

Speculative risk is highly affected by these factors:

- Price risk—Uncertainty about cash flows resulting from possible changes in the cost of raw materials and other inputs (such as lumber, gas, or electricity), as well as cost-related changes in the market for completed products and other outputs.

- **Credit risk**—Although a credit risk is particularly significant for banks and other financial institutions, it can also be relevant to any organization with accounts receivable.

Financial investments, such as the purchase of stock shares, involve a distinct set of speculative risks.

Insurance deals primarily with risks of loss, not risks of gain—that is, with pure risks rather than speculative risks. However, the distinction between these two classifications of risk is not always precise. Many risks have both pure and speculative aspects.

Distinguishing between pure and speculative risks is important because each must often be managed differently. For example, although a commercial building owner faces a pure risk from causes of loss such as fire, that owner also faces the speculative risk of the building's market value increasing or decreasing during any one year. Similarly, although an investor who purchases an apartment building to rent to tenants faces speculative risk because rental income may produce a profit or loss, the investor also faces a pure risk from causes of loss such as fire.

To properly manage these investments, the commercial building owner and the apartment owner must consider both the speculative and pure risks. For example, they may choose to manage the pure risk by buying insurance or taking other measures to address property loss exposures. The speculative risk might be managed by obtaining a favorable mortgage and maintaining the property to enhance its resale value.

Subjective and Objective Risk

When individuals and organizations must make a decision that involves risk, they start by assessing the risk. The assessment can be based on opinions, facts, or both.

Because it is based on opinion, **subjective risk** may be quite different from the actual underlying risk that is present. In fact, subjective risk can exist even where **objective risk** does not. The closer an individual's or organization's subjective interpretation of risk is to the objective risk, the more effective its risk management plan will likely be.

These are some ways that subjective and objective risk can differ:

- Familiarity and control—For example, although many people consider air travel (over which they have no control and likely low familiarity) to

Credit risk

The risk that customers or other creditors will fail to make promised payments as they come due.

Subjective risk

The perceived amount of risk based on an individual's or organization's opinion.

Objective risk

The measurable variation in uncertain outcomes based on facts and data.

carry a high degree of risk, they are much more likely to suffer a serious injury when driving their cars, where the perception of control and degree of familiarity are much greater.

- Consequences over likelihood—People often have two views of low-likelihood, high-consequence events. The first misconception is the "It can't happen to me" view, which assigns zero probability to such low-likelihood events as natural disasters, murder, fires, and accidents. The second misconception is overstating the probability of a low-likelihood event; this is common with people who were previously exposed to such an event. Generally, if the effects of a particular event can be severe, such as the potential devastation caused by a hurricane or earthquake, the perception of likely deaths resulting from the event is heightened. This perception may be enhanced by increased media coverage given to high-severity events.

- Risk awareness—Because organizations have different levels of risk awareness, they perceive risks differently. An organization that is not aware of its risks, for example, would perceive the likelihood of something happening as very low.

Both risk management and insurance depend on the ability to objectively identify and analyze risks. However, subjectivity is also necessary because facts are not always available.

Diversifiable and Nondiversifiable Risk

Diversifiable risk A risk that affects only some individuals, businesses, or small groups.

Diversifiable risk is not highly correlated—that is, its gains or losses tend to occur randomly and be isolated. Such risk can be managed through diversification, or spread, of risk.

An example of a diversifiable risk is a fire, which is likely to affect only one or a small number of businesses. So an insurer can diversify the risks associated with fire insurance by insuring many buildings in several different locations. Similarly, business investors often diversify their holdings instead of investing in only one business, hoping that successes will more than offset failures.

Examples of nondiversifiable risks include inflation, unemployment, and natural disasters such as hurricanes. Nondiversifiable risks are correlated. For example, interest rates can increase for all firms at the same time. So if an insurer were to insure firms against interest rate increases, it would not be able to diversify its portfolio of interest rate risks by underwriting a large number of insureds, because all of them would suffer losses at the same time.

Systemic risk The potential for a major disruption in the function of an entire market or financial system.

Systemic risks are generally nondiversifiable. For example, if excess leverage by financial institutions causes systemic risk resulting in an event that disrupts the financial system, this risk will have an effect on the entire economy and, therefore, all organizations. Because of the global interconnections in finance and industry, many risks that were once viewed as nonsystemic (affecting only one organization) are now viewed as systemic.

For instance, many economists view the failure of Lehman Brothers in early 2008 as a trigger event: highlighting the systemic risk in the banking sector that resulted in the financial crisis. Not understanding the systemic nature of risk posed by the securitization of mortgage obligations was at the root of AIG's risk management failure in backing a large number of collateralized debt obligations underwritten by banks. The high correlation and systemic risk were not recognized or managed.

Quadrants of Risk: Hazard, Operational, Financial, and Strategic

Although no consensus exists about how an organization should categorize its risks, one approach involves using risk quadrants:

- Hazard risks arise from property, liability, or personnel loss exposures and are generally the subject of insurance.

- Operational risks fall outside the hazard risk category and arise from people or a failure in processes, systems, or controls, including those involving information technology.

- Financial risks arise from the effect of market forces on financial assets or liabilities and include **market risk**, credit risk, **liquidity risk**, and price risk.

- Strategic risks arise from trends in the economy and society, including changes in the economic, political, and competitive environments, as well as from demographic shifts.

Hazard and operational risks are classified as pure risks, and financial and strategic risks are classified as speculative risks.

The focus of the risk quadrants is different from the risk classifications previously discussed. Risk classifications focus on some aspect of the risk itself, while the four quadrants of risk focus on the risk source and who traditionally manages it. For example, the chief financial officer traditionally manages financial risk, and the risk manager traditionally manages hazard risk.

Market risk

Uncertainty about an investment's future value because of potential changes in the market for that type of investment.

Liquidity risk

The risk that an asset cannot be sold on short notice without incurring a loss.

What Do You Know?

True or false: Risk quadrants isolate risks into single categories, thus allowing each risk to be treated according to its specific quadrant.

Feedback: False. In fact, many of the risks that pose the most potent threats and greatest opportunities actually fall into more than one risk quadrant. And the manner in which risks from all quadrants intersect to form an organization's holistic risk portfolio is a vital determinant of the strategies that can best mitigate negative outcomes and exploit positive ones.

Just as a particular risk can fall into more than one classification, a risk can also fall into multiple risk quadrants. For example, embezzlement of funds by an employee can be considered both a hazard risk, because it is an insurable pure risk, and an operational risk, because it involves a failure of controls. To learn more, see "Risk Quadrants."

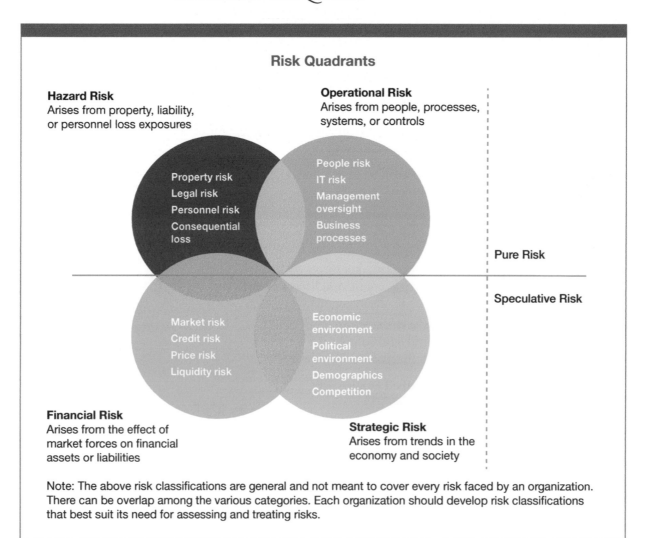

Risk Quadrants

Hazard Risk
Arises from property, liability, or personnel loss exposures

Property risk
Legal risk
Personnel risk
Consequential loss

Operational Risk
Arises from people, processes, systems, or controls

People risk
IT risk
Management oversight
Business processes

Pure Risk

Speculative Risk

Market risk
Credit risk
Price risk
Liquidity risk

Economic environment
Political environment
Demographics
Competition

Financial Risk
Arises from the effect of market forces on financial assets or liabilities

Strategic Risk
Arises from trends in the economy and society

Note: The above risk classifications are general and not meant to cover every risk faced by an organization. There can be overlap among the various categories. Each organization should develop risk classifications that best suit its need for assessing and treating risks.

[DA08677]

Organizations define types of risk differently. Some organizations consider legal risks as operational risk, and some may characterize certain hazard risks as operational risk. Financial institutions generally use the categories of market, credit, and operational risk (defined as all other risk, including hazard risk). Each organization should select categories that align with its objectives and processes.

Apply Your Knowledge

The New Company manufactures electronic consumer products. The company's manufacturing plant is highly automated and located in the United States. However, it purchases components from three companies in Asia. The majority of its sales are in the U.S., but European sales represent a growing percentage.

Describe the types of risk New Company would have in each of the four risk quadrants.

Feedback: In the hazard risk quadrant, New Company would have property damage risks to its plant and equipment resulting from fire, storms, or other events. It would also have risk of injury to its employees and liability risks associated with its products.

In the operational risk quadrant, New Company would have risks from employee turnover or the inability to find skilled employees. It would also have business process risk related to how it manages its supply chain and information technology risk related to its automated manufacturing process.

In the financial risk quadrant, New Company would have exchange rate risk related to its European sales. It would also have price risk for raw materials and supplies.

Strategic risks include competition, economic factors that could affect consumer demand, and the political risk arising from countries in which the company's component suppliers are located.

Handwritten margin notes:

Hazard
- property risk to plants, equip.
- employee injury · product liability

Ops
- Break down in workflow
- employee turnover
- supply chain management
- IT out w/ automation

Financial
- exchange rate risk for European countries
- price risk for prices of raw materials & cheaper prices for electronic goods

Strategic
- political strife in China (suppliers are from abroad) could upset supply chain
- competition → consumer demand
- age demographics

OBJECTIVES AND BENEFITS

Although it's rooted in concepts as old as business itself and is essentially intangible, holistic risk management (sometimes referred to as enterprise risk management, or ERM) isn't just a hypothetical ideal. When implemented, maintained, and continually improved, it provides tangible advantages that are a direct result of its objectives. A challenge for risk professionals is increasing their organization's awareness of holistic risk management's benefits. To learn more, see "How They Did It: Clorox."

Let's examine some of the most important benefits of holistic risk management.

How They Did It: Clorox

ERM is an evolving area, and a lot of people aren't familiar with it. Until there's broader understanding of what ERM practitioners do, soft skills such as getting alignment, buy-in, and support are key to launching a program.

Allison Zheng (Program Manager, Clorox), interviewed by Mike Elliott, March 2019, transcript, The Institutes, Malvern, Pa. [DA_13131]

What Do You Know?

True or False: Most organizations' sole risk management objective is to mitigate the effects of accidents.

Feedback: False. A holistic risk management approach entails the pursuit of a variety of objectives besides mitigating the effects of accidents.

Components

① Reduce downside risks
② Earnings stability
③ Anticipate & recognize emerging risks
④ Business/Ops continuity

Risk tolerance

Risk appetite

Amount of risk an organization is willing to take on in order to achieve an anticipated result or return.

Value at risk (VaR)

A technique to quantify financial risk by measuring the likelihood of losing more than a specific dollar amount over a specific period of time.

Tolerable Uncertainty

Risk is basically an expression of uncertainty about the future—and the greater that uncertainty, the greater the risk an organization faces. That's why defining and maintaining tolerable uncertainty, which means aligning risks with the organization's **risk appetite**, is essential to every holistic risk management strategy. This connects to risk management's fundamental purpose for organizations—to ensure that whatever might happen will be within the bounds of what was anticipated and can be effectively addressed.

To meet this objective, risk management programs should use measurements that align with the organization's overall objectives and take into account senior management's risk appetite. For example, **value-at-risk (VaR)** can be used to analyze various financial portfolios with different assets and risk factors. VaR can be calculated quickly and easily to determine risk-factor returns on a portfolio.

So what does tolerable uncertainty mean to you as a risk professional? Here are a few of its most important components.

Reduce Downside Risk

Downside risks, including losses and failures, are an inevitable aspect of any type of business or speculative risk. For example, a company faces downside risk whenever it introduces a new product. A financial institution faces downside risk every time it makes a loan or an investment. Operational risk includes risk to an organization's processes, and the downside risks include delays, errors, cost increases, and the failure of any aspect of the operation.

To reduce downside risks, organizations can use threshold limits, which can be applied to many types of risks. By monitoring risks with preset limits based on established risk criteria, triggers are established to alert management when the threshold has been breached. This threshold might be a certain number of faulty manufactured items within a certain amount of time (operational risk), a certain variation in interest rates on investments (financial risk), or the number of serious accidents within a specified time frame (hazard risk). When these thresholds are breached, management can review the situation and discuss changes before the losses become more significant and more difficult to manage. The risk management strategy an organization uses must be well thought out so that the strategy itself does not increase risk. Hedging is an example of a risk management technique that can be used to manage downside risk resulting from market volatility, but it must be well designed and executed.

Earnings Stability

Rather than strive for the highest possible level of current profits (or, for not-for-profit organizations, surpluses) in a given period, some organizations emphasize earnings stability over time. Maintaining earnings stability requires precise forecasting of fluctuations in asset values, liability values, and risk management costs (such as costs for insurance).

Anticipate and Recognize Emerging Risks

Analyzing the past will always be one of the most effective ways to predict the future—after all, past is prologue. However, the risks that offer the richest potential upside and the most calamitous downside are often those that either can't be anticipated at all or are deemed so improbable that the organization doesn't even consider them. For these risks, normal identification and monitoring will not work because the frequency and impact are usually completely unknown. An organization's risk radar should scan both the organization and the external environment for emerging risks. This radar should also be sensitive to the convergence of emerging internal and external risks.

Apply Your Knowledge

Learn more from an expert in the online video.

One indicator of emerging risks is the creation of new insurance coverages to treat them. Can you name some recently developed coverages that signal the emergence of new risks?

Feedback: Some of the emerging risks you may have suggested include risks associated with active shooters and risks associated with the sharing economy.

Business Continuity

For risk management purposes, an organization can be viewed as a structured system of resources, such as financial assets, machinery and raw materials, employees, and managerial leadership. The organization generates income for its employees and owners by producing goods or services that meet others' needs. Many risks can threaten an organization's survival. Hazard risk, which could destroy an organization's facilities or injure employees or customers, was traditionally viewed as a major threat to an organization's survival. Risk management professionals use techniques such as loss control and risk transfer to manage hazard risks.

However, the risks organizations face today are much broader than hazard risk. These risks include global competition, trade disputes, supply chain risks, and technology (vulnerability to computer attacks and inability to keep pace with technological developments). An organization's survival depends on identifying as many risks as possible that could threaten the organization and managing them appropriately. It also depends on anticipating and recognizing emerging risks, such as those related to climate change.

Continuity of operations is a key goal for many private organizations and an essential goal for all public entities. Although survival requires only that no risk occurrence (no matter how severe) permanently shut down an organization, the goal of continuity of operations is more demanding. To be resilient, an organization cannot interrupt its operations for any appreciable time. When an organization's senior management sets business continuity as a goal, its risk management professionals must have a clear, detailed understanding of the specific operations for which continuity is essential and the maximum tolerable interruption interval for each operation.

Profitability and Growth

Holistic risk management isn't just about staving off disaster or ensuring organizational survival. Ideally, risk management is integrated into every facet of an organization's strategy for profitability and growth. Here are some ways risk management aligns with this crucial organizational objective:

- Intelligent, strategic risk taking—Successful organizations usually take risks to grow and increase profit. This type of risk can create a positive or a negative outcome. Decisions about new opportunities should be based on the organization's risk appetite. An important benefit of risk management is that it provides organizations with a framework to analyze and manage the risks associated with an opportunity. For example, when an organization considers whether to expand into a new product line, risk management can help it decide whether the potential rewards are greater than the downside risks. If the organization decides to go forward with the new product line, risk management can assist in designing a process to manage the associated risks.

- Identification and management of cross-enterprise risks—In addition to recognizing and addressing emerging risks, holistic risk management can help identify and manage risks that affect multiple and often diverse areas of an organization. For example, supply chain risks have traditionally been viewed as operational risks. However, a supply chain interruption could also become a financial risk if it affects product sales and a reputational risk if it affects customer service. Holistic risk management provides an opportunity to recognize these cross-enterprise risks when making strategic supply chain decisions. An organization's risk radar can also detect risk indicators from one area of the organization that affect one or more additional areas. For example, an increase in customer service calls regarding a product may indicate a production problem.

- Improved capital allocation—A holistic risk management strategy empowers organizations to improve their capital allocation in two ways. The first is by reducing the cost of risk, freeing up capital for other purposes. The second way is by improving risk analysis for various strategic options so that capital is allocated where it is likely to produce the best reward for the risk.

[handwritten margin note: 1) reduce cost of risk = freed up capital 2) risk analysis to see which opp is likely to produce best results given its risk]

Legal and Regulatory Compliance

An important goal for risk management programs is to ensure that the organization's legal obligations are satisfied. Such legal obligations are typically based on these items:

- Standard of care owed to others
- Contracts entered into by the organization
- Federal, state, provincial, territorial, and local laws and regulations

Social Responsibility

Many organizations value social responsibility. This concept includes the organization's ethical conduct as well as the philanthropic commitments that the owners of the organization have made to the community and society as a whole. Beyond the altruistic interests of the organization's owners, many organizations pursue social responsibility because such activities enhance the organization's reputation. Risk management professionals should consider an

[handwritten margin note: → blowing trumpets for your alms-giving → capitalism @ is great!]

organization's societal commitments when developing its risk management program. γ

Reduced Cost of Risk

Cost of risk

The total cost incurred by an organization because of the possibility of accidental loss.

The **cost of risk** associated with a particular asset or activity is the total of these costs:

- Costs of accidental losses not reimbursed by insurance or other outside sources
- Insurance premiums and expenses incurred for noninsurance indemnity
- Costs of risk control techniques to prevent or mitigate accidental losses
- Costs of administering risk management activities

Effective holistic risk management aims to reduce the long-term overall cost of risk for the organization without precluding or otherwise interfering with the organization's achieving its goals or engaging in its normal activities. The reduction in the overall cost of risk can increase the organization's profits (or, for a not-for-profit organization, reduce the budget it needs for a particular activity). Risk management also supports safety while minimizing its cost.

Reduced Deterrent Effects of Hazard Risks

Risk management reduces the deterrent effects of uncertainty about potential future accidental losses by making these losses less frequent, less severe, or more foreseeable. The resulting reduction in uncertainty offers organizations these benefits:

- Alleviates or reduces management's fears about potential losses, thereby increasing the feasibility of ventures that once appeared too risky
- Increases profit potential by greater participation in investment or production activities
- Makes the organization a safer investment and therefore more attractive to suppliers of investment capital through which the organization can expand

Many new products and manufacturing processes have become attractive only after better ways of preventing and paying for accidental losses have reduced related uncertainty. Like an organization's senior managers, those who would provide the organization with funds seek assurances: stockholders or other investors seek assurance that their equity is safe and will generate future income; creditors seek assurance that the money they have loaned will be repaid on time with interest.

The security sought by these sources of new capital rests at least partly on confidence that the organization will prosper despite the accidental losses that might befall it. Consequently, an organization's ability to attract willing investors depends to a significant degree on the effectiveness of its risk management program to protect investors' capital against the cost of accidental losses.

BASIC RISK MEASURES

One of the more daunting tasks risk professionals face is developing actionable data about risk, which is inherently abstract and intangible. That's why some of the most valuable tools in risk professionals' toolboxes are methods for measuring risk, which can reveal essential attributes of threats and opportunities that empower them to imagine the best strategies for treatment.

There are basic measures that risk professionals use when they're assessing and quantifying the risks that they'll ultimately treat as part of their organizations' holistic risk management strategy.

What Do You Know?

How many basic risk measures can you name?

Feedback: There are numerous basic risk measures, but six commonly used ones are exposure, volatility, likelihood, consequences, time horizon, and correlation. These all attempt to quantify the risks an organization faces, which is essential to developing strategies to treat them.

Let's examine each in more detail:

- **Exposure**
- **Volatility**
- **Likelihood**
- **Consequences**
- **Time horizon**
- **Correlation**

Let's take a look at the first risk measure. To learn more, see "Understanding Exposure."

Understanding Exposure

Exposure provides a measure of the maximum potential damage associated with an occurrence. Generally, the risk level increases as the exposure increases, assuming the risk is nondiversifiable.

 See the corresponding online video.

[DA13056_1]

Exposure

Any condition that presents a possibility of gain or loss, whether or not an actual loss occurs.

Volatility

Frequent fluctuations, such as in the price of an asset.

Likelihood

A qualitative estimate of the certainty with which the outcome of a specific event can be predicted.

Consequences

The effects, positive or negative, of an occurrence.

Time horizon

Estimated duration.

Correlation

A relationship between variables.

For example, if a bank underwrites mortgages for subprime borrowers, the bank's aggregate credit risk level increases as the number of subprime mortgages increases because the overall exposure to default increases. An insurer that writes homeowners policies in coastal areas increases its exposure to windstorms as its coastal book of business grows. In these examples, the exposure can be quantified based on the number and amount of mortgages or the number of policies and policy limits. Other exposures, such as the risk of a data breach or loss of reputation, are not as easily quantified. However, even if an exposure cannot be readily quantified, an attempt should be made to qualitatively measure its effect on the organization to effectively manage the risk. For instance, the effect of reputational risk could be measured in terms of its potential influence on an organization's stock price, customer loyalty, and employee turnover. To learn more, see "Understanding Volatility."

Understanding Volatility

Volatility provides a basic measure that can be applied to risk outcomes. Risk increases as volatility increases. Volatility can often be quantified.

 See the corresponding online video.

[DA13056_2]

The CBOE Volatility Index, or VIX, created by the Chicago Board Options Exchange, provides a measure of stock market volatility. The volatility of energy prices, as another example, is a major risk for many organizations. Utilities, airlines, trucking companies, and other types of organizations that are highly dependent on fuel use strategies such as hedging to manage the risk associated with volatility in the price of oil and other fuels. However, organizations that may be only indirectly affected by energy price volatility, such as retailers whose customers have less disposable income when gas prices rise, may also want to assess and manage this risk through inventory and pricing adjustments. To learn more, see "Understanding Likelihood."

For example, a bank can probably quantify the likelihood of a loan default based on a prospective borrower's credit score and other characteristics. However, it would be more difficult for the bank to determine the likelihood of a cyberattack in which customer data is taken, resulting in liability. It would be even more difficult for the bank to predict the likelihood of a terrorist attack that could be catastrophic.

Similarly, it is easier to determine the likelihood that certain risks undertaken to improve an organization's performance will have a positive outcome than it is for others. If a bank decides to issue credit to borrowers with slightly lower credit scores than its current borrowers, the bank probably has sufficient

Understanding Likelihood

The likelihood of an occurrence is a key measure in risk management. The term "likelihood" is used rather than "probability" because probability analysis relies on the law of large numbers, which basically means that the larger the sample size, the more representative the probability of occurrence is of the whole.

When an adequate amount of historical data exists, insurers and some other organizations can use the law of large numbers to accurately determine the probability of various risk outcomes. However, most organizations need to determine the likelihood of an occurrence without the benefit of a probability analysis. The relationship between likelihood and consequences is critical for risk management in assessing risk and deciding whether and how to manage it. Therefore, organizations must determine to the extent possible the likelihood of an event and then determine the potential consequences if the event occurs.

 See the corresponding online video.

[DA13056_5]

data to determine the likelihood of a positive outcome. However, if the bank decides to expand into a new and unfamiliar region, it may be more difficult to predict the likelihood of a successful outcome. To learn more, see "Understanding Consequences."

Understanding Consequences

Consequences are the measure of the degree to which an occurrence could positively or negatively affect an organization. The greater the consequences, the greater the risk. In assessing the level of risk, a risk professional must understand, to the extent possible, both the likelihood and the consequences. If there is a low likelihood of an occurrence with minor consequences, it may not be necessary for an organization to actively manage the risk.

 See the corresponding online video.

[DA13056_6]

As an example, a bank may decide that the likelihood of employees taking office supplies for personal use is low, and the consequences if this occurs are minor. Therefore, the bank may decide not to manage this risk.

Risks with high likelihood and minor consequences should usually be managed through an organization's routine business procedures. To illustrate, there is a significant likelihood that a customer will be a few days late in making a loan payment. The consequences of payments that are a few days late are relatively minor. However, the bank should manage this risk through normal business procedures such as assessing late charges or sending reminder notices if a payment has not been received by the due date.

Risks with potentially major consequences should be managed even if the likelihood of their occurrence is low. For instance, the risk of a fire at a bank, although unlikely, must be managed. Risks with significant likelihood and major consequences require significant, continuous risk management. For example, an international bank faces exchange rate risk that could result in considerable losses. The bank may use hedging strategies and other techniques to modify this type of risk. To learn more, see "Understanding Time Horizon."

Understanding Time Horizon

The time horizon of an exposure is another basic measure that is applied in risk management. A risk's time horizon can be measured in various ways. The time horizon associated with an investment risk such as a stock or bond can be determined by specified bond duration or by how quickly a stock can be traded. Longer time horizons are generally riskier than shorter ones. For example, a thirty-year mortgage is usually riskier for a bank than a fifteen-year mortgage. A business strategy that involves purchasing real estate and building new structures is not easily reversed and is, therefore, riskier than one that involves only a new advertising campaign.

    See the corresponding online video.

[DA13056_3]

Although an organization may have little or no control over the time horizon of a risk, the organization should evaluate and manage this risk just as it would manage other risks over which it has no control, such as weather-related risks. For example, diversification in financial investments can help manage the risks associated with the time horizon of those investments. An insurer that matches the durations of its assets (investments) and liabilities (loss reserves) neutralizes the risks associated with time horizon. When real estate prices are highly volatile, an organization may defer an expansion strategy that involves a long time horizon, such as purchasing or building new facilities. To learn more, see "Understanding Correlation."

Understanding Correlation

Correlation is a measure that should be applied to the management of an organization's overall risk portfolio. If the gains or losses from two or more risks tend to move in the same direction, the two risks are correlated. The greater the correlation, the greater the combined risk. For example, if a bank makes mortgage loans primarily to the employees of a local manufacturer and business loans primarily to that same manufacturer, the bank's loan risks are highly correlated. The failure of the manufacturing business would likely be catastrophic for the bank's entire loan book of business. If a manufacturer contracts with three major suppliers in the same earthquake-prone region in Asia, the manufacturer's supply-chain risks are highly correlated.

 See the corresponding online video.

[DA13056_4]

SUMMARY

A process for managing risk focuses on potential opportunities as well as potential threats. This ongoing process includes scanning the environment, identifying risks, analyzing risks, treating risks, and monitoring and reviewing the process.

Classifying the various types of risk can help organizations manage risk. Some of the most commonly used classifications are pure and speculative risk, subjective and objective risk, and diversifiable and nondiversifiable risk. An organization's risks can also be categorized into quadrants as hazard risk, operational risk, financial risk, and strategic risk.

A properly implemented holistic risk management strategy enables an organization to maintain tolerable uncertainty, drive profitability and growth, ensure legal and regulatory compliance, pursue social responsibility, and reduce the cost of risk and the deterrent effect of hazard risks.

Effective risk management should quantify risks and the results of risk management efforts to the extent possible. The basic measures applied to risk management include exposure, volatility, likelihood, consequences, time horizon, and correlation.

Identifying and Analyzing Costly Risks

3

Educational Objectives	Outline

▶ Evaluate the holistic approach to identifying risks.

▶ Apply each of the following team-oriented techniques to identify an organization's risks:

- Facilitated workshops

- Delphi technique

- Scenario analysis

- HAZOP (hazard and operability study)

- SWOT (strengths, weaknesses, opportunities, and threats) analysis

▶ Apply the risk analysis process.

▶ Apply the following accident analysis techniques:

- Sequence of events (domino theory)

- Energy transfer theory

- Technique of operations review (TOR) approach

- Change analysis

- Job safety analysis

▶ Apply the root cause analysis process.

Identifying and Analyzing Costly Risks

3

HOLISTIC RISK IDENTIFICATION

Businesses have always insured against common hazard risks, such as fire, flood, property damage, employee accidents, and theft. However, organizations are subject to a myriad of risks beyond those hazards that can inflict not only physical damage but also strategic, financial, and operational damage. That's why it's important to understand how to take a more holistic approach to managing risk—and to foster the kind of communication and collaboration needed to make that approach successful.

Traditionally, risk management has been associated with preventing property damage and injuries: Companies install alarms and sprinkler systems to prevent and minimize fire damage. They issue helmets, goggles, and gloves to factory and labor-intensive workers. And in areas where weather is a severe risk, companies construct special buildings or barriers to combat wind, rain, or hail threats.

But the holistic approach to managing risk is much broader in scope, examining all areas of the business, not just hazard risks. It encompasses the analysis and predictability of business processes and organizational decisions. It mandates taking a broader view of all possible results a company may be exposed to, as well as the collaboration of internal and external stakeholders to identify, assess, and treat risks. It's critical that all stakeholders communicate with not only each other but also their supervisors, the organization's risk manager, and the board of directors to ensure that the organization is truly following a holistic risk management approach.

What Do You Know?

True or false: It's important for an organization to insure against common hazard risks, and this approach to risk management should be conducted separately from holistic risk management.

Feedback: False. Traditional risk management practices that focus on common hazard risks are a part of holistic risk management; the two should not be separated. Holistic risk management examines all areas of the business, including hazard risks.

Technological advancements continue to provide risk managers with more sophisticated tools to gather and analyze data and to track and report on the safety and movement of people and products. As a result, organizations can now assess the potential outcomes of a wider scope of business activities. With this greater analysis capability, organizations can minimize business risks and potentially even turn them into financial and reputational gains. After all, while risk is often defined as the possibility of suffering harm or loss, an alternate definition focuses on both the upside and downside of risk, opening up the possibility that the outcome of risk-taking can be positive. Thus, managing risk also involves looking at what might be gained by a certain decision or action. E'

B' Defining Enterprise-Wide Risks

The premise of holistic risk management is that all business decisions and operations carry some risk. With this in mind, organizations look beyond hazard risks to also assess risks from the other three quadrants of risk:

- Strategic risk—Uncertainties associated with the organization's long-term goals and management decisions
- Operational risk—Uncertainties associated with the organization's procedures, systems, and policies
- Financial risk—Uncertainties associated with the organization's financial activities

Today's conception of risk incorporates the idea that taking risks is fundamentally necessary for growth. For example, a software company may create a new product for a new market (a strategic risk). The time, cost, and market uncertainties involved may prove disastrous, or such a risk could generate new revenue and elevate the company to a Fortune 500 or better listing.

As that example implies, strategic decisions may carry a greater risk dynamic, positive or negative, than the other categories. Entertaining a merger with a complementary business, for example, could disrupt employee morale and customer relations, which could eventually drive the bottom line into the red. But on the other hand, the merger might create new revenue streams and a financial windfall. Analyzing the risk variables and potential outcomes can only increase the odds that the result will be positive.

Banks are a good case study for operational risks. They have a lot of inherent operational risks related to compliance issues, legal issues, credit policies, customer service procedures, software tools, and many other facets of their operations. To learn more, see "How They Did It: TruMark Financial."

Analyzing and managing financial risks can be as simple as monitoring cash flow and interest rates or as complex as managing foreign exchange transactions. Financial risks can also involve the cost of raw materials, depreciating equipment, asset investments, loans, revolving lines of credit, and liquidity (of assets).

How They Did It: TruMark Financial

Obviously, there are several risks that are common to a financial institution of our size: cybersecurity, business continuity, succession planning, and talent management. I think virtually every company lists these as key risks.

Customer expectations are also changing at a rapid pace, and we need to position ourselves to be more operationally efficient and innovative—our failure to do so would be a strategic failure. Though we need to consider our small scale, recognizing that we aren't Google, we must still make sure we are structured in a way that takes advantage of some of the technological advancements and new customer experience models.

Kelly Botti (Chief Risk Officer, TruMark Financial), interviewed by Mike Elliott, July 2019, transcript, The Institutes, Malvern, Pa. [DA13148]

Taking a holistic approach to financial risk may uncover inconsistencies in how a company manages loss retention. For example, an organization that is exposed to millions of dollars of risk in foreign exchange markets may find that it retains only $100,000 per loss under its property insurance policy.

Another benefit of effective holistic risk management [→ HRM] is that it can help organizations better absorb losses. For example, through a holistic approach, gains in one area of a large organization can be used to offset losses in another, rather than making each area fend for itself. Therefore, an organization can mitigate the negative effects of risk by analyzing and managing its risks as a whole rather than individually.

[handwritten margin note: HRM helps ~~spread~~ to offset losses in one risk area ~~the~~ by increasing chances of gain in other areas]

Technology's Effect on Holistic Risk Management

Risk management has benefited tremendously from technological advancements, in particular the increasing capabilities to capture, store, and analyze data.

The ever-expanding universe of historical data can empower decision making by uncovering previously imperceptible risk factors. The ways that technology and risk management intersect to achieve this can seem complex, but the basics are simple: vastly more and better data, coupled with newer, sophisticated software tools that analyze, extrapolate, and predict outcomes. This process is often referred to as predictive modeling.

Apply Your Knowledge

Learn more from an expert in the online video.

Think of all of the data that your organization collects and stores. In what ways can your organization benefit from using that data to perform predictive modeling and manage risk?

Feedback: Some of the benefits you listed might include empowering decision making by uncovering risks that are not yet known or predicting potential outcomes of business decisions.

Innovations in risk data collection are largely the result of smart products that sense their environment, process data, and share it instantly (and often wirelessly). The network of such devices is called the Internet of Things (IoT).

IoT devices and their interactions generate much of the data used in advanced analytics and predictive modeling. To learn more, see "IoT Devices in Use."

IoT Devices in Use

Telematics in automobiles
Create a picture of an insured's driving habits by measuring acceleration, speed, braking, and distance traveled

Sensors in buildings
Monitor things such as heat, moisture, noise, and air quality

Drones
Take photos or video of difficult-to-reach areas to assess damage and danger

Smartphones and tablets
Connect with others through voice, text, and video, as well as provide a host of other services, including global positioning system (GPS) tracking

Health trackers
Measure heart rate, steps walked, and sleep patterns

Robots
Assess damage and monitor hazards and environmental conditions

High-definition cameras with sensors
Scan and inspect buildings, bridges, and other structures for signs of erosion and other risks

[DA13008]

Cloud computing enables organizations to store and share all this data through wireless internet and networking services. But because of the risk of cyberthreats, the data needs to be trusted and protected—that's where blockchain technology comes into play. Blockchain technology is a giant leap forward in digital record keeping. It's a decentralized data-storage technology and real-time ledger that contains a secure history of transactions. It facilitates secure transactions without the need for a third party.

Thanks to their security, blockchains can eliminate the need to verify the accuracy of risk management data. As a result, instead of spending time trying to double-check past data, risk managers can spend more time on forward-looking functions, such as predictive analysis or forecasting.

The bottom line is that risk managers need to embrace these technical and often complex issues. The future of holistic risk management will be fueled by the capture, storage, and analysis of data.

Measuring Risk Variables

The interactions between risk factors have a significant impact on risk management decision making. To assess these interactions, risk managers use statistical and mathematical measurements such as variance, covariance, and correlation. Variance and covariance, despite the similar names, are actually quite different. Covariance refers to the measure of how two random risk variables will change in relation to each other, and it's used to calculate the correlation (linear relationship) between the variables. Variance refers to the spread of the data set—or how far apart the numbers are in relation to the mean (average). These statistical measures are particularly useful when calculating the probability of future events or performance.

Analyzing how one risk factor affects (or does not affect) another is particularly valuable in risk assessment. For example, correlation and covariance are useful for selecting sources of risk for a financial portfolio. The terms convey the direction and strength of the association between two variables, such as two types of investments.

A positive covariance indicates that both variables (such as the returns on two investments) tend to move upward or downward at the same time. An inverse, or negative, covariance means that they move counter to each other (one rises while the other falls). The typical relationship between interest rates and bond values is an example. When interest rates rise, bond values decrease (and vice versa). Purchasing one investment that has a negative covariance with another can be a way to balance or minimize risk in a portfolio.

Risk professionals measure correlation and covariance for several purposes:

- Identify and quantify relationships among various sources of risk
- Communicate the degree of uncertainty in a risk portfolio
- Prioritize investments in loss control

- Optimize financing for multiple sources of risk
- Evaluate the effectiveness of a risk management program

Another approach to solving complex problems and predicting outcomes is the Monte Carlo simulation. It's a statistical computer model that simulates the effects that various types of uncertainty may have on a process. Its name comes from the famous gambling destination in Monaco and reflects the role that chance plays in this modeling technique.

In a Monte Carlo simulation, a computer randomly selects values for each variable and generates thousands of possible scenarios. The results are assembled into probability distributions representing possible outcomes.

This statistical evaluation may be able to uncover the effectiveness of the risk management program itself. By comparing cost variables between operations and financial risk assessments, a risk manager may be able to pinpoint strengths or weaknesses in risk evaluation processes. That may be a much more complex undertaking, but it can be a worthwhile exercise.

RISK IDENTIFICATION AS A TEAM

Incorporating individuals from multiple areas of an organization into the risk identification process can bring more risks to light as well as reveal how those risks are interconnected. So knowing how to use various team-oriented techniques to identify risks is extremely valuable.

Effective team approaches to identifying risks include facilitated workshops, the Delphi technique, scenario analysis, HAZOP (hazard and operability study), and SWOT (strengths, weaknesses, opportunities, and threats). Each technique should be chosen and customized based on the specific project, process, and operation.

What Do You Know?

Identify reasons it's important to take a team-oriented approach to identifying risks.

Feedback: Taking a team-oriented approach to identifying risks can provide diverse perspectives on risks. Plus, when individuals from multiple teams or departments are included in the process, it can also reveal how risks are connected across the organization, reducing the likelihood that risks from those areas will be overlooked.

Facilitated Workshops

In a facilitated workshop, a neutral party (the facilitator), who has no stake in the outcome or participation responsibilities, administers the risk workshop and propels the group to achieve its goal.

When risk management professionals meet with an organization's leaders, key employees, and other stakeholders in a facilitated workshop, the group discussion can help identify risks in a dynamic way. The facilitator should initiate a discussion or brainstorming session that allows ideas to flow freely from participants. He or she can then design workshops to encourage follow-up discussion and further brainstorming.

It's wise to include representatives from diverse groups in the organization during these workshops because discussion of the interconnectedness and cascading effects of risks provides valuable information on risk levels and priorities. The discussion can identify both opportunities and downsides arising from risks. The facilitated workshop technique can be used for a specific project or process, as well as to identify those risks that affect overall organizational objectives.

If facilitated workshops are used to identify all organizational risks, the facilitator must be skilled in risk identification and management as well as group communication and be prepared for a long-term project. If the facilitator is a consultant, he or she can meet with the team at defined intervals after the team has worked independently on identifying the risks in each of the risk quadrants.

Delphi Technique

The Delphi technique—which is named after the myth of the all-knowing Oracle at Delphi—uses the opinions of a select group of experts to identify risks. Typically, these experts don't meet but respond to a survey or inquiry instead.

The standard Delphi technique involves submitting two rounds of queries to the selected experts. First, each expert responds to a question, and the combined answers, which remain anonymous, are presented to the group. The same question is then posed again to the experts, who are instructed to consider revising their responses based on the results that were reported to the group. This question-and-response cycle continues for a predetermined number of rounds or until a consensus is reached.

The Delphi technique was originally used to forecast new developments, such as innovations in technology. Now it's used for a wide range of projects and processes.

There are a few benefits to using this technique. For starters, it's typically cost-effective because it doesn't require the resources necessary to assemble a facilitated workshop of experts. In addition, by keeping responses anonymous, it can eliminate group bias, as well as encourage participants to give their honest opinions without fear of repercussions.

However, one disadvantage is that the experts' opinions may be limited to their current thinking on a subject. In other words, unless prompted, the experts may fail to render a more forward-thinking opinion. For example, if an organization is considering a new product or project, the current expert opinion may not be as useful as the opinion of a group of potential (or future) product users or the community that proposed the idea.

Scenario Analysis

Scenario analysis identifies risks and predicts the potential consequences of those specific risks.

For example, windstorm is identified as a risk. The outcomes associated with wind damage and the flooding that often accompanies windstorms aren't limited to the hazard risks of property damage and bodily injury. They also include business interruption, disruptions in customer relations, and possibly reputational risk based on how an organization responds during and after a flood. For example, in the months following Hurricane Harvey, which triggered massive flooding in the Houston metropolitan area, businesses had to cope with property damage, power loss, and long-term business interruption.

A scenario analysis can help identify a range of potential consequences and prioritize risks. An organization should assemble an internal cross-functional team to gain a multidimensional view of a risk's potential consequences.

For example, an operations manager at a manufacturing facility in Houston may be primarily concerned with damage to a facility and employee safety in the event of a flood. A member of the legal team may be concerned with liability if chemicals stored at the facility leak into floodwaters. A financial representative may be concerned about the effect on the prices of raw materials if supply chain disruptions ensue. The benefit of a scenario analysis is that it brings all of these concerns together, so they can be addressed as a whole.

However, a potential disadvantage is that the risk identification process may be limited by the imagination and brainstorming capabilities of the team selected. This could lead to overlooking key risks or consequences of risks. Inviting cross-functional teams into the process can reduce the chances of this, but it won't eliminate it, especially if members of the analysis team have never experienced a particular risk.

HAZOP

The term HAZOP is derived from hazard and operability study, which is a comprehensive review of a process or system. A team of subject matter experts and stakeholders identifies the risks associated with a given process and recommends a solution.

HAZOP is primarily used to design complex, scientific systems such as those used in engineering, chemical, mechanical, electronic, and computer operations. But it can be adapted to analyze certain organizational strategies and initiatives. To learn more, see "Steps in the HAZOP Process."

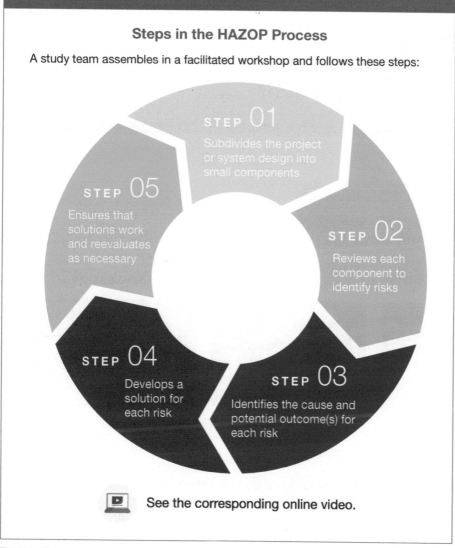

Steps in the HAZOP Process

A study team assembles in a facilitated workshop and follows these steps:

STEP 01 — Subdivides the project or system design into small components

STEP 02 — Reviews each component to identify risks

STEP 03 — Identifies the cause and potential outcome(s) for each risk

STEP 04 — Develops a solution for each risk

STEP 05 — Ensures that solutions work and reevaluates as necessary

See the corresponding online video.

[DA13015]

Because this process is comprehensive and involves experts on the subject at hand, it's ideal for projects and systems where virtually all risks must be eliminated.

SWOT Analysis

SWOT is an acronym for strengths, weaknesses, opportunities, and threats. This is a team approach that's useful in analyzing a new project or product. The strengths and weaknesses are internal environmental factors to be considered. The opportunities and threats are external environmental factors.

Different team members, representing different organizational functions, may analyze specific quadrants. For example, the Marketing and Legal departments may analyze the opportunities and threats. The Research, Operations, and Financial departments may analyze the internal strengths and weaknesses. To learn more, see "SWOT Analysis."

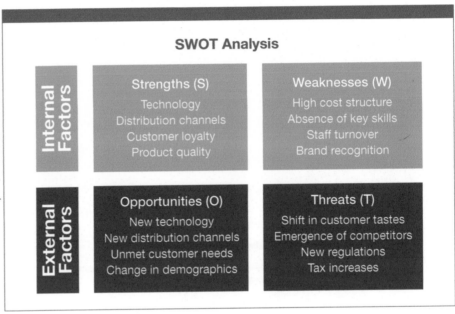

[DA08766]

A SWOT analysis is useful when there is a specific goal, such as determining whether engaging in a new product or project is feasible. It's less useful for analyzing current processes and procedures to identify risks unless there is a specific objective, such as whether a procedure conforms to new regulations or customer specifications. A goal is necessary to keep the SWOT analysis from becoming too general or failing to provide actionable information.

A SWOT analysis ideally concludes with a "go" or "no go" recommendation for a specific project that notes whether weaknesses or threats can be converted into strengths or opportunities. For example, say Widget Warehouse is planning to launch a new product. But one month before the launch, a competitor launches a similar product (a threat). Using the SWOT analysis, Widget Warehouse should consider whether its new product is different enough to distinguish Widget Warehouse from the competitor and gain market share and/or a better reputational standing with consumers (opportunities). To learn more, see "Performing a SWOT Analysis."

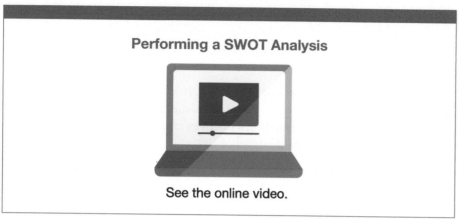

Performing a SWOT Analysis

See the online video.

[DA03626_2]

Apply Your Knowledge

Delmar AeroFab Inc. is designing a part for a commercial aircraft that cannot have any defects. Which of these team-oriented approaches to risk identification should it adopt?

→ *comprehensive & exhaustive risk elimination is characteristic of HAZOP*

a. Facilitated workshops
b. Delphi technique
c. HAZOP
d. SWOT

Feedback: *c.* The company should adopt the HAZOP approach. Because this process is comprehensive and involves experts on the subject at hand, it's ideal for projects and systems where virtually all risks must be eliminated.

INTRODUCTION TO RISK ANALYSIS

Before getting involved with risk control or prevention, an individual or organization needs to understand what risks it actually faces. This is where risk analysis, enhanced by enterprise-wide communication among internal stakeholders and decision makers, comes into play.

In order to properly handle a particular risk, an organization has to understand its source, possible consequences, and likelihood. It doesn't do any good knowing that your home could suffer water damage without also knowing where the water could come from, how likely it is to happen, and how to prevent it. Communicating and collaborating with experts, whether internal or external, helps provide a strong basis of knowledge when it comes to determining the possible frequency and severity of risks being faced.

What Do You Know?

Risk analyses are generally either qualitative or quantitative. How would you explain the difference between the two?

Feedback : Qualitative assessment measures a risk by the significance of consequences; it may use such ratings as high, medium, and low. Quantitative analysis assigns specific values to consequences and their probabilities to reach a numeric indication of the level of risk.

The Nature of Risk Analysis

As part of its overall approach to risk analysis, an organization might analyze the risk related to a potential event, product line, project, or process. After identifying a risk, the organization would note the range of possible consequences and determine the probability of each. The consequences of those risks relate to how each one might affect, positively or negatively, the ability of the organization to accomplish its objectives.

An identified consequence may be so unlikely or insignificant that it requires little or no further assessment. In contrast, a single event may trigger multiple far-reaching consequences that could affect many organizational objectives. For more complex consequences, several methods of analysis may be required to determine the level of risk involved.

Some risk analyses focus on the consequences of a specific event, such as a hurricane or power failure. Others may focus on a process (such as manufacturing) or a system (such as automated inventory tracking) and examine the risks associated with each step of the process or each component of the system.

Qualitative and Quantitative Analysis

Depending on the type of risk, the data available, and the organization's needs, a risk assessment may be qualitative, quantitative, or a combination of the two.

Qualitative analysis measures a risk by the significance of consequences; it may use such ratings as high, medium, and low. A clear, written explanation of the agreed-upon bases for each qualitative determination should be included in any qualitative assessment.

Quantitative analysis assigns specific values to consequences and their probabilities to reach a numeric indication of the level of risk. This approach may not be feasible, or even useful, for every risk if the organization lacks historical data or because of other uncertainties related to the risks being analyzed. In such cases, an organization may choose to incorporate some qualitative analysis into the process, too.

Both qualitative and quantitative approaches may include estimates of probability to assess risk. Probabilities are usually based on historical data relating to occurrences arising from the same types of risk as those being analyzed. If such occurrences have been infrequent or if historical data is otherwise lacking, the resulting probability estimates will probably be uncertain. In such cases, an organization may base probability estimations on predictions or expert opinions. Several structured processes have been developed to incorporate expert opinions into probability estimations involving risk. Predictive techniques, such as decision tree analysis and event tree analysis, assign numerical values to various components related to a risk and combine them to produce a probability estimate.

What Do You Know?

Qualitative and quantitative analyses both have their upsides and downsides when it comes to assessing risk. Having reviewed some of the benefits of each, what do you think some of the drawbacks are?

Feedback: While qualitative analyses provide a good basis for quickly determining whether a particular risk poses a low-level or high-level threat, they don't provide much help in determining exactly what costs those threats might entail. What one person considers a high-level threat might be a low-level threat in someone else's opinion.

Assessing Controls

To accurately determine its level of risk, an organization must examine the effectiveness of its current **risk control** measures. Every current technique designed to prevent or control a specific risk should be identified. The organization should verify whether each technique is capable of achieving the intended level of treatment or control and whether its effectiveness can be demonstrated when required. Verification depends on the existence of records and documentation of the control's performance in relation to the risk.

Control assessment can be quantitative, qualitative, or both. Although such information need not be detailed, it is useful in helping an organization decide whether to retain a control, improve it, or replace it with a different control method.

Risk control

A conscious act or decision not to act that reduces the frequency and/or severity of losses or makes losses more predictable.

TRADITIONAL ACCIDENT ANALYSIS

Accidents happen. There's no way to avoid that, unfortunately. But one marginal benefit they offer is in providing an opportunity to examine why they happened and, through that, perhaps the ability to learn how to avoid a repeat occurrence in the future.

Often, an accident investigation focuses on either an unsafe act or an unsafe condition, but the causes of an accident can be much more complicated than that, and multiple factors could be involved. It is up to risk management professionals to look past the surface of an accident to find its root cause and to prevent repeat occurrences in the future.

What Do You Know?

While there can be an unlimited number of specific causes of accidents, they can generally be sorted into three basic categories. What do you think those categories of accident causes are?

Feedback: The three basic categories of accident causes are poor management, safety policy, and personal or environmental factors.

There are five theories or approaches to understanding accident causation, relating to elements that are direct, indirect, and basic:

- Sequence of events (domino theory)
- Energy transfer theory
- Technique of operations review (TOR) approach
- Change analysis
- Job safety analysis

β'

Sequence of Events (Domino Theory)

The sequence of events theory proposes that these five accident factors can form a chain of events that, like dominos, lead in succession to the resulting accident and injury:

1. Ancestry and social environment, such as inherited psychological disorders and dysfunctional social environments

2. Fault of person, such as impulsiveness, violent temper, nervousness, or a refusal to adapt to safe practices

3. An unsafe act and/or a mechanical or physical hazard, such as improper use of machines or equipment, or poor maintenance of surroundings, such as slippery floors or faulty railings

4. The accident itself

5. The resulting injury

Because each of the earlier links of the domino theory leads directly to the next, removing any of the four factors that occur before the injury should, in theory, prevent the resulting injury from occurring. Removal of the third domino, the unsafe act and/or mechanical or physical hazard, is usually the best way to break the accident sequence and prevent injury or illness.

Considering its emphasis on human fault, the domino theory is most applicable to situations within human control. This theory, therefore, has limited applicability to accidents caused by natural disasters. Although people can attempt to protect themselves and their property from a natural disaster such as a hurricane, preventing the cause of the accident is not within their control. However, the domino theory is well-suited to accidents caused by human carelessness.

Energy Transfer Theory

The **energy transfer theory** posits that the basic cause of accidents is energy out of control. Its approach to preventing accidents or reducing the resulting damage focuses on controlling released energy and/or reducing the harm caused by that energy. The basic strategies of the energy transfer theory deal with maintaining safe distances between objects that may move at great speed, such as separating pedestrians and motor vehicles, and ensuring that objects that have the potential to move at great speeds also have the ability to slow themselves down or stop themselves completely, such as equipping elevators with emergency brakes or installing physical barriers within buildings to prevent the spread of fires or floods. To learn more, see "Ten Basic Strategies of Energy Transfer."

E'

→ what a bunch of bull! So, #2, that is, the fault of the person, is fundamentally a disorder or a result of your environment (#1, no sin, no inherent wickedness ⇒ either a disorder, or society's fault.

↳ how can you be culpable for violence, if a violent temper is fundamentally a product of your environment or a disorder? You can't help where you are raised, or how your body is dysfunctional.

Energy transfer theory

An approach to accident causation that views accidents as energy that is released and that affects objects, including living things, in amounts or at rates that the objects cannot tolerate.

Ten Basic Strategies of Energy Transfer

1. Prevent the marshaling of the energy by eliminating the production of high-powered vehicles

2. Reduce the amount of energy marshaled by limiting the speed of vehicles

3. Prevent the release of built-up energy by keeping elevators from falling or reckless drivers from having access to automobiles

4. Modify the rate or spatial distribution of the release of energy by reducing the slope of ski trails or installing explosion-relieving walls

5. Separate, in space or in time, the energy being released from a susceptible structure by establishing separate lanes for pedestrian and vehicular traffic or by controlling the time interval between landings and takeoffs at airports

6. Interpose a physical barrier between the energy and the susceptible structure by requiring fire doors in public buildings or requiring workers to wear protective clothing

7. Modify the contact surface or basic structure that can be affected by installing breakaway highway light poles or by requiring front and side airbags in automobiles to cushion occupants' impact

8. Strengthen the susceptible structure that might be damaged by the energy by requiring special building construction in earthquake zones or building codes that require hand rails on stairwells to be able to withstand the weight of multiple users at once

9. Move rapidly to detect and evaluate damage and to counter its continuation or spread by giving first aid or protecting property in imminent danger of fire

10. Take long-term action (after the emergency period) to reduce further damage by rehabilitating injured persons or salvaging damaged property

---

William Haddon Jr., MD, "On the Escape of Tigers," American Journal of Public Health and the Nation's Health, December 1970, pp. 2229–2234. [DA13007]

Technique of Operations Review (TOR) Approach

Technique of operations review (TOR)

An approach to accident causation that views the cause of accidents to be a result of management's shortcomings.

Another approach to accident causation is the **technique of operations review (TOR)**, which focuses on preventing accidents caused by ineffective management. TOR establishes five basic principles of risk control:

- An unsafe act, an unsafe condition, and an accident are all symptoms of something wrong in the management system.

- Certain circumstances, unless identified and controlled, may produce severe injuries.

- Safety should be managed like any other organizational function, with management setting achievable goals and planning, organizing, leading, and controlling to achieve them.

- Management must specify procedures for accountability if safety efforts are to be effective.

- The function of safety is to locate and define the operational errors that allow accidents to occur.

TOR tries to identify particular faults of an organization's management and groups these faults into categories such as inadequate coaching, failure to take responsibility, unclear authority, and inadequate supervision, among others. It also helps identify accident causes and suggests corrective actions. Managers must then recognize their own (or their colleagues' or subordinates') faults and correct them, which may help eliminate most, if not all, accidents.

Learn more from an expert in the online video.

Change Analysis

As opposed to the other techniques, which review accidents that occurred in an effort to discover their causes, **change analysis** asks a series of what-if questions regarding a possible change in process that has yet to occur. It then projects the consequences for the changes and for all feasible combinations of changes to reveal the risks that could arise because of the changes that went into effect. For example, suppose an automobile manufacturer is considering using hybrid gas and electric engines instead of gas-powered engines for its automobiles. Risk management professionals can ask how the change will affect the safety of the drivers, the employees assembling the automobiles, the operators of service stations, and perhaps the general public.

As another illustration, risk management professionals may join the human resources department in asking, "If the company changes to a flextime arrangement that allows employees to have a workweek consisting of four ten-hour days, how will this change affect the frequency or severity of automobile or train accidents that our employees suffer while commuting?"

Change analysis can also apply to various combinations of changes in systems. To illustrate, the automobile manufacturer considering the hybrid gas and electric engine option may recognize that an automobile's safe performance depends partially on the automobile's weight. Change analysis can evaluate the safety implications of switching from gasoline to hybrid engines, changing the weight of the vehicles, and using various combinations of weight changes and hybrid engine options. This analysis may reveal that a particular combination of engine options and weight changes is safer than any engine option or weight change alone.

Change analysis

An analysis that projects the effects a given system change is likely to have on an existing system.

Job Safety Analysis

Job safety analysis (JSA)

An analysis that dissects a repetitive task, whether performed by a person or machine, to determine potential hazards if each action is not performed.

Job safety analysis (JSA) is one of the most universally applicable and versatile techniques for analyzing the cause of accidents. Each job (activity or operation) is broken down into individual sequential steps. Hazards associated with each step are identified, controls are defined, and responsibility for implementing each step is assigned (provided that the added benefit of the safety procedure outweighs its costs). JSA applies best to repetitive human tasks performed in an environment sufficiently stable to allow most hazards to be foreseen, such as for positions along an assembly line or in an office where employees spend a majority of their day working at their desks. Repetitive tasks and person/machine systems are so common that JSA is applicable in almost every case in which a person must act safely to avoid causing bodily injury or property damage.

ROOT CAUSE ANALYSIS

Accidents are often the result of a series of events or decisions, but many of these can go unrecognized, hidden behind the convenience of declaring that the most obvious event or decision in the process is the sole cause. Root cause analysis (RCA) is a process that enables the risk management professional to dig past the obvious causes of an accident to find other factors that played a role.

By addressing the factors at the beginning of a chain of events that led to an accident, it may be possible to limit the chances that a similar accident will occur in the future. For example, if a customer at a restaurant slips on a puddle of water that had gathered in the middle of the floor, it's easy enough to say that the staff needs to be more aware of such things in the future. But what factors led to the puddle's formation? Why didn't anyone notice the puddle before the accident occurred? By using RCA to find the answers to these questions, the restaurant can stop such a chain of events before it even begins and prevent an accident from occurring.

What Do You Know?

Focusing on the example of the customer who slipped on a puddle in the restaurant, what do you think some of the possible root causes of the accident might be?

Feedback: Using RCA to examine why the water had puddled on the floor in the first place, a risk professional might find that an employee failed to follow procedures that called for mopping floors only before and after business hours or that the employee was improperly trained on how to properly remove all the water. It could also be possible that the waitstaff in the area was given too much work to be able to report maintenance issues like the water or that water pitchers are overfilled by practice, which causes water to regularly spill from them as they're carried. Identifying these possible causes and taking appropriate action would prevent issues such as the water puddle earlier in the process, rather than relying on staff to notice the hazard sooner.

The Nature of Root Cause Analysis

Root causes have four basic characteristics:

- A root cause is expressed as a specific underlying cause, not a generalization. For example, identifying operator error or equipment failure as a root cause of an event is not sufficient because management cannot address such vague causes. The root cause of such an event should be expressed as something specific, such as "operator removed machine guard."

- A root cause can be reasonably identified. In the machine-guard example, it would be necessary to know why the operator removed the machine guard. Was it because the guard was not working properly? Did the supervisor demand faster production, and the guard hampered that? Did the employee want to get the work done faster so that he or she could leave work early?

- A root cause must be expressed as something that can be modified. For example, weather conditions could not be considered root causes because such events are beyond human control. If an employee was injured because a lightning strike caused a power failure, the lightning strike could not be considered a root cause because management cannot control the weather. However, the root cause could be the absence of a backup generator.

- A root cause is something that can be prevented through effective recommendations. Identifying and mitigating the actions, inactions, conditions, or behaviors that caused a harmful event can prevent reoccurrence of the event. By addressing the root cause of a problem, risk managers can help prevent future incidents.

Harmful events generally are associated with one of three basic causes of loss: physical, human, or organizational. A physical cause is a failure of a tangible or material item, such as damage to a vital part on a manufacturer's production line. When human error or inaction lies at the root of an accident, it is considered to be a human cause of loss (for example, the maintenance department did not perform the proper maintenance on the manufacturer's production line). Organizational causes of loss stem from faulty systems, processes, or policies (such as procedures that do not make it clear which maintenance employee is responsible for checking and maintaining the manufacturer's production line). To learn more, see "Root Cause Analysis Approaches."

Root Cause Analysis Approaches

Root cause analysis (RCA) encompasses a variety of tools, philosophies, and processes. There are several broadly defined RCA approaches, identified according to their basic approach or field of origin:

- Safety-based RCA originated from accident analysis and occupational safety and health.

- Production-based RCA evolved from quality control procedures for industrial manufacturing.

- Process-based RCA is similar to production-based RCA, but it also includes business processes.

- Failure-based RCA stems from failure analysis and is used primarily in engineering and maintenance.

- Systems-based RCA combines these four approaches with change management, risk management, and systems analysis concepts.

[DA08696]

Steps in the Root Cause Analysis Process

The RCA process is a systematic way to determine root cause.

The first step is to collect data. Root causes associated with an event cannot be identified without complete information about the surrounding circumstances, facts, and causes.

Causal factors

The agents that directly result in one event causing another.

The second step in the process is to chart **causal factors**. This provides the structure to organize and analyze the data gathered during the investigation. It also helps identify gaps and deficiencies in knowledge as the investigation progresses. Usually, the most readily apparent causal factor is given the most attention during the charting process, but more than one causal factor can be associated with an event. Take an employee who is injured on a manufacturer's production line: Was the injury caused by lax maintenance, a missing machine guard, inadequate training, or all of these?

Step three of the RCA process is to identify the root cause. Mapping or flowcharting can help determine the underlying reason(s) for each causal factor identified in the previous step. For example, if equipment difficulty is identified as a causal factor, the map or flowchart is used to identify whether the difficulty was caused by equipment design, reliability, installation, misuse, or some other cause (in which case additional flowcharts can be used until the causal factor is determined).

The fourth step of the RCA process is to determine and implement recommendations. After a root cause has been identified, attainable recommendations for preventing its recurrence are generated. Implementing these attainable recommendations will ensure that the effort necessary to perform the RCA process has not been wasted and will help prevent the event(s) that caused the RCA to be performed from occurring again.

RCA is typically used after an event has occurred, but it also can be used to predict events that could harm the organization. By using RCA in this fashion, organizations can learn to solve problems before they become major events, rather than just reacting to them as they occur.

Root Cause Analysis Example

George drives a delivery truck for New Space Furniture. New Space hired George recently, but he previously worked in the same role for another furniture store. While making a delivery one rainy afternoon, he approached a yellow traffic light. He applied the truck's brakes, but according to George's statement, they failed to "catch." His truck slid through the intersection after the light turned red and struck another vehicle. The delivery truck sustained a dented front fender and a flat tire. The other vehicle was declared a total loss by the driver's insurance company. Both drivers were uninjured. The risk manager for New Space must now determine all causal factors and root causes associated with George's accident.

The first step is to collect data by taking statements from George, the other driver, witnesses, and first responders who investigated the accident scene to determine road conditions. The delivery truck brakes were examined by a mechanic to determine whether they were functioning properly.

The next step is to chart the causal factors. By starting with what is known to be true, investigators can work backwards to determine the causal factors. To learn more, see "Causal Factor (CF) Charting."

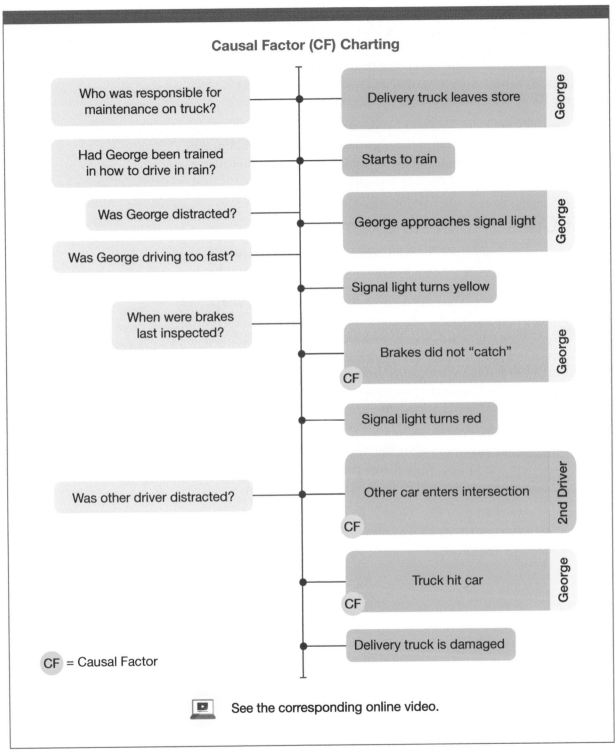

Causal Factor (CF) Charting

- Who was responsible for maintenance on truck? — Delivery truck leaves store (George)
- Had George been trained in how to drive in rain? — Starts to rain
- Was George distracted? / Was George driving too fast? — George approaches signal light (George)
- Signal light turns yellow
- When were brakes last inspected? — Brakes did not "catch" (CF) (George)
- Signal light turns red
- Was other driver distracted? — Other car enters intersection (CF) (2nd Driver)
- Truck hit car (CF) (George)
- Delivery truck is damaged

CF = Causal Factor

See the corresponding online video.

[DA08693]

After identifying all causal factors, the root causes are investigated. Each causal factor is inserted into a root cause map to determine its root cause. To learn more, see "Root Cause Mapping."

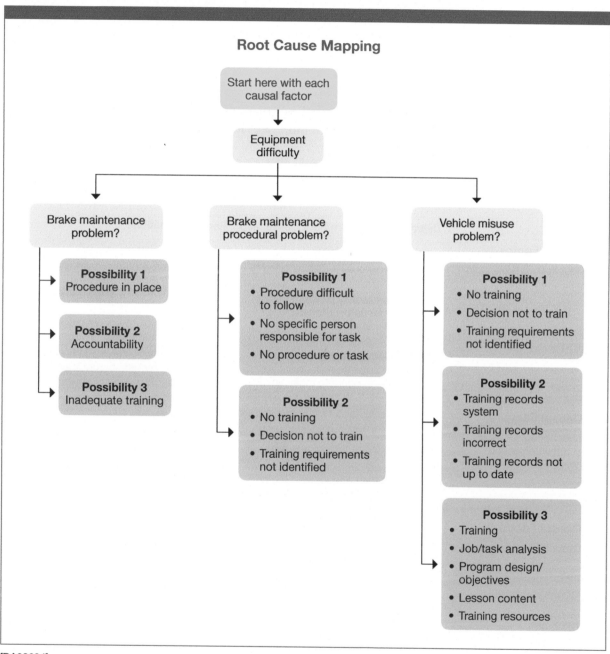

[DA08694]

Apply Your Knowledge

The fourth step in the RCA process would be to develop recommendations that management can implement to prevent an accident like George's from recurring. Using the three factors identified in the causal factor charting and the determinations made for each one in the root cause mapping, come up with some recommendations on how management can help prevent future accidents.

Feedback: The root cause summary table contains examples of recommendations that could be made, but there could be others that have not been included as well. To learn more, see "Root Cause Summary Table."

Root Cause Summary Table

	Determinations From Root Cause Map	Recommendations
Causal Factor 1		
Description: Brakes did not "catch"	Equipment difficulty—Brakes failed to engage.	Reexamine preventative maintenance procedure to replace brake pads, drums, and fluid on predetermined basis.
	Equipment reliability program design less than adequate—Procedure to inspect/maintain brakes was not adequate.	Assign personnel to ensure proper maintenance completed.
	Active implementation less than adequate—Supervisor did not implement procedure to maintain brakes.	Implement policy—Drivers to review maintenance records before leaving facility.
Causal Factor 2		
Description: Other car enters intersection	Personnel difficulty—George was drinking coffee at time of accident.	Implement policy prohibiting eating/drinking while driving.
	Standards, policies, or administrative control less than adequate—George had not been trained in defensive driving.	Develop/implement driver training policy that covers defensive driving.
Causal Factor 3		
Description: Truck hit car	Personnel difficulty—George was not able to avoid hitting other car.	Consider alternative strategy for delivering merchandise.
	Administrative/management systems—All product is delivered on company vehicles.	Implement accident policy covering whom to contact.
	Standards, policies, or administrative controls less than adequate—Inadequate hiring/training practices in place for drivers.	

[DA08695]

SUMMARY

Organizations are subject to a myriad of risks beyond traditional insurable hazards like fire, flood, and property damage. So it's important to adopt a more holistic approach to managing strategic, operational, and financial risk. This holistic approach will be fueled by the capture, storage, and analysis of data and incorporates advanced mathematical measurements and techniques.

Adopting a team approach to identify risks can help organizations uncover risks that wouldn't necessarily be apparent to an individual. It can also provide diverse perspectives on risks, as well as reveal how risks are interconnected. Effective team approaches include facilitated workshops, the Delphi technique, scenario analysis, HAZOP, and SWOT. The best approach varies depending on the circumstances and goals of the organization.

Organizations use risk analysis to determine their levels of risk and how best to treat identified risks. A risk analysis can include qualitative assessment, quantitative analysis, or a combination of those methods. As part of risk analysis, various approaches can be used to determine the probabilities of assorted consequences of a risk. To accurately determine its level of risk, an organization must examine the effectiveness of its current risk control measures.

The choice of a specific accident analysis technique depends, in part, on the assumptions made about how accidents are caused, prevented, or made less severe. Because different sets of assumptions imply different causes (some primarily unsafe human acts and others unsafe conditions), differing theories of accident causation suggest distinct ways of removing those accident causes.

The root cause analysis process involves four steps:

1. Collect data
2. Chart causal factors
3. Identify root causes
4. Determine and implement recommendations

Leveraging Tech and Insurance

4

Leveraging Tech and Insurance

4

RISK TREATMENT FUNDAMENTALS

Identifying and analyzing risks are critical parts of an organization's holistic risk management strategy. But they are exactly that—parts of a larger strategy. In the grand scheme of things, they can mean little if effective means for managing and treating those risks aren't then selected, communicated, and implemented.

Imagine for a moment that your physician diagnoses you with an illness and tells you that it could lead to significant health complications or even death if left untreated. Knowing this is really of little value to your physical health unless that knowledge leads to an effective treatment plan. Or, let's say that you start making and selling products out of your home and discover that demand for your goods is far greater than you ever thought possible. This information really only benefits you if it leads to a plan to increase production to fulfill this unexpected demand.

The same can be said for organizational risk. Knowing what risks (positive or negative) your organization faces and the outcomes they can lead to will not help your organization if it doesn't take a proper course of treatment. When properly selected, communicated throughout the organization, and implemented, risk treatment can mitigate the effects of negative risks or maximize the positive outcomes of opportunities. The key is first selecting the overall risk treatment technique that's appropriate for a specific risk and then developing a plan to ensure that it's carried out properly.

Risk management professionals can help executives and managers make decisions that propel an organization to achieve its strategic goals by explaining the risk treatment process and helping to apply it throughout different areas of the organization. The ability to suggest appropriate risk treatment techniques for various types of risks and to explain why one treatment or a combination of treatments may be most effective can be especially valuable to decision makers—as can monitoring the environment for changes that might prompt the need to reevaluate risks and risk treatments.

Risk assessment involves identifying and analyzing risks. **Risk treatment** involves making decisions based on the results of a risk assessment. It may help to think of risk treatment as risk-response planning. For each risk identified as needing treatment, the goal is to select one or multiple treatment options that best help the organization achieve its strategic objectives.

Risk treatment is a continual process that entails examining each risk treatment option in terms of whether it leads to a tolerable level of **residual risk**

Risk treatment

The selection and implementation of actions to help manage or mitigate a risk.

Residual risk

The level of risk remaining after actions are taken to alter the level of risk.

or helps the organization maximize the potential benefits of an opportunity. It also involves selecting, communicating, and implementing risk treatment options and measuring the effectiveness of each treatment.

Treatment techniques aren't mutually exclusive. In fact, many risks call for a combination of techniques. Appropriate treatments will often vary from risk to risk, and the cost of each treatment option should be weighed against its potential benefits.

What Do You Know?

Can you identify the five most common techniques risk management professionals use to treat risks?

Feedback: Generally, risk treatment techniques fall under the categories of avoidance, modification, transfer, retention, or (for opportunities) exploitation. This discussion will explore these techniques and when to use each.

Avoidance
Modification
Transfer
Retention
Exploitation (for opportunities)

Successful risk management depends on effective communication: Risk professionals need to inform decision makers and stakeholders of not only the overall strategy but also the steps needed to implement it and how its success can be measured. After selecting a treatment technique or combination of techniques, risk management professionals must create a risk management plan that indicates the proposed actions, priorities, resource requirements, responsible parties, and monitoring requirements. It's also important to continually review risk treatment plans as part of the overall risk management process because risks change as an organization's operations change in response to economic, legal, regulatory, and technological factors.

Risk Treatment Techniques

Risk treatment techniques apply to hazard, operational, financial, and strategic risks. In general, these techniques fall into five categories. To learn more, see "Risk Treatment Techniques."

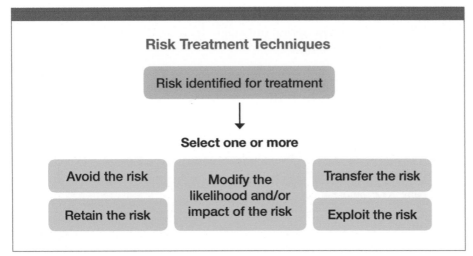

[DA08744]

For each risk identified as needing treatment, risk management professionals can choose to take one or more of these actions:

- Avoid the risk—Stopping or canceling the activity that would cause the risk. An organization may exercise risk **avoidance** if a risk is deemed too high to take on in any form or amount.

- Modify the risk—Increasing or decreasing an event's likelihood and/or consequences that will result in positive or negative outcomes. For example, for hazard risks, **loss prevention** actions (such as installing theft-prevention systems) are taken to reduce overall loss frequency. And **loss reduction** actions (such as installing sprinkler systems to reduce the severity of fires) are taken to reduce the impact of risks.

- Transfer the risk—Sharing the risk with, or moving it entirely to, another party. Purchasing insurance is a prime example of **risk transfer**. Risk can also be transferred by outsourcing a process to a contractor, who then takes on the risks associated with that process.

- Retain the risk—Accepting and absorbing some or all of the consequences of the risk. Risk **retention** is often used only after other treatment techniques have been considered, and it's often used in conjunction with other techniques such as risk modification and risk transfer. Typically, retention is used when the potential negative consequences associated with it are low. In addition, any risk that is retained should be carefully analyzed so that the organization fully understands the extent of that risk. Organizations can also choose to retain more risk in order to exploit an opportunity.

- Exploit the risk—Taking actions to maximize the expected gains of opportunities. For example, an organization could modify the likelihood of an event to increase the opportunity for financial gains. It could also share the opportunity with another party that may be able to contribute additional resources, which could increase the likelihood of generating more business. However, actions to exploit risks can create more risks, which must then be identified, analyzed, and possibly treated.

Avoidance

A risk control technique that involves ceasing or never undertaking an activity so that the possibility of a future loss occurring from that activity is eliminated.

Loss prevention

A risk control technique that reduces the frequency of a particular loss.

Loss reduction

A risk control technique that reduces the severity of a particular loss.

Risk transfer

The shifting of risk from one individual or organization to another.

Retention

A risk financing technique that involves assumption of risk in which gains and losses are retained within the organization.

Treatment selection should also include a cost-benefit analysis to ensure that the benefits of a treatment option outweigh the related costs. To learn more, see "Risk Treatment in Action."

Risk Treatment in Action

Let's take a look at an organization's strategic goal, an action being considered that could help the organization achieve that goal, some of the risks that action would create, and how the organization could apply the risk treatment techniques to address those risks.

Company: XYZ Metal Fabricators, Inc.

Strategic goal: increase business by adding new metal products

Action being considered: adding a heat-treatment area to its existing production facility, which would allow XYZ to expand its product offerings

Risks that action would create: increasing the chance of fire (negative risk) in the production facility and expanding production capabilities (opportunity risk)

Possible treatment techniques:

- Avoid the risk—If it's determined that the risk of fire is too great to take on in any form, XYZ could simply avoid the risk by deciding not to build the heat-treatment area.

- Modify the risk—The frequency of fire losses could be modified through loss prevention actions such as limiting the hours of operation for the heat-treatment area. The severity of fire losses could be modified through actions such as adding an advanced fire-suppression system to the area.

- Transfer the risk—XYZ could transfer the risk of fire to another party in one of two ways. The first is by obtaining an insurance policy to cover some or all of its losses in the event of a fire, transferring the risk to the insurer. Second, XYZ could hire a contractor to perform the heat-treatment process off site, transferring the risk to the contractor.

- Retain the risk—Because the potential consequences of a fire are significant, XYZ will want to transfer some of the risk before deciding to retain a smaller portion of the risk. For example, by selecting an insurance policy with a deductible, XYZ is retaining a portion of the risk (the deductible). It's also retaining the risk that some of its operations will be shut down in the event of a fire, but it could transfer this risk by purchasing business interruption insurance.

- Exploit the risk—XYZ could exploit the opportunity of expanding its production capabilities by not only adding to its product line but also offering its heat-treatment services to other organizations that aren't direct competitors. This would allow XYZ to increase business by adding customers through new products and by becoming a provider of heat-treatment services to a new customer segment.

   See the corresponding online video.

[DA13059]

The risk treatment techniques, strategies, and measures an organization selects will vary by industry, organizational size, the specific risks faced, and other factors. To learn more, see "How They Did It: TruMark Financial."

How They Did It: TruMark Financial

As we implement our operational risk management program, we intend to assign risk treatment categories to individual operational risks. They include risk transfer, risk acceptance, and risk mitigation. As we move forward in our maturity, we will assign risk treatment categories across the board and employ a formal method for making risk treatment decisions during the next chapter of TruMark's ERM maturity.

Kelly Botti (Chief Risk Officer, TruMark Financial), interviewed by Mike Elliott, July 2019, transcript, The Institutes, Malvern, Pa. [DA13149]

The Prouty Approach

One way to select a risk treatment technique is to utilize the Prouty Approach. This approach, which takes its name from its pioneer, Richard Prouty, analyzes a risk's loss likelihood and impact to determine a proper treatment. Prouty believed that when a risk's likelihood and impact could be accurately estimated, risk managers could use a matrix to determine which risk treatment method would be best for the risk. In this approach, risks are typically divided into four broad categories of loss likelihood and three broad categories of loss impact.

These are the four categories of loss likelihood:

- Almost nil: extremely unlikely to happen
- Slight: could happen, but not likely
- Moderate: happens occasionally
- Definite: happens regularly

These are the three categories of loss impact:

- Slight
- Significant
- Severe

Risk managers can chart on the matrix where a risk would fall based on its likelihood and impact. Although these categories are subjective, they provide risk management professionals with a means of communicating and justifying the priority that they believe should be placed on a risk as well as a means of providing risk treatment suggestions. The Prouty Approach is similar in concept to a heat map, which shows risk levels and recommended treatments in a color-coded matrix. To learn more, see "Prouty Approach Matrix."

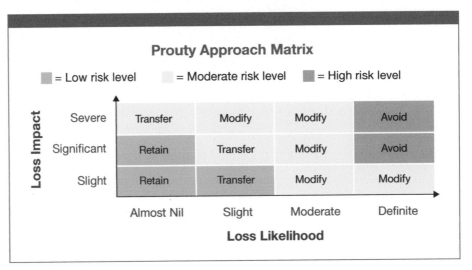

[DA01675]

Activities with losses that have a slight chance of occurring and are of low impact (depicted in green) tend to be retained and accounted for in the annual budget. At the other extreme, an activity with a high likelihood and intolerable loss impact (depicted in red) is typically avoided because it's too dangerous to undertake. Risks that fall in the middle (depicted in yellow) typically call for modification.

Developing a Risk Treatment Plan

Once an organization selects a risk treatment technique, it needs to develop a risk treatment plan to outline how the organization will implement and monitor the technique.

To be effective, a treatment plan must contain each of these elements:

- Explanation of treatment technique—outline the specific treatment option selected
- Proposed actions—document the actions proposed for implementing the selected treatment and how they'll be prioritized
- Resource requirements—identify the resources required to carry out the selected treatment

- Roles and responsibilities—determine who will be involved in every action step as well as who will be accountable for ensuring that the entire plan is implemented and monitored correctly
- Timeline—establish the dates by which action steps need to be executed and/or reevaluated
- Monitoring requirements—indicate how performance will be measured, monitored, and reported to upper management

THE EVOLUTION OF RISK TREATMENT

Risk financing, which entails transfer or retention of risk, is a form of risk treatment that is needed to pay for the cost of an organization's risks—and technology is dramatically changing the risk financing environment. Risk management professionals who understand the impact of technology on this area will be better positioned to select the most appropriate financing for their organizations' risks.

To achieve strategic objectives, every organization must find ways to pay for the corresponding risks and treatments. So **risk financing** must be part of every organization's holistic risk management strategy.

The more risk an organization retains to pursue opportunities, the more funds it must allocate to finance those risks. These funds are then used to apply the risk treatments of avoidance, modification, transfer, and retention.

Technological advancements have affected all types of risk treatment, with modification and transfer being affected most. In addition, technology has spurred significant improvements in processing risk-related financial transactions.

Because technology, and its risk management ramifications, evolves too fast for any single person to keep track of, organizations that use risk committees composed of cross-functional decision makers and stakeholders and discuss emerging risks and potential technological treatments are in a better position to take full advantage of emerging technologies. To learn more, see "How They Did It: Direct Rail."

Let's take a look at technology's influence on risk modification, risk transfer, and risk-related financial transactions.

Technology's Impact on Risk Modification

In the past, risk management focused on examining the causes of past losses in order to identify and implement ways to prevent future losses. Today, thanks to advances in data capture, data storage, and data analytics, risk management has become more forward-looking. Large datasets about past events gathered using computers, **Internet of Things** (IoT) devices, sensors, wearables, and telematics devices allow organizations to accurately identify

Risk financing

A risk management technique that includes steps to pay for or transfer the cost of losses.

Internet of Things (IoT)

A network of objects that transmit data to computers.

How They Did It: Direct Rail

First, the managing director set up a risk committee consisting of the executive directors, and I was asked to be a member. The risk committee considered the following questions: What risks are keeping us awake at night? What are the biggest risks to fulfilling our mission, strategy, and business plan? As part of this process, the risk committee identified opportunities as well as threats.

Richard James (Head of Risk, Direct Rail Services), interviewed by Mike Elliott, July 2019, transcript, The Institutes, Malvern, Pa. [DA13143]

patterns of risk, model risk, and predict risk. In some cases, risk can be predicted so accurately that it can be modified to the point of being nearly preventable. This can create significant cost savings for both organizations and insurers. To learn more, see "Preventing Risk." ⌒

Preventing Risk

Let's take a look at an example of technology's ability to predict risk to the point of nearly rendering it preventable.

A risk for a distributor of frozen groceries is that the freezers in its warehouse will stop running overnight (when nobody is on-site to notice). This could cause inventory to thaw and spoil. But that risk can be modified by placing IoT temperature sensors in the freezers. Those sensors could detect when the temperature in a freezer is starting to climb (a telltale sign that a freezer's compressor is starting to fail) and then trigger a backup compressor to kick on and/or send a warning to management that the freezer needs to be fixed immediately to prevent lost inventory.

This early warning system could allow the distributor to reduce the amount of insurance it has to purchase to cover potential losses. Similarly, an insurer may charge a lower premium because the distributor has installed the IoT sensors.

While this risk may seem completely preventable through the use of IoT sensors, there is still a small risk that the sensor could fail. Thus, the distributor will need to select a treatment (like insurance) for the remaining risk.

 See the corresponding online video.

[DA13061]

The advancements in forecasting could result in minimal financing being required to retain, transfer, or modify negative risks. However, risk management professionals must factor in that there is a cost associated with forecasting technology. For example, the sensors used the by the distributor in the exhibit would have to be purchased, installed, and maintained.

E¹

Technology's Impact on Risk Transfer   *B¹*

Risk transfer is the area most people think of when it comes to risk financing. Typically, it involves purchasing insurance that shifts the risks associated with an organization's product, process, or action to an insurer. Risk transfer has been significantly altered by the evolution of technology.   *y*

Insurers' growing access to big data coupled with advancements in **machine learning** and artificial intelligence (AI) have made it easier for them to not only predict and plan for risk but also to develop products that specifically address certain risks.

Machine learning

Artificial intelligence in which computers continually teach themselves to make better decisions based on previous results and new data.

Apply Your Knowledge

Learn more from an expert in the online video.

Insurance plays a big role in risk financing by facilitating the transfer of risk. Identify ways advancements in big data are changing how insurers operate.

Feedback: Advancements in big data are changing how insurers operate by helping insurers stand in their customers' shoes, better understand what's driving risk, develop a risk appetite, and price insurance policies more accurately.

These advancements have also helped insurers price insurance policies more precisely, so organizations managing risk don't have to pay for what they don't need. For example, insurers can now use telematics devices and sensors to monitor their customers' behaviors and environments and then customize policies to more closely align with customers' actual risks. To learn more, see "Insurers Embrace IoT."

Technology has also facilitated insurers' abilities to create alternative products. For example, parametric insurance and microinsurance, which cover risks associated with small events or one-time events such as a specific trip or project, are now more prevalent. In the past, the problem with these products was that they generated a relatively low premium for the administrative burden associated with them, so insurers were hesitant to offer them. But technological advancements have eased the administrative burden and

Insurers Embrace IoT

Usage-based Insurance

For commercial auto and truck insurance policies, Progressive created a usage-based program called Smart Haul. It uses IoT electronic logging devices in vehicles to track things driving behavior, location, distance traveled and other data. Progressive can then use the data to customize policies for customers.

Predicting and Preventing Losses

Property and casualty insurer Chubb partnered with Hartford Steam Boiler Inspection and Insurance Company to provide business insurance customers with IoT sensors that will monitor things like temperature, vibration, and humidity to detect when damage may occur so it could be prevented. At the launch of the partnership, Chubb's chief risk officer said the initiative would help transition the insurance model from "repair and replace" to "predict and prevent."

[DA13062]

expense of these products by enabling applications, data, and premiums to be collected and processed electronically.

Using real-time data and AI, insurers can push product offers to potential customers that are specifically tailored to the requirements of those individuals or organizations when they need them—and the payment options and policy information can be delivered to a mobile device, eliminating paperwork.

Technology's Impact on Financial Transactions

The faster an organization can recoup its financial losses and regain the position it was in before the loss occurred, the better. Technology is constantly speeding up this recovery process. Smart contracts and blockchain technologies are the forefront of this acceleration.

Smart insurance contracts are self-executing contracts that will initiate a loss payment as soon as the parameters for the contract have been reached. For example, as soon as it's verified that a manufacturing facility with flood insurance is located in an area that experienced a flood, the contract will trigger a claim payment to the facility without the need for an intermediary or third party to process the payment. This can dramatically increase the speed of loss payments, as well as reduce administrative costs for insurers.

Blockchain technologies can be the infrastructure upon which smart contracts are built and implemented. Say, for example, your business has flood insurance and loss payments can be triggered through a smart contract on a blockchain. If the blockchain receives a signal that a flood has occurred in your area (this could come from IoT sensors or a weather service), the blockchain could instantly determine whether your business is covered for a flood loss. Having detected that your business has coverage, a loss payment could be deposited directly into your organization's bank account. The claim, verification of coverage (claim investigation), and payment could be completed within seconds rather than days or weeks.

Apply Your Knowledge

Learn more from an expert in the online video.

Based on what you know about technology's growing influence on risk financing, summarize how technology is changing, or will change, how risk is financed through insurance?

Feedback: Some of the ways technology will affect how risk is financed through insurance include increasing speed and automation, reducing paperwork, implementing smart (self-executing) contracts, and creating more policies that specifically address the needs of individual customers.

RISK TREATMENT APPLICATIONS

Once a risk has been identified and analyzed, a treatment technique must be selected and applied to the risk. The risk quadrant(s) that the risk falls into can determine which treatment is best, so risk management professionals need to be prepared to apply various treatments.

Typically, treating and controlling risk involves one or a combination of these techniques: avoidance, modification, transfer, retention, or (for opportunity risks) exploitation. Selection of the best technique(s) may depend on whether the risk is a hazard, an operational, a financial, or a strategic risk. Risk management professionals will likely treat risks differently depending on which quadrant(s) they fall into.

What Do You Know?

Duplication is one of the additional techniques risk management professionals can apply to control risk. Can you describe it?

Feedback: Duplication is a risk retention and modification technique in which exposure units are duplicated to create backups, spares, or copies of critical property, information, or capabilities. Duplication, separation, and diversification are all additional techniques addressed in this section.

Let's take a look at different hazard, operational, financial, and strategic risks and how an organization might apply various risk treatments.

Hazard Risk: Creating a New Product

Say a toy manufacturer is planning to produce a new toy that contains several small parts. The biggest risk associated with the toy is that the small parts, if broken off the toy, could create choking hazards for small children. As a result, the manufacturer could face large products liability claims related to choking.

The various treatment options that the manufacturer could choose from include these:

- Avoid the risk—The manufacturer could simply avoid the risk by deciding not to produce the toy. This option would likely be selected if the potential cost of the products liability claims and the negative impact the claims would have on the company's reputation would outweigh the revenue generated from the sale of the toy. However, this option eliminates the opportunity to increase sales using the toy.

- Modify the risk—By redesigning the toy to contain fewer small parts, the manufacturer would lower the likelihood that a child will choke on them. This is an example of loss prevention. Loss reduction, on the other hand, wouldn't apply in this scenario because the manufacturer is unlikely to reduce the severity of a choking hazard.

- Transfer the risk—Products liability insurance could be purchased to shift the financial consequences of a products liability claim to an insurer.

- Retain the risk—Part of the risk could be retained by the manufacturer through a deductible for the products liability insurance. The bigger the deductible it's willing to retain, the less the manufacturer will pay in insurance premiums. The manufacturer wouldn't want to retain all of the risk because the full financial consequences of products liability claims related to choking could be devastating to the business.

- Exploit the risk—The manufacturer could exploit this opportunity by producing a product that none of its competitors offer. This could be done by producing a one-of-a-kind product or by making the toy safer than similar toys produced by competitors.

Operational Risk: Data Breach

Now, suppose a large retailer collects and stores a lot of personal information about its customers—name, address, phone number, email, credit card number, and so forth. This organization faces a large data security risk. If its data were to be breached, it would face significant damage to its reputation as a trustworthy keeper of customer information, potentially driving customers away.

Two treatment options that this retailer may want to explore include separation and duplication. To learn more, see "Additional Loss Control Techniques."

Additional treatment options that the retailer could choose from include these:

- Avoid the risk—The retailer could elect not to store any customer data. But this would hurt its marketing and customer service efforts, likely leading to a decline in business. So this isn't a viable option.
- Modify the risk—By upgrading its security systems, the retailer could help prevent data breaches. Duplication and separation, as outlined in the exhibit, could also reduce the likelihood and/or severity of data losses. The retailer may even reduce the impact of a data breach by developing protocols that outline steps its employees must take following a breach. For example, notifying affected customers and issuing a public statement may help salvage the retailer's reputation.
- Transfer the risk—Cyber insurance could be purchased to shift some of the financial risk associated with data breach recovery to an insurer. The risk can't be fully transferred to an insurer because the organization will always retain reputational risk. The retailer could also transfer some of the risk by hiring a third-party data storage company, which would be responsible for handling and securing the customer data.
- Retain the risk—The retailer could choose to retain all of the risk. In addition to reputational damage, this would include all recovery costs.
- Exploit the risk—The more data the organization collects (within the law), the greater a competitive advantage it can create for itself. However, risk grows exponentially as data collection increases.

Additional Loss Control Techniques

Additional loss control techniques that risk management professionals may want to consider include:

Separation

Separation is a type of modification and retention that disperses a particular asset or activity over several locations. Separation of exposure units can reduce an organization's dependence on a single asset, activity, or person, making individual losses smaller. Two examples are dividing existing inventory between two separate warehouses or manufacturing a component in two separate plants.

In the retail scenario, storing customer data in multiple locations or on multiple servers could reduce the potential consequences of a data breach by ensuring that a single breach doesn't compromise data pertaining to all of the retailer's customers.

Duplication

Duplication is a type of modification and retention that duplicates exposure units. These duplicates aren't used unless the primary asset is damaged or destroyed. Like separation, duplication can reduce an organization's dependence on a single asset, activity, or person, making individual losses smaller. Duplication is appropriate if an entire asset or activity is so important that the consequences of its loss justify the expense and time required to maintain the duplicate. An example of duplication is maintaining duplicate accounting records.

In the retail scenario, by duplicating the data and storing it on a second server, the retailer significantly reduces the risk of losing customer data.

One drawback to consider with both approaches in this case is that separation and duplication create an additional risk: that the second server could be breached.

[DA13063]

Financial Risk: Extending Credit to Customers

Organizations that extend credit to customers face financial risks related to those customers' failure to repay debts. For example, if a financial organization provides loans to small businesses that have existed for fewer than five years, this organization has a credit or default risk that the businesses that borrowed money won't succeed and won't be able to repay their loans.

The various treatment options that the financial institution could choose from include these:

- Avoid the risk—The financial institution could choose not to provide loans to small businesses that have existed for fewer than five years. Instead, it may wish to extend loans only to more mature businesses. However, this would eliminate the opportunity to gain from the fees and interest payments that would be earned on loans that don't go into default.

- Modify the risk—Both loss prevention and loss reduction techniques can be used to modify the credit risk. For example, the institution could reduce the frequency of losses by altering its underwriting guidelines so that loans are provided only to businesses with great credit ratings and financial positions. The institution could also reduce the severity of losses by reducing the dollar value of the loans it's willing to make.

- Transfer the risk—One of the common ways financial risks can be transferred is through **hedging**. It normally involves making an investment to reduce the risk of adverse price movements in an asset. But in this case, the financial institution can hedge its risk through a credit **derivative**, which transfers the credit risk to a third party in exchange for a fee paid to that third party.

- Retain the risk—If multiple loans going into default won't result in devastating losses to the financial institution, it could choose to retain the risk.

- Exploit the risk—The financial institution could exploit the opportunity by becoming the preferred financial partner to small businesses on the rise. By helping these businesses early in their development, the institution could build lasting relationships with them, which could lead to more profitable business in the future.

Hedging

A financial transaction in which one asset is held to offset the risk associated with another asset.

Derivative

A financial instrument whose value is derived from the value of an underlying asset, which can be an index, an asset, yield on an asset, weather conditions, inflation, loans, bonds, an insurance risk, or other items.

Strategic Risk: Entering a New Market

Finally, let's say an electronics manufacturer plans to launch a product in a foreign market. This manufacturer faces a strategic risk that the product may not sell well in the new market if the economic, political, or competitive environment changes in a way that lowers demand for the product.

The various treatment options that the manufacturer could choose from include these:

- Avoid the risk—The manufacturer could avoid placing the product in the foreign market. However, this would eliminate the opportunity to benefit from the product's being exposed to a new group of customers.

- Modify the risk—In this scenario, **diversification** could be applied to reduce the severity of the product failing in the new market. Diversification prevents a single event or series of events from derailing an organization from achieving its strategic goals. In this case, the manufacturer could release the product in several new markets (or release several products within the same market) to reduce the chance that this product launch could significantly harm the organization.

- Retain the risk—If lower-than-expected demand for the product in the new market wouldn't significantly harm the organization, it could elect

Diversification

A risk control technique that spreads loss exposures over numerous projects, products, markets, or regions.

to retain the potential financial consequences of launching the product and later having to pull it from that marketplace.

- Exploit the risk—The manufacturer could exploit the sales opportunity by launching the product in the foreign market, which we can assume hasn't yet been saturated by competing products. This could allow the manufacturer to gain a foothold and establish a strong reputation in the marketplace, giving it an advantage over competitors that may later seek to enter the same market.

Typically, a strategic risk can't be transferred—or the cost to transfer the risk exceeds the expected return.

USING INSURANCE TO TREAT RISK

Insurance is often the best technique for financing losses with high severity and low frequency. For that reason and others, insurance is a key component of most risk financing plans. The self-insurance plan of a large corporation, for example, might consist of a $1 million retention per occurrence, with insurance covering the part of any loss that exceeds the retention, up to the applicable limit of insurance. Another organization might be comfortable retaining up to $100,000 per occurrence by way of large deductibles on its insurance policies.

In this section, we consider insurance as a risk management technique, the risks that are generally insurable, and the ability of insurance to meet common risk financing goals.

What Do You Know?

True or false: Insurance is often used to finance speculative risks.

Feedback: False. Insurance is normally used only to finance pure risks, which entail a chance of loss or no loss. Speculative risks, which present the possibility of loss, no loss, or gain, are generally not insurable.

Insurance as a Risk Management Technique

Insurance

A risk management technique that transfers the potential financial consequences of certain specified loss exposures from the insured to the insurer.

Insurance enables an organization to transfer some of its loss exposures to an insurer through a legal contract called an insurance policy. The insurer agrees to pay for all losses that are covered by the policy, subject usually to a deductible and one or more limits of insurance. The insurer also agrees to pay for certain services, such as investigating claims and defending the insured against liability claims. The insured, or policyholder, agrees to pay a sum, called the policy premium, that's ordinarily much smaller than the policy limit(s).

In addition to being a transfer technique, insurance also involves sharing the costs of losses. The insurer pools the premiums paid by its insureds, and insureds who experience covered losses are paid from the pooled funds. In this way, the total cost of losses is shared by all the insureds whose premiums were pooled.

Most insurance policies can be characterized as guaranteed cost insurance, in which the premium is specified at policy inception, when the policy takes effect. The cost of the insurance is guaranteed in that the insurer does not modify the premium at the end of the policy period based on the insured's loss experience during the policy period.

→ - they may NR or increase ded., etc
- also, premium may be Δ'ed, but it won't be for loss experience, but would be a customer-wide premium/rate increase.

Learn more from an expert in the online video.

Insurable Risks and Loss Exposures

A significant limitation of insurance as a risk financing technique is that it is not available for some types of risks. One approach to categorizing risks is shown in the exhibit. Insurable risks are mainly confined to hazard risk and operational risk, while financial risk and strategic risk are generally uninsurable. To learn more, see "Risk Quadrants."

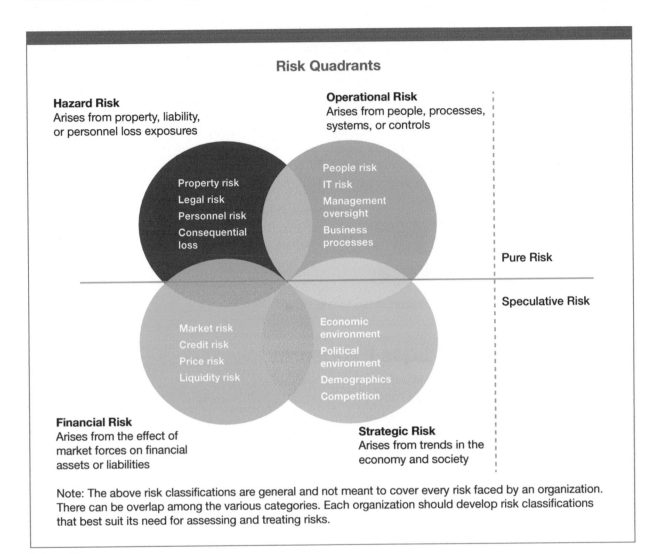

Risk Quadrants

Hazard Risk
Arises from property, liability, or personnel loss exposures

Operational Risk
Arises from people, processes, systems, or controls

Property risk
Legal risk
Personnel risk
Consequential loss

People risk
IT risk
Management oversight
Business processes

Pure Risk

Speculative Risk

Market risk
Credit risk
Price risk
Liquidity risk

Economic environment
Political environment
Demographics
Competition

Financial Risk
Arises from the effect of market forces on financial assets or liabilities

Strategic Risk
Arises from trends in the economy and society

Note: The above risk classifications are general and not meant to cover every risk faced by an organization. There can be overlap among the various categories. Each organization should develop risk classifications that best suit its need for assessing and treating risks.

[DA08677]

In general, insurers are willing to insure a loss exposure that has all or most of these characteristics:

- *It's associated with pure risk*—Pure risk entails a chance of loss or no loss, but no chance of gain. A speculative risk, in contrast, presents the possibility of loss, no loss, or gain. With few exceptions, insurance for speculative risks is not available. For example, a real estate developer can purchase insurance covering damage by fire and other causes of accidental loss to an apartment complex while it's being constructed, because that's a pure risk: the complex is either damaged or it's not damaged before construction is completed. The developer would not be able to obtain insurance guaranteeing that the apartment complex will be sold for a certain amount of profit, because that's a speculative risk.

- *It's accidental from the insured's standpoint*—Theft of property, for example, is not an accidental loss from the thief's standpoint but is an accidental loss from the standpoint of an insured whose property has been stolen. So a property owner can purchase insurance against loss resulting from theft of the owner's property. Similarly, a fire caused by lightning is accidental from the insured's viewpoint, but a fire started by the insured to burn down his building so he can collect under his insurance policy is not an accidental loss from the insured's standpoint and therefore would not be covered by his commercial insurance.

- *It's definite and measurable*—Losses must be definite in time, cause, and location so that the insurer can determine whether they are covered under the policy. For example, commercial property policies that include coverage for theft commonly exclude missing property when the only evidence of the loss is a shortage disclosed on taking inventory, with no physical evidence showing what happened to the missing property. The frequency and severity of the expected losses must be measurable so that the insurer can determine an appropriate policy premium.

- *It's one of a large number of similar exposure units*—The loss exposure must be common enough that the insurer can pool a large number of homogeneous, or similar, exposure units, which enables the insurer to predict losses accurately and determine appropriate premiums. For example, the majority of insurers may be unwilling to insure losses arising from an emerging technology in its initial stage of adoption, for which no credible loss data exists. Insurance might (or might not) be available from a specialty insurer with underwriters who are experienced at assessing emerging technology risks.

- *It's not catastrophic*—Insurers prefer to provide insurance for a loss exposure that is not subject to an adverse event that would simultaneously affect many other similar loss exposures and result in a catastrophic loss for the insurer. For example, if all the homes and businesses in a particular city were insured by the same insurer, the insurer would probably suffer a financial disaster if a hurricane leveled the city. Instead, the insurer must diversify the homes and businesses it insures so that it does not have a large concentration of insureds in any one geographic area.

- *It's economically feasible to insure*—Insurers seek to cover only loss exposures that are economically feasible to insure. Providing insurance to cover small losses doesn't make sense when the expense of providing the insurance probably exceeds the amount of potential losses. Similarly, most insurers are not willing to insure losses that are almost certain to occur. For example, an insurer that has been asked to provide directors and officers liability insurance will probably exclude any claims that have already been made against the applicant's directors and officers but are awaiting litigation. The premiums required to cover such losses would probably exceed the potential amount of the anticipated losses.

Ability to Meet Risk Financing Goals

Before using guaranteed cost insurance for risk financing, an organization should consider the extent to which such insurance meets the organization's risk financing goals. To learn more, see "Ability of Guaranteed Cost Insurance to Meet Risk Financing Goals."

Ability of Guaranteed Cost Insurance to Meet Risk Financing Goals

Risk Financing Goal	How Guaranteed Cost Insurance Meets the Goal
Pay for Losses	Insurance can meet this goal, provided the loss exposures are covered by the guaranteed cost insurance policies.
Maintain Liquidity	Insurance can meet this goal because the organization requires less liquidity with guaranteed cost insurance compared with retention or other risk financing measures.
Manage Uncertainty	Insurance can meet this goal because much of the uncertainty about future losses is transferred to the insurer.
Comply With Legal and Regulatory Requirements	Insurance can meet this goal, especially regarding loss exposures that are required (by law or contractual obligation) to be transferred.
Minimize the Cost of Risk	Insurance can meet this goal, but it is not ideal because insurance premiums are designed to cover not only expected losses, but also insurer administrative costs, adverse selection and moral hazard costs, premium taxes, and any social loadings.

[DA12702]

Guaranteed cost insurance is effective in paying for losses, maintaining liquidity, managing uncertainty, and complying with legal and regulatory requirements. It's less effective than retention in minimizing the cost of risk, which helps to explain why retention, along with insurance, is a key component of most risk financing plans. An additional benefit of guaranteed cost insurance is that an organization can generally deduct insurance premiums for income tax purposes.

Learn more from an expert in the online video.

NONINSURANCE CONTRACTUAL RISK TRANSFER

Most organizations purchase insurance to transfer the financial consequences of some of their accidental losses to an insurer. In addition, most organizations are parties to noninsurance contracts—such as leases, construction contracts, and purchase agreements—that may include risk transfer provisions. When an organization enters into a contract, it may either transfer its loss exposures to the other party or assume the other party's loss exposures.

In a noninsurance contractual risk transfer, one party (the transferee), which is not an insurance company, accepts another party's (the transferor's) loss exposures or financial consequences of the transferor's loss exposures as an incidental aspect of another business transaction. These agreements fall into two categories:

- A noninsurance transfer for risk control shifts loss exposures to the transferee to reduce the frequency and/or severity of the transferor's losses arising from the loss exposures.

- A noninsurance transfer for risk financing transfers only the financial consequences of the transferor's loss exposures.

A crucial difference between the two categories becomes apparent when a transferee becomes insolvent or otherwise unable or unwilling to fulfill the contractual transfer terms. In a noninsurance transfer for risk financing, an insolvent transferee provides no protection to the transferor, who must then pay for its own accidental loss. In a noninsurance transfer for risk control, a bankrupt or uncooperative transferee may continue to be responsible for losses arising from the transferred loss exposures, preserving the transferor's protection.

What Do You Know?

True or false: In many jurisdictions, anti-indemnity statutes forbid broad form hold-harmless agreements in construction contracts.

Feedback: True. In jurisdictions having such laws, a broad form hold-harmless agreement in a construction contract is void.

[Handwritten margin note, top right: — transfer of risk which reduces severity/frequency of potential losses]

Noninsurance Transfers for Risk Control

A noninsurance transfer for risk control can take various forms. Four common types of noninsurance transfers for risk control are leasing, contracting for services, a waiver or exculpatory clause, and a disclaimer of warranties.

Leasing

Certain losses that can arise from property ownership do not exist for a lessee occupying the property. These losses include accidental damage to the property and liability to third parties resulting from hazards on the property. A lessee does not normally bear responsibility for such losses. However, two important exceptions apply: The lease obligates the lessee to return the property to the lessor in the same condition in which it was received or the lessee is at fault in causing harm to others.

[Handwritten margin note, left: So, the lessee/tenant is the transferor of risk to the lessor/landlord (transferee) — if leak in the building — if HVAC breaks down — if fire causes damage / loss exposure is for the landlord, not the tenant]

An organization that leases property instead of owning it practices risk control by allowing the property owner to retain the risks related to property ownership.

Contracting for Services

An individual or organization that performs a particular activity is generally held primarily responsible for any losses caused by that activity. An organization can transfer this loss exposure by contracting with another organization to perform the activity. This noninsurance transfer method is called contracting for services, or simply subcontracting—even though the transferor need not be an independent contractor, and the transferee need not be a subcontractor.

Liability loss exposures associated with an activity are not easily transferred, especially those that involve harm to third parties. For example, if negligence by a property owner's landscaping contractor creates a hazard that injures a visitor on the owner's property, the contractor would be primarily liable. However, the injured visitor could sue the property owner as the party responsible for the property's condition.

Because courts seek to compensate those who are injured, they favor restricting the rule exempting the person who hires an independent contractor (the principal) from liability for the independent contractor's torts. So they have established some exceptions to this rule:

- The principal is directly liable for negligence in selecting the contractor, giving directions, or failing to stop any unnecessary dangerous practices of which the principal was aware.

- The principal's responsibility for certain duties to be performed safely cannot be delegated to another party. The owner of an apartment building, for example, cannot transfer to a contractor its duty to keep common areas safe.

- If the subcontracted work is inherently dangerous to others (such as blasting or excavating near a public highway), the principal that hired the contractor can be held liable for a third-party injury caused by the contractor's negligence.

Waiver or Exculpatory Clause

An individual or organization can relinquish its right to sue another party through a **waiver**. An **exculpatory clause (exculpatory agreement)** is similar to a waiver. Both waivers and exculpatory clauses can function as effective risk control mechanisms.

Waivers or exculpatory clauses in various contracts can transfer responsibility for liability loss exposures. For example, in a particular jurisdiction, the applicable law allows a real property lessee (tenant) to sue a lessor (landlord) for failing to maintain premises suitable for people to live in. However, if the lease agreement between the two contains a provision stating that the lessee waives its right to sue the lessor for this reason, the lessor no longer faces that exposure.

Disclaimer of Warranties

Sellers of property often assert disclaimers of warranties. A disclaimer in a sales contract may deny any express warranties made during the property's sale. It may also deny implied warranties, such as the implied warranty of fitness for a particular purpose (or, that the seller is aware of the particular purpose for which the buyer will use the property and that the property is suitable for that purpose) and the implied warranty of merchantability (or, that the property is suitable for the purpose for which most buyers use it).

This is an example of disclaimer language used in a software sales contract: [Seller's property] is provided "as is." To the maximum extent permitted by law, [seller] disclaims all warranties of any kind, either express or implied, including without limitation, implied warranties of fitness for a particular purpose and merchantability. E¹

Noninsurance Transfers for Risk Financing B¹

— reduces the financial risk incurred w/ potential loss

Noninsurance transfers for risk financing are accomplished through **hold-harmless agreements**, which are commonly included in various types of contracts and agreements, such as construction contracts, maintenance contracts, rental and lease agreements, purchase orders, and sales agreements.

An example of a hold-harmless agreement is this provision in a lease of premises: "To the fullest extent permitted by law, the lessee shall indemnify, defend, and hold harmless the lessor, agents, and employees of the lessor from and against all claims arising out of or resulting from the leased premises."

The party that uses a hold-harmless agreement to transfer the financial consequences of loss to a second party is commonly referred to as the indemnitee; the second party, which agrees to indemnify the indemnitee, is referred to as the indemnitor. To increase the likelihood that it will have the necessary financial resources, the indemnitor may need to demonstrate

Waiver

The intentional relinquishment of a known right.

Exculpatory clause (exculpatory agreement)

A contractual provision purporting to excuse a party from liability resulting from negligence or an otherwise wrongful act.

Hold-harmless agreement (or indemnity agreement)

A contractual provision that obligates one of the parties to assume the legal liability of another party.

proof of financial responsibility, such as through a certificate of insurance. Commercial general liability insurance policies and commercial auto liability policies commonly include coverage for liability assumed under an insured contract.

Hold-harmless agreements can be classified according to the extent of responsibility they transfer. For example, assume the contracting parties are Building Owner and General Contractor. They may adopt any one of these three forms:

- Limited form—General Contractor agrees to indemnify Building Owner only for claims that result from General Contractor's own negligence, often referred to as sole fault.
- Intermediate form—General Contractor agrees to indemnify Building Owner only for claims that result from General Contractor's sole fault or from both parties' joint fault.
- Broad form—General Contractor agrees to indemnify Building Owner for losses that result from General Contractor's sole fault, both parties' joint fault, or Building Owner's sole fault.

Many jurisdictions have anti-indemnity statutes that prohibit broad form, intermediate form, or both broad and intermediate form hold-harmless agreements contained in construction contracts. In some jurisdictions that do not have anti-indemnity statutes, judicial rules (established by courts) limit the use of hold-harmless agreements. The purpose of these statutes and rules is to prevent a party with greater bargaining power from taking advantage of the other party to a contract, who is often less able to assume the other's liability. Because the statutory prohibitions and judicial rules vary by state, determining the legality of a proposed hold-harmless agreement in the applicable jurisdiction before including it in a contract is essential.

The handling of punitive damages under hold-harmless agreements also varies. In some jurisdictions, the indemnitor's payment of punitive damages is included automatically within a hold-harmless agreement. In others, punitive damages are included only if specified. In still others, contractual transfer of the obligation to pay punitive damages is illegal.

In some cases, organizations use hold-harmless agreements to finance loss exposures that are not economically feasible to insure. However, in many cases, an organization using a hold-harmless agreement to finance a particular loss exposure also has insurance that includes coverage for that exposure.

For example, a paving contractor hired to resurface a shopping mall's parking lot agrees to an intermediate form hold-harmless agreement in the owner's favor. The owner also has coverage under its commercial general liability insurance policy for bodily injury and property damage liability claims arising out of the contractor's work.

A shopper is injured by mobile equipment operated by an employee of the contractor and sues both the contractor and the owner. In accord with the hold-harmless agreement, the contractor indemnifies the owner for its share of a settlement paid to the claimant. The owner did not need to use its own insurance for this claim, ultimately reducing its cost of risk.

Before using a hold-harmless agreement as a risk financing measure, an organization should evaluate its ability to meet common risk financing goals. To learn more, see "Ability of a Hold-Harmless Agreement to Meet Risk

Ability of a Hold-Harmless Agreement to Meet Risk Financing Goals

Risk Financing Goal	How a Hold-Harmless Agreement Meets the Goal
Pay for losses	The agreement can meet this goal provided the loss exposures are covered by the agreement and the other party has the financial ability to pay losses subject to the agreement.
Maintain liquidity	The agreement can meet this goal because the organization requires less liquidity with a hold-harmless agreement compared with retention or other alternative risk transfer measures.
Manage uncertainty	The agreement can meet this goal subject to the extent of the agreement.
Comply with legal and regulatory requirements	The agreement can't be used to comply with a law or regulation requiring insurance, a surety bond, or a qualified self-insurance plan.
Minimize the cost of risk	The agreement can meet this goal subject to any other contractual demands the other party requires before accepting the hold-harmless agreement.

[DA12715]

Financing Goals."

LARGE DEDUCTIBLE PLANS

Many organizations that purchase insurance reduce their cost of risk by assuming significant retentions through large deductible plans.

A large deductible plan is an insurance policy with a significant per occurrence or per accident deductible, such as $100,000 or more. Such plans are typically used to treat workers compensation, automobile liability, and general liability loss exposures.

What Do You Know?

True or false: A large deductible operates in the same way as a self-insured retention (SIR).

Feedback: False. Large deductibles and SIRs both require insureds to retain covered losses up to a specified amount. However, there's a key difference in how they apply. With large deductibles, the insurer adjusts and pays the entire loss and then bills the insured for the deductible amount. With SIRs, the insured is responsible for adjusting and paying its own losses up to the SIR amount.

Purpose and Operation of Large Deductible Plans

Large deductible plans allow an organization to pay a reduced insurance premium for retaining losses below the deductible level. The organization transfers the financial consequences of losses that exceed the deductible to the insurer.

As losses occur, the insurer settles each claim and then periodically bills the insured organization for the amount of the loss (and possibly also the claims handling expense) up to the deductible. In this way, the organization benefits from deferring cash outflows for its retained losses compared with paying a premium up front. Organizations that choose large deductible plans usually make a commitment to controlling losses they would otherwise retain. To learn more, see "Operation of a Large Deductible Plan."

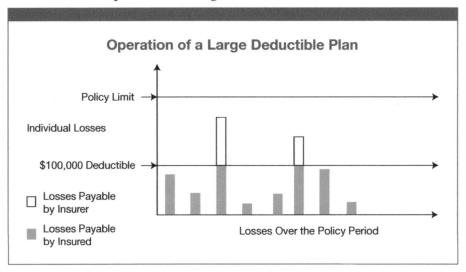

Operation of a Large Deductible Plan

[DA01498]

The insured organization usually must provide the insurer with a form of financial security, or collateral, such as a letter of credit, to guarantee payment of covered losses up to the deductible level. Often, at the request of the insurer, the insured will also set up a trust fund for reimbursing the insurer.

Large Deductible Versus Self-Insured Retention

Large deductibles are distinct from SIRs. Both require the insured organization to retain a relatively large amount of loss, but with SIRs, the insured organization is responsible for adjusting and paying its own losses up to the SIR amount. Organizations with SIRs frequently outsource these tasks to independent claims adjusting organizations.

Under a large deductible plan, the insurer adjusts and pays all claims for loss, even those below the deductible level, and then seeks reimbursement from the insured. In effect, the insurer guarantees the payment of all claims. Accordingly, a large deductible plan gives the insurer direct control over individual claims that start out small but have the potential to exceed the deductible level.

Use of Large Deductible Plans

Large deductible plans are commonly used for workers compensation, auto liability, and general liability policies. Workers compensation deductibles can apply on a per person and/or per accident basis, while auto liability deductibles usually apply on a per accident basis and general liability deductibles on a per occurrence basis.

Such plans can also include an aggregate deductible, which caps total deductible payments over a period of time (usually one year). The exhibit shows how large deductible plans can be tailored to meet an insured organization's loss expectations and financial ability to retain accidental losses related to workers compensation. To learn more, see "Example of a Large Deductible Plan."

Under a large deductible plan, the amount that the insurer incurs to adjust losses, including legal defense costs, can be either inside or outside the deductible. If inside, or included, the insurer adds it to the amount of the loss to determine the total amount subject to the deductible. If outside, it is not added to the amount of the loss but usually prorated between the insured and insurer based on the size of the loss.

Benefits of Large Deductible Plans

An organization's motive for having a large deductible plan is to reduce its cost of risk. Even though most of the premium reduction is offset because

Example of a Large Deductible Plan

Assume that a large deductible plan applied to workers compensation incorporates the following:

- A deductible of $100,000 for each injured person

- A deductible of $250,000 per accident, regardless of the number of persons injured

- An annual aggregate deductible of $350,000

Assume six employees are injured in a single year, with four employees injured in a single accident. The table below shows the cost of the losses for each employee.

Accident No.	Employee No.	Amount of Loss	Amount Payable Under Deductible
1	1	$150,000	$100,000
1	2	85,000	85,000
1	3	70,000	65,000
1	4	10,000	0
2	5	50,000	50,000
3	6	60,000	50,000
		$425,000	$350,000

Under this large deductible plan, the insured organization would reimburse the insurer $100,000 for Employee 1 (subject to the per person deductible) and a total of $250,000 for Employee 1 through Employee 4 because they were involved in a single accident. In addition, the insured organization would reimburse the insurer for an additional $100,000 for Employee 5 and Employee 6 together, with the annual aggregate deductible capped at $350,000.

 See the corresponding online video.

[DA01499]

the organization must pay for its losses under the deductible, reducing the premium helps for two main reasons:

- States impose various charges, such as premium taxes and residual market loadings. A residual market loading is an amount charged to make up for losses in a state-sponsored plan to insure high-risk exposures, such as an assigned risk plan for auto insurance. A residual market loading is calculated based on a percentage of premium.

- An insurance premium includes charges for the insurer's overhead costs and profit.

A large deductible plan can significantly reduce the cost of risk compared with other insurance plans by helping organizations avoid substantial premium taxes, residual market loadings, and insurer overhead and profit charges. Some jurisdictions minimize these benefits by enforcing premium taxes and residual market loadings on the retained-loss portion of large deductible plans.

Large deductible plans also allow insured organizations to benefit from the cash flow available on their reserves (funds set aside) for retained losses. An insured organization is not required to reimburse the insurer for the deductible amount until the insurer has paid covered losses.

Workers compensation, auto liability, and general liability losses are often not paid until several months or even years after they are incurred. Because the insured organization retains its funds until claims are actually paid, a large deductible plan enhances the insured organization's cash flow.

As with any risk financing plan with a retention component, losses under a large deductible plan may be higher than expected, lowering an organization's net income and cash flow. However, by keeping its per occurrence (or accident) and annual aggregate deductibles at prudent levels, an organization can manage such uncertainty.

Ability to Meet Risk Financing Goals

Before adopting a large deductible plan, an organization should evaluate the plan's ability to meet common risk financing goals. To learn more, see "Ability of a Large Deductible Plan to Meet Risk Financing Goals."

Ability of a Large Deductible Plan to Meet Risk Financing Goals

Risk Financing Goal	How a Large Deductible Plan Meets the Goal
Pay for losses	The plan meets this goal because the insurer pays for losses as they become due, including losses less than the deductible for which the insured eventually reimburses the insurer.
Maintain liquidity	The plan meets this goal because liquidity is maintained if the deductible level is carefully selected.
Manage uncertainty	The plan meets this goal because the organization can effectively manage cash flow uncertainty if the deductible amount is chosen carefully.
Comply with legal and regulatory requirements	The plan meets this goal because it can meet legal requirements for purchasing insurance because an insurer issues a policy guaranteeing that all covered claims will be paid.
Minimize the cost of risk	The plan may meet this goal because it can avoid a substantial amount of premium taxes, residual market loadings, and insurer overhead and profit charges.

[DA12716]

SUMMARY

Following a risk assessment, an organization needs to make risk treatment decisions based on the results of that assessment. Generally, risk treatment techniques fall under the categories of avoidance, modification, transfer, retention, or (for opportunities) exploitation. These techniques can be applied to hazard, operational, financial, and strategic risks. Many risks call for a combination of treatment techniques, which can be selected, communicated, and justified using the Prouty Approach. After selecting a treatment technique, the organization must create a risk treatment plan.

Risk financing must be a part of every organization's holistic risk management strategy. It's necessary to help an organization pay for the cost of the risks it takes in order to achieve its strategic goals. The risk financing environment has evolved significantly because of the influence of advancing technology, particularly for the areas of risk modification and risk transfer. In addition, technology has increased the speed with which financial transactions involving risk can be processed.

To properly control risk, the right treatments must be selected. Typically, this involves applying one or more of these techniques: avoidance, modification, transfer, retention, or (for opportunity risks) exploitation. Risk management professionals will likely select the treatment(s) based on whether the risk is a hazard, an operational, a financial, or a strategic risk, so it's important to understand how various treatments can be applied to those risks.

Insurance is a key component of most risk financing plans. It enables an organization to transfer loss exposures to an insurer that will pay all losses covered under an insurance policy in return for the insured's payment of the policy premium. Insurable risks are mainly confined to hazard risk and operational risk, while financial risk and strategic risk are generally uninsurable. In general, insurers are willing to insure a loss exposure that has all or most of these characteristics: It's associated with pure risk; it's accidental from the insured's standpoint; it's definite and measurable; it's one of a large number of similar exposure units; it's not catastrophic; and it's economically feasible to insure. Before using insurance, an organization should consider the extent to which insurance meets its risk financing goals.

A noninsurance contractual risk transfer can be classified as either a noninsurance transfer for risk control or a noninsurance transfer for risk financing. A noninsurance transfer for risk control shifts loss exposures to the transferee to reduce the frequency and/or severity of the transferor's losses. A noninsurance transfer for risk financing transfers only the financial consequences of loss exposures; if the transferee defaults, the transferor ultimately retains responsibility. Common types of noninsurance transfers for risk control include leasing, contracting for services, waiver or exculpatory clauses, and disclaimers. Noninsurance transfer for risk financing is accomplished through hold-harmless agreements, also known as indemnity agreements.

Under a large deductible plan, an insured organization retains losses up to a substantial deductible and transfers the consequences of covered losses that exceed the deductible to the insurer. The insurer provides claims handling services on all claims, paying the full covered amount of losses and then billing the insured organization for the amount of loss (and possibly the claims handling expense) falling under the deductible. If carefully designed, a large deductible plan can meet common risk financing goals.

E^1

Preparing for Hazards

5

B^1

Preparing for Hazards

SOURCES OF PROPERTY RISK

After identifying the property risk exposures an organization faces, a risk management professional will need to consider the sources of risk that could affect those exposures. For example, once it's determined that a fleet of delivery vehicles is usually parked in a lot that floods easily in severe storms, the next step would be to figure out how to deal with that flooding issue.

Categorizing sources of risk can help provide a framework for managing the risk exposures. However, no approach to categorizing sources of risk is infallible, and some sources could fall into more than one category. Nonetheless, physical risks can generally be broken into two categories: natural and human.

What Do You Know?

How might risk management address natural risk sources?

Feedback: Because natural risks can't be controlled, the most effective risk management strategies for treating them entail the use of loss reduction methods to control their effects.

Natural Risk Sources

As the term suggests, natural risks occur randomly in nature, including windstorms, floods, earthquakes, and volcanic eruptions, as well as any fires, explosions, and smoke that arise from them or from lightning strikes. Although natural risk sources encompass natural disasters that affect whole communities, they also include events that affect just one organization, such as a building collapse caused by snow accumulating on the roof. Freezing, sinkholes, and vermin infestation are among the less-common natural perils known to cause property damage. To learn more, see "Natural Risk Sources—Acts of Nature."

Occurrences of natural risk sources are largely beyond human control. Consequently, risk management has little, if any, effect on reducing the likelihood of an event. However, organizations can implement loss reduction measures to control the consequences of any such events.

Natural Risk Sources—Acts of Nature		
Cave-in	Landslide/mudslide	Rust
Drought	Lightning	Temperature extremes
Earthquake	Meteors	Tidal waves
Erosion	Mildew	Tides
Evaporation	Mold	Uncontrollable vegetation
Fire	Perils of the air (e.g., icing and clear-air turbulence)	Vermin
Flood		Volcanic eruption
Hail	Perils of the sea (e.g., icebergs, waves, sandbars, and reefs)	Water
Humidity extremes		Wind (e.g., tornadoes, hurricanes, and typhoons)
Ice	Rot	

[DA13019_1]

For example, a manufacturer located in Nebraska may not think that hurricanes and earthquakes present much of a threat to its operations. However, a risk management professional who takes a global view of company operations will understand that the materials vital to the manufacturer's operations come from a supplier located in south Florida. Additionally, some of its main customers reside in Japan, where there is a substantial risk that an earthquake could disrupt supply lines. Proper planning in regard to secondary suppliers and market-scaling abilities could help the manufacturer maintain its operational health in spite of natural disasters beyond its control.

Learn more from an expert in the online video.

Human Risk Sources

Human risk sources include deliberate acts of individuals or groups, as well as events that are not deliberate but involve some element of human intervention. Examples include terrorism, vandalism, and explosion. To learn more, see "Human Risk Sources—Acts of Individuals or Groups."

Risk control techniques can usually manage the likelihood and consequences of human risk sources to some extent. For example, adopting security measures and limiting access available to the general public could help protect the previously mentioned manufacturer from on-site vandalism and terrorism risks.

Human Risk Sources—Acts of Individuals or Groups

Arson	Industrial contamination	Strikes
Chemical leakage	Labor union strikes (direct effects)	Terrorism
Collapse		Theft, forgery, fraud
Discrimination	Machinery breakdown	Toppling of high-piled objects
Electrical overload	Molten materials	
Embezzlement	Pollution (smoke, smog, water, noise)	Vandalism, malicious mischief
Explosion	Power outage	Vibration
Expropriation (confiscation)	Riot	War
Fire and smoke of human origin	Sabotage	Water hammer
	Shrinkage	
Human error	Sonic boom	

[DA13019_2]

NATURAL DISASTER LOSS CONTROL

Although it is generally impossible to control events such as windstorms, tornadoes, earthquakes, and floods, risk managers can attempt to mitigate and limit the losses they cause. By doing so, they have a chance to protect not only an organization's property but also its continuity and the livelihoods of the people it employs.

Natural catastrophes often strike with little warning, so organizations need to have plans in place to deal with the possible losses before a catastrophe actually happens. Because they each create different sorts of damages and losses, risk managers should have specific pre-loss and post-loss plans for windstorms, tornadoes, earthquakes, and floods.

What Do You Know

It's fairly easy to come up with examples of how a local catastrophic weather event could damage an organization's property and threaten its operations, but can you explain why a risk manager might be concerned with catastrophes that take place in other regions or areas of the world?

Feedback: It's not just local catastrophes that organizations need to worry about; risk managers should keep in mind how catastrophes in other parts of the world can affect their organization. For example, a supplier of parts for a manufacturer in New England could be affected by a windstorm or tornado in Oklahoma, or a key customer in India could be affected by flooding during the rainy season. Maybe the weather on the other side of the globe won't affect an organization's physical health, but that doesn't mean that it can't affect financial health.

Windstorm

A **windstorm** produces high winds or violent gusts of wind with little or no rain. Some can be tracked for days, giving those in its path time to batten windows, anchor outdoor property, or stock up on disaster supplies, but others occur rapidly and less predictably. These storms might allow only enough time to find immediate shelter. Disaster recovery plans for this source of risk should therefore reflect not only weather conditions but also the difference in warning times.

The greatest threat from windstorm is building damage, such as collapse of roofs and outside structures. Pre-loss actions for windstorm include these:

- Design buildings and outside structures to withstand anticipated wind loads. The design should reflect location conditions in which wind velocities might exceed the average.
- Use storm shutters and blinds that are rated to handle higher wind loads.
- Keep roof and wall systems, including roof tie-downs, in good repair and provide adequate supports for outside structures.
- Secure materials and equipment located outside the facility.

After a windstorm, a risk manager will want to have his or her organization ready to use any spare construction materials, such as plywood panels, tarpaulins, and plastic sheets, to temporarily repair buildings and reduce any further losses that could result if the building or equipment is exposed to the elements. There should also be arrangements in place to have security on premises to prevent looting or vandalism.

Tornado

A **tornado,** or cyclone, is a rotating column of air in a funnel-shaped vortex. A tornado extends downward from a cloud and rotates at speeds of up to 300 miles per hour (mph). Tornadoes affect most of the continental United States east of the Rocky Mountains, but high-frequency areas include the central Plains, east central Arkansas, northern Mississippi and Alabama, and central Indiana.

Nothing can prevent property losses when a tornado makes direct contact, but bodily injury can be reduced by taking shelter. Most structures are not designed to withstand a tornado's violent winds. Reinforced concrete construction has withstood tornado-force winds in some instances, but constructing all buildings this way is neither practical nor economical. Installing underground shelters, however, has proved to be an effective way to provide a safe place during evacuation.

Unfortunately, the severity of the tornado damage may not leave any meaningful post-loss options beyond preserving life and clearing rubble. If the devastation is not total, appropriate post-tornado procedures include beginning a search-and-rescue process, making temporary repairs to avoid additional property damage (all while being careful of downed power lines), and, when safety has been ensured, beginning salvage procedures.

Ɏ

Earthquake

Location is a key factor in mitigating earthquake damage and injuries for two reasons. First, people and property located farther away from volcanic areas and major geological faults (where earthquakes tend to concentrate) are less likely to experience detectable earthquakes than those located nearer to such areas. Second, stable earth can absorb seismic waves better than unstable ground can, so people and structures suffer less harm. Because earthquakes themselves can't be prevented, selecting an appropriate geographic region and a specific site within that region are crucial to earthquake risk control. Evaluating the earthquake loss exposure at a specific site normally requires a detailed geologic analysis.

The design of a building or other structure is another pre-loss action. A building in an earthquake zone should be constructed to ride atop the ground without damage. These are the two major types of earthquake-resistant construction (though many buildings in earthquake-prone areas incorporate features of both):

- **Box action design** buildings are stiff and can withstand considerable ground motion. However, an intense earthquake can sever their foundations or other anchors.
- **Frame action design** relies on the building's ability to absorb the energy of the earth movement.

During and immediately after an earthquake, post-loss actions should focus on caring for the injured, protecting the uninjured, and safeguarding endangered property. Less-intense aftershocks typically occur during the seventy-two hours after a major earthquake. Weakened buildings, underground piping, and utilities should be reinforced to the extent feasible without endangering the people doing this work. Any buildings that are not designed to withstand earthquake forces should be left temporarily unoccupied, and people should stay clear of areas where debris could fall. And during aftershocks, people may not want or be able to return to their homes, so it might be necessary to provide temporary housing for people until the aftershocks cease. Apart from preventing any imminent additional injury or damage, post-loss restoration efforts should wait until the danger of further seismic activity passes.

Box action design

Earthquake-resistant construction, used in buildings under three stories tall, that integrates roof and floor diaphragms that can flex to transmit and distribute the forces an earthquake exerts on a structure.

Frame action design

Earthquake-resistant construction that relies on the resilience of steel or specially designed reinforced concrete to absorb energy while undergoing considerable distortion and return to their original shapes.

Flood

Both inland and coastal areas can be subject to flooding from heavy rainfall, melting snow, or tidal surges. Oceanic earthquakes can cause tsunamis or tidal waves, which can travel at up to 600 mph in deep water. As a tidal wave enters coastal shoals, its velocity drops sharply, but its wave height increases—some tidal waves crest at over 100 feet. Tidal waves occur most frequently in the Pacific Ocean basin. To learn more, see "Pre-Loss Actions Can Prevent Flood Damage."

Pre-Loss Actions Can Prevent Flood Damage

See the online video.

[DA13058]

Though damage from all types of flooding may be extensive, pre-loss actions such as these can prevent property risk exposures resulting from flooding:

- Evaluate location of operations. Flood-prone or coastal areas may not be the best location from a risk management perspective.
- Analyze existing structures in flood zones for their ability to withstand normally expected events.
- Use temporary levees (or landscaping that incorporates levee features), shutters for building openings, and barriers.
- Stock disaster supplies, including portable power equipment, to maintain vital utility services.
- Place main electrical service equipment on upper floors of buildings, above historical flood-stage heights.

Many floods indirectly cause fires through electrical shorts, flammable liquids floating on top of the water, or flammable gas that escapes from broken piping. These are some pre-loss actions that can minimize flood-related fire loss exposure:

- Allow no open flames or nonwaterproof electrical wiring near or in a flood-exposed structure.
- Protect flammable-gas piping (whether utility or process services) from mechanical damage and install shutoffs or disconnects above expected flood-stage heights.
- Prevent flood water from entering buildings, by either having no lower-level openings or covering those openings against water entry.

Post-loss actions for flood emergencies can begin once flood waters have receded. These include actions such as assessing the damage (paying particular attention to building foundations), making temporary repairs of any building openings, starting salvage operations, clearing any clogged drains, and cleaning and inspecting all production and electrical equipment before restarting them.

LIFE SAFETY

A building's fire safety encompasses more than just the materials the building is made of and how its floor plans are laid out—who occupies the building and why also play a role. Fire loss control requires a great deal of advance planning because fires occur without warning and can create smoke that can blind occupants and be fatal if inhaled. In contrast, there is usually some advance warning of other risk events, such as an impending windstorm.

Factors such as the health and mobility of a building's occupants may affect their safety in a fire or other risk event. Risk management professionals must be familiar with their clients' buildings and their occupants to ensure the occupants are adequately protected against the risk of fire.

What Do You Know?

There are four human characteristics that affect an individual's susceptibility to injury or death caused by a building fire. How many can you name?

Feedback: The four human characteristics that affect an individual's susceptibility to injury or death caused by a building fire are age, mobility, awareness of the fire, and knowledge of the building.

Human Characteristics

Life safety engineers have identified six characteristics of individuals and groups of individuals that affect their susceptibility to injury or death caused by a building fire.

These are the four characteristics that affect individuals:

- Age—Occupants who are very old or very young may have limited mobility and altered awareness, which can hinder any evacuation plans in place.
- Mobility—If the occupants have physical conditions that make it difficult for them to move or be moved, their fatality rate in a fire will likely be higher.

- Awareness of the fire—The survival rate of the occupants may be affected by whether they are awake, sober, distracted, or otherwise unalert at the time of the fire.
- Knowledge of the building—Familiarity with a building can save lives in a fire, but there are many types of commercial buildings, such as malls or medical offices, where the occupants may be less familiar with the building, and will not partake in fire drills or study evacuation routes.

Additionally, these two characteristics affect groups of individuals:

- Density—Less crowded buildings enable occupants to quickly escape.
- Crowd control—Occupants who are subject to discipline and control are less likely to panic during a fire than those who are not familiar with a fire escape plan. However, risk management practices in regard to a fire should be different for an office building with regularly scheduled fire drills than for an elementary school where each teacher is responsible for many children.

Building Occupancies

In addition to being affected by human characteristics, life safety is also determined by a building's occupancy, or how the building is used. Occupancy classes are relevant to life safety because, for example, each has certain features that affect an occupant's safe exit from a building. Therefore, life safety risk control techniques and measures are determined based on both the characteristics of a building's occupants and how the building is used. To learn more, see "Classes of Occupancy."

Fire Safety Standards

Based on the general characteristics of both building occupants and occupancy, safety engineers developed specific fire safety standards for buildings. These standards are codified in the Life Safety Code, which is published by the National Fire Protection Association (NFPA).

Risk management professionals must ensure that the buildings owned or occupied by their organization comply with the provisions of the Life Safety Code (or local ordinances). Although these provisions are detailed and vary significantly among classes of occupancy and types of building structure, risk management professionals should be familiar with the fundamental requirements. To learn more, see "Life Safety Code Loss Reduction Risk Control Measures."

Life safety concerns have been the principal factors driving the development of fire, electrical, plumbing, and building codes that regulate the construction of buildings in the United States. These codes are also designed to protect building property itself from damage by fire, wind, water, and other hazards.

B¹

Classes of Occupancy

Life safety engineers have identified these twelve classes of occupancy and related concerns:

- Assembly—Generally contains large numbers of people who are unfamiliar with the spaces.

- Educational—Includes large numbers of young people.

- Daycare—Contains both young and senior occupants who are supervised by adults other than their relatives or legal guardians.

- Healthcare—Contains occupants who are incapable of self-preservation and unable to use exits, regardless of the number provided.

- Ambulatory Healthcare—Similar to healthcare occupancies.

- Detention and Correctional—House occupants are incapable of self-preservation because of imposed security.

- Residential—Includes occupants who are asleep for a portion of the time they occupy the building and may be unaware of an incipient fire that could trap them before egress occurs. Such occupancies include dwellings, rooming houses, hotels, dormitories, and apartment buildings.

- Residential Board and Care—Provides sleeping accommodations where residents also receive personal care services by caretakers who live with them.

- Mercantile—Contains large numbers of people who gather in a space that is relatively unfamiliar to them and often also contains sizable quantities of combustible contents.

- Business—Generally has a lower occupant density than mercantile occupancies, and the occupants are usually more familiar with their surroundings.

- Industrial—Exposes occupants to a wide range of processes and materials of varying hazard.

- Storage—Relatively low human occupancy in comparison to building size, and by varied hazards associated with the materials stored.

E¹

Life Safety Code Loss Reduction Risk Control Measures

The Life Safety Code requires that every building or structure should use these loss reduction risk control measures:

- Construct, arrange, equip, maintain, and operate buildings and structures to avoid undue danger to the lives and safety of occupants. (Dangers include fire, smoke, fumes, or resulting panic.)

- Provide a sufficient number of exits so that occupants can promptly escape in case of fire or other emergency.

- Design exits so that they do not rely on any one single safeguard. Provide additional safeguards, such as fire extinguishers and sprinklers, in case any single safeguard fails.

- Provide the appropriate kind, number, location, and capacity of exits. (To determine what is appropriate for a building or structure, consider the occupancy, number of persons exposed to a fire cause of loss, the fire protection available, and the height and type of construction.)

- Arrange and maintain exits to provide free and unobstructed egress from all parts of the building or structure while occupied. (No lock or fastening should prevent free escape.)

- Make exits clearly visible or conspicuously indicate the route to the exit so that every physically and mentally capable occupant can determine the direction of escape.

- Arrange and clearly mark doorways or passages that do not lead to exits so that occupants do not become confused. Make every effort to avoid having occupants mistakenly travel to dead-end points.

- Provide a minimum of two means of egress wherever occupants could be endangered by attempting to escape through a single means of egress blocked by fire or smoke.

- Arrange separate means of egress to reduce the possibility that more than one could become impassable at the same time.

- Incorporate adequate and reliable lighting for exits.

- Install fire alarms that alert occupants to danger and that facilitate orderly fire-exit drills.

- Enclose or protect vertical exits and other vertical openings between floors to protect occupants while exiting and to prevent the spread of fire, smoke, or fumes.

VALUING PHYSICAL PROPERTY

In order to properly protect an asset from risk, a risk manager needs to know that asset's worth. Several methods may be used to determine a property's value, and each has its own strengths.

Depending on the purpose of the valuation, organizations can value their property in various ways. For example, property could be insured for either its book value, which could diminish over time, or its replacement value, which may remain steadier. Some of the typical approaches to valuing property include these:

- Book value
- Replacement cost
- Market value
- Economic value

Book Value

An asset's **book value** is calculated on the accounting assumption that a portion of that asset's useful life has expired. Generally, a long-term asset's book value is lower than its market value because inflation will increase the market value while depreciation will decrease the book value. Consequently, risk management professionals do not rely solely on book value for valuing property. It may, however, serve as a starting point in determining an accurate value.

The book value of a property is based on its **historical cost**. Financial statements use the historical cost method for most assets. However, this does not mean that the financial statements simply show the original cost of those assets. For example, for a piece of real estate, the historical cost includes the building's total original purchase price, including the value of the land it occupies, plus real estate commissions, closing costs, and any other legitimate business expenses attributable to that purchase. Any capital improvements to the building are added to the original purchase price as funds are expended. For example, if an organization originally purchased its building ten years ago for $250,000 (including closing costs and other related expenses) and spent $5,000 to reroof the building, the historical cost is $255,000.

Replacement Cost

Replacement cost can be used to value buildings and personal property. Generally, a risk management professional depends on qualified property appraisers to estimate replacement cost.

Book value (net depreciated value)
An asset's historical cost minus accumulated depreciation.

Historical cost
The original cost of a property.

Replacement cost
The cost to repair or replace property using new materials of like kind and quality with no deduction for depreciation.

Buildings

A building's replacement cost is the cost of constructing a new building to replace an existing building that has been damaged or destroyed. Construction costs to replace a building can be estimated with a high degree of accuracy. Appraisers may use a simplified method, often called the unit-cost method of appraisal, in which they apply average local costs on a square- or cubic-footage basis to estimate replacement costs. They may also use a more detailed method in which they apply average local costs for each major building element to obtain a more precise estimate, called the segregated costs, of the building's replacement cost.

Some buildings might have little economic value but high replacement costs. That is particularly true of construction styles featuring large and ornate structures and of structures specifically designed for uses that are obsolete because of technological advances. For example, Airbus's introduction of the A380 airplane with a seven-story tall tail created the need for hangars to be built to larger specifications.

Personal Property

Although estimating the replacement cost of personal property is usually not as difficult as it is for buildings, it can be more time-consuming and require more specialized knowledge because many separate items of property can be involved in one loss exposure. Valuing an organization's personal property begins by creating an inventory of all furniture, fixtures, equipment, vehicles, supplies, and other tangible property that the organization owns or uses at each of its facilities. This inventory may be developed from several sources, including purchase records, values reported on insurance policies, personal inspections, and discussions with the organization's personnel.

The next step in the valuation process is to determine how to establish property replacement cost. Replacement cost differs depending on the type of business: manufacturer, wholesaler, or retailer. Every damaged or destroyed piece of inventory could be valued at its production cost (for the manufacturer), its purchase price from the manufacturer (for the wholesaler), or its purchase price from the wholesaler (for the retailer). The production costs or purchase prices that are relevant for the manufacturer, wholesaler, or retailer are the current costs or prices that are required to replace the inventory. The time of replacement could be some time after the inventory suffered the loss. For example, if the event that damaged the inventory also severely damaged the premises and forced its temporary closure, lost inventory may not be replaced until the facilities are reopened. At that time, the cost of replacing the inventory could be different from the costs or prices at the time the loss occurred.

Functional Replacement Cost

Functional replacement cost

The cost of replacing damaged property with similar property that performs the same function but might not be identical to the damaged property.

Risk management professionals use **functional replacement cost** when valuing property that is easily affected by technological changes. For example, an organization may network all of its computers through a server that it purchased several years ago. When purchased, the server was the latest model, but now it is technically obsolete (although it continues to perform its essential functions). Consequently, that model is no longer produced. The risk management professional therefore has to consider the cost of a server that is available in the current market and that can perform the necessary functions. This need not be the latest model.

Apply Your Knowledge

Goshen International operates a call center that supports several retailers. The company is located in a building that was constructed one year ago. Goshen's state-of-the art automated call system and related technology provide the company with a competitive advantage over similar types of businesses. How would Goshen's risk management professional value the company's physical property?

Feedback: Goshen's risk management professional could use several methods to establish the value of the company's physical property. The book value or the historical cost of the building would be relevant because the building is only one year old with a low amount of accumulated depreciation. The most appropriate method for valuing the building would be replacement cost, which may require the services of a qualified appraiser. Replacement cost would also be appropriate for personal property such as furniture, fixtures, and equipment. For the automated call system, the risk manager may consider using functional replacement cost. Although the current technology is state-of-the-art, it may quickly become obsolete, and newer technology may actually be less costly to replace in the future.

Market Value

Unlike some of the valuation standards previously discussed, **market value** may be more appropriate in risk management because property that must be replaced will usually be replaced at the going price in today's marketplace.

Perhaps the most appropriate use of market value is for valuing products that are relatively indistinguishable from one another, such as agricultural products, oil, or precious metals. These nonspecialized products are considered commodities and are traded as such in organized exchanges. Consequently, these products have a determinable daily market value. Risk management professionals should use a product's market value on the date of loss to determine the most appropriate valuation standard for such property. For example, if the grain in a warehouse is lost in a fire, the measure of that loss is the market value of the grain on the date of the fire.

Risk management professionals tend to use market value for other assets as well. For example, automobiles are typically valued at "Blue Book." This

Market value

The price at which a particular piece of property could be sold on the open market by an unrelated buyer and seller.

refers to the *Kelley Blue Book*, available online, which lists various makes and models of automobiles and the accessories that affect their price and states a wholesale and retail value for each kind of car based on market conditions. Other online services also offer vehicle values by type, mileage, condition, and zip code.

Economic Value

Economic value

The amount that property is worth based on the ability of the property to produce income.

Economic value focuses on the effect that the loss of the property would have on the organization's future income and, therefore, the property's contribution to the organization's overall value and net worth.

Assume, for example, that a particular metal stamping machine generates an annual output that has an income value of $100,000 after deducting all expenses. If this machine has an expected remaining life of ten years, its economic value is the present value of $100,000 that will be received annually over each of the next ten years.

Another example of economic value at risk of loss is the leasehold value of a rental property. A portion of a property's value to its owner/landlord consists of its economic value—that is, the present value of the future rental income for which it could be rented in the existing rental market. To secure the economic value, the owner/landlord must relinquish occupancy (or possession) of the rented property during the period for which the tenant has rented it. Relinquishing this right of present occupancy to secure a rental income tends to reduce the value of the landlord's ownership, but also tends to increase the landlord's economic value interest. For the landlord, the total value of the property is the total of the ownership value interest and the economic value interest.

MANAGEMENT LIABILITY RISK

In addition to property risks, an organization's risk manager must also consider liability risks. These risks result from a person's or an organization's legal responsibility for the consequences of an action they have taken or that was taken on their behalf. To differentiate the two, consider a pizza shop. An obvious property risk is that its cooking operations could cause a fire in the shop. The actions of the shop's management, meanwhile, create liability risk, such as hiring a delivery driver who isn't legally allowed to drive. Like property risks, liability risks are hazard risks that require a holistic risk management strategy.

When it comes to risk, there are times an organization can be its own worst enemy. It needs to carefully manage the actions of its management team, its employment practices, and its fiduciary responsibilities to avoid incurring damages that could destabilize the organization and keep it from reaching its goals.

While it would be impossible to note all the management liability risks the average organization faces, a few rise high enough in importance to warrant a closer look. Risks relating to the activities of an organization's directors and officers, its employment practices, and its fiduciary duties can lead to lawsuits and reputational damage. More often than not, education and awareness can help mitigate some of these risks.

What Do You Know?

Sometimes, a corporation will settle claims against its directors and officers even if it believes it has defenses to the claims. Why might it do this?

Feedback: Defense costs and the amount of time required to prepare an adequate defense can be substantial. Therefore, corporations in many situations settle claims against their directors and officers, even when their liability is not clear.

Directors and Officers Liability

Properly managing the risks posed by managerial decisions and actions requires an understating of the roles directors and officers play within an organization. While these roles can vary from organization to organization, in general, boards of directors establish corporate policy and appoint executive officers—such as the chief executive officer (CEO), president, secretary, treasurer, and so forth—to run the day-to-day operations. Although noncorporate entities also have boards of directors with the same responsibilities, the titles of their officers may differ.

Duties

When directors and officers fail to fulfill their responsibilities and duties as required under the law, they can be held liable for losses that result. The major responsibilities of corporate directors include these:

- Establishing the corporation's basic goals and broad policies
- Electing or appointing the corporate officers, advising them, approving their actions, and auditing their performance
- Safeguarding and approving changes in the corporation's assets
- Approving important financial matters and ensuring that proper annual and interim reports are given to stockholders
- Delegating special powers to others to sign contracts, open bank accounts, sign checks, issue stock, obtain loans, and conduct any activities that may require board approval
- Maintaining, revising, and enforcing the corporate charter and bylaws

- Perpetuating a competent board by conducting regular elections and filling interim vacancies with qualified persons
- Fulfilling their fiduciary duties to the corporation and its stockholders

The fiduciary relationship is the most important aspect of the corporation when it comes to analyzing the directors and officers (D&O) liability risk exposures. In addition to performing specific functions, directors and officers occupy a position of trust for stockholders and the general public. Breach of **fiduciary duty** is a common source of risk for directors and officers. These are some of those fiduciary duties:

Fiduciary duty

The duty to act in the best interests of another.

- Duty of care—Directors and officers are expected to act in good faith and in what they reasonably believe is the organization's best interest. They're expected to approach their responsibilities with informed judgment and the degree of care that any person in a similar position would believe to be reasonable.
- Duty of loyalty—Directors and officers cannot take business opportunities away from the company they work for. In other words, the CEO of a company cannot direct a client of his company to a failing competitor owned by his nephew. They must also remain loyal to stockholders in the sense that they cannot use insider information to profit from the sale or purchase of company stock.
- Duty of disclosure—Material facts must be disclosed to all people who have a right to know them and would not otherwise have access to them. For example, directors and officers have a duty to make public disclosures of facts that are material to stockholders, bondholders, and potential investors in the securities of the corporation.
- Duty of obedience—Some authorities also impose a duty of obedience (that is, obedience to the law) on directors and officers. Directors and officers are required to perform their duties according to federal and state law as well as the terms of the corporate charter.

Treatment for Directors and Officers Risks

If a corporation's stakeholders believe that they have suffered financial or other types of harm because of the actions of the directors or officers, they may take legal action. A typical risk is that investors will file a lawsuit if the corporation's stock price drops significantly. Another example is a suit against a charity that sells an old building used to house the homeless and replaces it with a modern facility: those who believe that the old building was adequate might sue the directors for wasting the charity's assets.

Lawsuits arising from D&O risks can create significant defense and settlement costs. Perhaps even more serious are the amount of time key executives must devote to defend against the lawsuits and the potential reputational harm to the corporation. Although D&O liability insurance can transfer some of the financial risk involved in the cost of defending these suits, it cannot restore a corporation's reputation. Loss of a corporation's reputation can damage customer relationships, hinder access to the capital markets, and make it difficult to attract highly qualified executives. Therefore, risk control should be a central part of the management of D&O loss exposures.

Risk Related to Employment Practices

Employers face employment practices liability (EPL) risks under a variety of national and local laws. These are the major types of EPL risks organizations can face:

- Discrimination—Discrimination does not need to be intentional to occur, creating an ever-present risk that isn't easily controlled. While overt discrimination is easily observable, disparate treatment and disparate impact may be more difficult to identify. Disparate treatment results when one individual is treated differently than others in similar situations (such as a female employee being berated for poor punctuality when male employees are not), and disparate impact occurs when policies that apply to everyone inadvertently exclude a certain group (such as requiring all employees to attend a particular religious service, which creates a disadvantage for potential employees who follow a different faith).

- Wrongful termination—Many wrongful termination claims involve charges of discrimination, but it is possible to bring them for other reasons. Traditionally, the legal doctrine of employment at will has allowed employers or employees to terminate the private-employment relationship with or without cause at any time.

- Sexual harassment—Employees who make unwanted sexual advances or demands create significant financial and reputational risks for their organization, especially in light of social media and the #MeToo movement. Some sexual harassment risks come from the perception that the employer created a hostile work environment, which exists when an employee is subjected to such severe or pervasive sexual harassment that it alters the conditions of his or her employment and creates an abusive working environment. Isolated incidents, however, are insufficient to establish a hostile work environment. In determining whether a workplace is a hostile work environment, courts consider such relevant factors as the frequency of the discriminatory conduct, its severity, and whether it unreasonably interferes with the employee's work performance.

- Retaliation—This risk arises from the possibility that a member of an organization's management team will retaliate against an employee because of a legitimate action taken by the employee. Retaliation claims may be combined with claims of discrimination based on race, gender, age, or another protected classification. Retaliation can also be alleged by employees who, for example, believe that they were discharged because they filed a workers compensation claim, testified against the employer in a legislative or court hearing, or were whistleblowers (who are protected by many federal and state laws).

These classifications are not mutually exclusive. An employee may allege that a particular situation involves more than one employment-related offense. Additionally, in recent years, employees have made EPL claims that do not fall within the context of discrimination, wrongful termination, sexual harassment, or retaliation.

For example, costly litigation has ensued after firms have closed plants or otherwise discharged large numbers of employees at one time. Another example is class action lawsuits on behalf of employees who allege that they did not receive overtime compensation. Many such claims have resulted in substantial awards. Employee claims have also arisen from objectionable email or website material sent by other employees.

To manage EPL risks, organizations can establish hiring practices that comply with federal and local standards, regulations, and laws. Additionally, they should take these actions:

- Document the company's policies and procedures clearly and concisely in the employee handbook.
- Provide employees with a formal policy regarding sexual harassment and discrimination, and document its receipt. The policy should be reviewed and updated as needed.
- Conduct annual employee performance reviews. If unacceptable behavior occurs, initiate interim reviews to correct it.
- Follow a documented termination procedure.
- Conduct and document exit interviews.
- Investigate all allegations of harassment or discrimination immediately.

Risks Related to Fiduciary Duties

Fiduciary liability risks arise mainly out of the possibility that beneficiaries of an employee benefit plan (such as active employees or retirees) may file a lawsuit against the plan officials (or fiduciaries) for breach of their fiduciary duties. For example, if an employee retirement plan that is heavily invested in company stock loses millions of dollars in value, the plan participants may file class action fiduciary liability lawsuits against the fiduciaries of these plans.

The duties of a plan fiduciary are comparable to those of a corporate director:

- Loyalty—A fiduciary's actions must be solely in the best interests of the plan and all its participants and beneficiaries.
- Prudence—A fiduciary must carry out his or her duties with the care, skill, judgment, and diligence of a prudent person familiar with such matters.

- Diversification—A fiduciary must ensure that the plan's investments are sufficiently diversified to minimize the risk of large losses.

- Adherence—A fiduciary must act according to the plan documents and applicable law. If the plan document is not in compliance with the law, the fiduciaries must follow the law and bring the plan document into compliance.

These duties imply a relatively high standard of care. The duty of loyalty may present difficult issues for fiduciaries who also are officers, directors, or employees of the employer that sponsors the plan. They cannot take the potential effect on the employer into consideration when making a decision as a prudent independent fiduciary.

If a fiduciary breaches a duty and the breach causes loss to a benefit plan, the fiduciary is personally liable to the plan for the full amount of the loss. Meanwhile, an employer may be held vicariously liable for breaches of fiduciary duty committed by its employees or agents. The employer, however, if vicariously liable, might be able to recover its share of the damages from the employee or agent.

Of particular concern from an American insurance point of view, the Health Insurance Portability and Accountability Act of 1996 calls for the protection of employee medical information and subjects the employer and fiduciaries to penalties for failure to comply.

Apply Your Knowledge

Discuss the reasons that risk control should be a central part of the management of D&O loss exposures.

Feedback: Claims against corporate directors and officers can create significant defense and settlement costs. Key executives must devote significant amounts of their time defending against claims and the potential loss of reputation for the corporation. Although D&O liability insurance can transfer some of the financial risk of these suits, it cannot restore a corporation's reputation. Loss of a corporation's reputation can damage customer relationships, hinder access to the capital markets, and make it difficult to attract highly qualified executives. Therefore, risk control should be a central part of the management of D&O loss exposures.

HUMAN RESOURCE RISK

An organization faces many liability risks arising from its employees and their behavior.

While it may be true that an organization's employees are its greatest asset, they can also be one of its greatest risks when it comes to potential liability. For example, despite whatever preventive measures an employer may take, job-related injuries will occur. Nonetheless, risk managers must try to limit the hazard risks presented in the course of employment, whether in the form of workplace injury or illness or a key employee's retirement or resignation.

What Do You Know?

Identify the difference between work-related injuries and illnesses.

Feedback: An on-the-job injury is usually caused by an external physical force, resulting in a laceration; a fracture; a contusion; or, if things really go wrong, an amputation. By contrast, a work-related illness usually develops more slowly as a result of an organic or inorganic agent being absorbed, ingested, inhaled, or injected by an employee.

Assessing Human Resource Risk

Although human resource risks originate from many sources, three are prevalent:

- Work-related injury and illness
- Retirement and resignation
- Work-related violence

Work-Related Injury and Illness

Usually, injuries are caused by an external physical force exerting stress on the human body, such as a box falling off a shelf and landing on an employee. Illnesses, in contrast, tend to happen more gradually than injuries, resulting over time as a consequence of exposure to a harmful foreign agent (through ingestion, inhalation, or something similar). This distinction is relevant because the types of risk controls applied to reducing the frequency or severity of particular disabilities depend on whether those disabilities are caused by sudden external events (injuries) or prolonged exposure to harmful conditions (illnesses).

These major categories of work-related injury are most prevalent in the manufacturing and retail fields, but risk managers in any organization should keep them in mind:

- Machinery and equipment use—Includes all mechanical devices that employees use or come in contact with on the job. As technology has advanced, sensors have had a role in enabling these machines to recognize when an injury may occur and to alert the user of the danger.

- Materials handling—Because raw materials, works in process, and finished goods can be heavy, bulky, and awkward to move, they have considerable potential for causing injury. New technologies such as wearable devices that monitor posture, weight load, and so forth can alert employees and their managers when a risk of injury exists.

- Vehicle fleet operations—Risks to drivers, passengers, and the vehicles themselves are based on many causes. To assess the risks within an organization's control, telematics can measure how safely an organization's drivers operate their vehicles, as well as record the operational health of the vehicles in case repairs or tune-ups should be done.

- Physical condition of premises—If floors, steps, and other surfaces are not properly maintained, they could cause injuries due to slips and falls. Risk managers should consider the four elements of construction, occupancy, protection, and external exposures when assessing the risks employees face on an organization's property. Fortunately, many kinds of sensors and alarms are available, such as water sensors that notify management when hazardous puddles have formed and gas detectors that monitor the air quality in a building, helping to avoid hazards such as carbon monoxide poisoning.

A personal inspection is a valuable method to help determine the extent of workplace hazards. Risk management professionals can use personal inspections to identify workplace hazards that may lead to the death or disability of employees who were not identified by the other methods of assessing personnel loss exposures. Personal inspections also provide risk management professionals with an opportunity to discuss with employees any other issues that may affect employee performance or morale.

Illness risks present a cause of concern for risk managers because organizations can be held liable for the conditions or environmental and operational factors that caused the illnesses. To learn more, see "Sources of Work-Related Illness Risk."

Retirement and Resignation

When an employee retires or resigns, the loss to the organization is the future value that the individual would have provided to the organization. For example, the resignation or retirement of a vice president who has specialized institutional knowledge of an organization's finances could result in a greater loss than the resignation of an entry-level employee. Either employee's replacement could reduce the organization's loss risk, but some will remain

Sources of Work-Related Illness Risk

Long-term
chemical exposure

Noise levels

Ergonomic stress

Radiation

Temperature
extremes

Poor air quality

[DA13104]

until the replacement employee reaches the same level of proficiency as the person who departed.

While some resignation risks and causes of dissatisfaction may be resolved with a cost-effective or feasible change, such as shifting the employee to a new position or assigning new responsibilities, not all of the possible reasons for an employee's resignation are within an organization's control. An employee may leave to start a business or because a better position was offered elsewhere, or may move to another town for personal reasons. It's possible he or she might just be dissatisfied in the current job for various reasons that may not be controllable by the employer. Part of assessing the risks regarding resignation is determining which of them are controllable and which are not.

For larger corporations or business entities, retirement and resignation risks must also be considered from an enterprise-wide perspective. Occasional reviews of the workforce's demographics can illuminate the risks of, in the case of a predominantly young workforce, potential mass resignations as employees seek new employment opportunities and career advancement or, within an older workforce, a wave of retirements.

Work-Related Violence

Workplace violence can occur despite an employer's best efforts to comply with its duty to provide a safe working environment. This duty includes protecting employees and visitors from both physical violence and mental harm caused by people they come in contact with during their working hours.

Beyond the obvious risks of death, disability, and injury, workplace violence can also create financial consequences, such as lost productivity, compensation for lost time, and lawsuits filed by the victim's family. Less obvious are the risks stemming from ongoing harassment or threats. Employees may become so fearful or ill that they cannot work, taking frequent sick days, filing workers compensation disability claims, or even filing lawsuits against the employer.

In addition to violence that can occur within the workplace, some organizations face the risk that employees will be kidnapped for ransom. While the most obvious and serious risk in this regard is that kidnap and ransom can result in serious injury or death to the kidnapped employee, the employer additionally suffers a loss, either temporary or permanent, of the employee's services, which results in a reduction of manpower for the organization. The severity of the loss depends on whether the kidnapped employee is a key person or someone whose services are more easily replaced.

Treating Human Resource Risk

Risk management professionals who are familiar with an organization's structure and procedures may select from a variety of risk control techniques to mitigate risks arising from work-related injury and illness:

- Avoidance—Reduces the probability of an activity's future loss to zero. For example, a tool manufacturer learns that the application of a rust-proof coating on its tools will emit toxic vapors. The manufacturer could simply avoid using the product, thus protecting employees from potential related harm.

- Loss prevention—Can be used when avoidance is impossible or undesirable. Safety engineering, which focuses on physical risk controls, and workplace design, which coordinates a work environment's physical features, devices, and working conditions to reduce injury risk, are two methods available to prevent injuries.

- Loss reduction—If a risk cannot be avoided, organizations will have plans in place to help restore an injured or physically limited (temporary or otherwise) individual to his or her highest attainable level of functional independence in self-care, vocational, and recreational activities.

- Separation and duplication—Separation involves arranging an organization's activities and resources so that no single event can cause simultaneous losses to all of them. For example, an organization might use separate buildings at different locations, maintain separate routes for its delivery trucks, or use several suppliers for key raw materials. Duplication involves creating backup facilities or assets to be used only if the primary activity or asset suffers a loss. An example of duplication is cross-training employees so that each has a variety of skills. Duplication helps to offset the adverse financial effects of employee injuries and illnesses. If one employee is disabled by a work-related injury or illness, a cross-trained employee with acceptable skills can temporarily replace the disabled employee.

These risk control techniques may be less effective when it comes to risk regarding resignations and retirements. For instance, although separation and duplication may help limit losses caused by the resignation or retirement of a key employee, it will never be able to remove the risk that the key employee will leave.

An organization should be concerned when the frequency of employee departures increases. Determining the cause of these departures is essential because it may indicate problems within the workplace. For example, a worker who is treated poorly by a manager may find the work environment intolerable and resign. When this occurs, a risk management professional needs to determine whether this is an isolated incident or other workers have similar impressions of the manager. Problems may be identified through an exit interview with the departing employee. Exit interviews can reveal whether other workers have resigned for similar reasons; the issue may concern just one manager or may be prevalent throughout the division or company.

Another consideration is whether the manager's behavior may have been illegal. Can the employee claim mistreatment because of discrimination based on gender, age, race, or a disability? If so, the organization may be liable under various federal and state laws. Aside from the immediate short-term loss of the productivity of the employee who leaves, there is the long-term potential of a more severe loss exposure with employment liability.

Apply Your Knowledge

Identify the four categories of risk control techniques that may be applied to work-related injury and illness.

Feedback: The four categories are avoidance, loss prevention, loss reduction, and separation and duplication.

SUMMARY

Risk management professionals should consider the risk sources that may affect identified property risk exposures. Categorizing risk sources can provide a framework for managing those exposures. Although no approach to categorizing risk sources is completely satisfactory, categorizing according to natural or human factors encompasses many risk sources that might affect property.

An impending natural disaster requires that appropriate pre- and post-loss actions be taken to ensure the organization's survival and continuing operating efficiency. Risk managers should develop disaster recovery plans for windstorms, tornadoes, earthquakes, and floods.

Risk management professionals must be familiar with their clients' buildings and their occupants to ensure the occupants are adequately protected against the risk of fire. It is important to know the minimum building design requirements for adequate fire safety. Many of these requirements focus on ensuring that a building has enough exits and that they are properly located and clearly visible.

Risk management professionals need to value an organization's property so that the magnitude of a property loss can be considered as part of the risk assessment. Most organizations own a significant amount of property, making it difficult to track the values of all but the most significant items. Typical approaches to valuing property include book value, replacement cost, market value, and economic value.

The actions of an organization's directors and officers, its employment practices, and its fiduciary duties are all sources of managerial risks that can lead to extensive financial losses and reputational damage. Education, awareness, and proper documentation of each are key to controlling these risks and protecting the organization.

Risk managers are responsible for trying to limit the hazard risks presented in the course of employment, whether in the form of workplace injury or illness or a key employee's retirement or resignation.

Uncovering Operational Risks

6

Educational Objectives	Outline

- ▶ Categorize an organization's operational risk.

- ▶ Utilize risk indicators to track the level of an organization's operational risk.

- ▶ Apply a risk and control self-assessment to assess an organization's operational risk.

- ▶ Assess the role of blockchain technology and robotic process automation in controlling operational risk.

Operational Risk Categories

Operational Risk Indicators

Self-Assessing Operational Risk

Emerging Technology and Operational Risk

Summary

Uncovering Operational Risks

6

OPERATIONAL RISK CATEGORIES

It's impossible for an organization to exist without encountering some form of operational risk—even by just hiring its first employee, it accepts the possibility that the hiring decision could help it meet its goals or wind up costing it dearly. Given this reality, it's the risk manager's responsibility to help the organization navigate through these organizational risks to meet its goals.

Operational risk is integrated into every activity of an organization; therefore, it should be evaluated based on the organization's strategic objectives, risk appetite, and risk tolerance. Organizations can benefit when they categorize their specific operational risks and develop a framework for managing them. In a risk classification framework, operational risks can often be divided into categories such as these from Basel II, an international standard for banking regulations:

- People
- Process
- Systems
- External events

} Basel II op? risk classification

People

This category typically includes all the employees of an organization, as well as its contractors, vendors, clients, and any other group of people the organization chooses to put in this category. While selecting the right employees provides an organization with the opportunity to grow, each person also presents downside risk. And although many of the risks associated with people are insurable, not all of the consequences of these risks are.

For example, discrimination or harassment by managers can be insured under employment practices liability coverage, but highly publicized discrimination cases can cause reputational damage to the organization and discourage highly qualified candidates from applying for employment. Likewise, employee theft and dishonesty may be insurable, but rogue trading and other types of risky conduct employees may engage in are often not. In 2017, for example, Wells Fargo confirmed that its staff had created millions of fake accounts since 2002 and charged customers the related fees. They also enrolled thousands of customers in online bill payment without authorization, and they imposed unneeded auto insurance on about half a million auto loans and repossessed more than one-third of those autos for noncompliance with the insurance mandate. Wells Fargo blamed unrealistic sales goals, indicating a culture of risky operational conduct from management down through certain staff members.

Individuals and organizations also cannot receive coverage for risks and opportunities that are not taken. For example, an employee who refuses to customize a product or service for a key customer may cost the organization an important customer and the corresponding revenue—there are no insurance coverages for the loss of that revenue.

Errors made during the course of business can lead to significant cost, either in aggregate or as a result of one particularly costly error. Errors and omissions (E&O) and liability insurance can cover some of these errors but rarely cover errors that do not affect a third party. For example, if a bank employee incorrectly keys in a payment amount that exceeds the actual payment, this error would not be covered by insurance. If the customer notices and reports the error, the bank could suffer reputational loss.

Another important factor in managing people risk is the significance of the organization's culture. Some organizational cultures encourage risk taking, while others prefer risk avoidance. Cultures are mainly informal and therefore can be difficult to change. In addition to observation and informal employee feedback, employee surveys can be effective in providing a basis for making changes when necessary. To learn more, see "Strategies to Mitigate People Risk."

Strategies to Mitigate People Risk

Recruitment—Recruitment allows organizations to seek candidates who best match the organization's needs and culture.

Selection—Selection procedures, such as checking references and criminal backgrounds when legally permitted, help mitigate people risk.

Training and development—Training and development should address the risks related to a given job position. For example, managers should be trained to interact appropriately with other employees.

Performance management—Employee performance should be reviewed periodically, and managers should provide ongoing feedback.

Incentives—Incentive programs can be developed to encourage appropriate employee risk taking and discourage inappropriate behaviors.

Succession planning—Organizations should maintain a plan for replacement of staff in crucial executive positions, such as chief executive officer and chief financial officer, as well as in roles that perform essential functions of the organization.

[DA12690]

Process

Process risk typically includes the procedures and practices organizations use to conduct their business activities. Managing these risks involves a framework of procedures and a mechanism to identify practices that deviate from those procedures. Risk often stems from the possibility that a practice will depart from procedure. Occasionally, such departures are creative and present a new and potentially more effective method. However, many create a negative risk. For example, speeding up a production process by skipping inspection procedures can result in unacceptable product failures that would have severe consequences.

An organization's procedures should be based on best practices and designed with the highest levels of quality and safety for both the products and employees. They should also be monitored continually with the intention of diagnosing issues and improving or redesigning the process when necessary. For instance, hospitals track rates of infection to determine whether a potential source of infection exists and should be addressed within the facility. To learn more, see "Reduction of Operational Risk Through Blockchain."

Apply Your Knowledge

Which one of the following best describes the management of process risk?

a. Process risk is best managed through training and development and performance management.

b. Process risk is best managed through a framework of procedures and a mechanism to identify nonconforming practices.

c. Process risk is best managed by developing procedures to manage market and credit risk.

d. Process risk is best managed by using best practices acquired from competitors without their knowledge.

Feedback: *b.* Process risk is best managed through a framework of procedures and a mechanism to identify nonconforming practices.

Systems

Systems risk concerns the function of technology, its intentional or accidental failure, and security. The evolution of technology and the software it uses is one of the factors that led to greater recognition of operational risk. For example, a data breach at a financial organization in which customer records are stolen can cause a loss that might threaten the organization's very existence.

Reduction of Operational Risk Through Blockchain

The development of blockchain and increasing applications for its use promise new ways to reduce operational risk. Blockchain was developed as a tool for financial transactions, such as trading cryptocurrency, that also protects the private information of the parties involved. It offers a simplified, efficient, transparent transaction that is permanently recorded and date-stamped in a distributed ledger. These transactions differ from banking transactions because blockchain transactions are verified and approved by all parties in the affected network, removing the need for central bank clearing and for the time and labor to process the transactions. Blockchain is a peer-to-peer method for performing any contract, and it establishes ownership of the property throughout its useful life.

In financial markets, blockchain is ideal for stock trading, catastrophe bond trading, real estate and other property ownership and sales, and other legal contracts that become self-executing and self-enforcing. Blockchain can simplify insurance premium collection and claim payment transactions, and it offers a streamlined approach to captive insurance and self-insurance policies by simplifying complex transactions, reducing operating costs, and adding transparency.

The benefits of exchanging data through blockchain also make it a game changer for nonfinancial transactions. It can authenticate ownership rights to art forms while managing royalty payments. Insurers can use it for policyholder acquisition and servicing. Governments can use it for efficient insurance regulatory and compliance monitoring. Manufacturers can apply it to improve supply-chain communications and ensure proof of origin and ownership. It can simplify and authenticate electronic voting and can streamline payroll processing. Blockchain offers potential with the Internet of Things, such as for managing information and requesting supplies for smart appliances; sharing operating and driver information on connected vehicles; and confirming digital identities for use in birth, marriage, and death certificates, driver's licenses, passports, and other documents. The medical field can use radio-frequency identification (RFID) devices with a blockchain to securely share patients' medical information among providers in a network while creating transparency for the providers and the patient and eliminating the need for manual handling of patient files and a central database. And insurers and legal authorities can use blockchain to identify property and detect and deter fraud.

[DA12691]

Equipment failure also presents risk for an organization's continuing operations. While some aspects of this risk are insurable, others aren't. The potential loss of customers and market opportunity, for example, are not insurable.

External Events

For organizations whose definition of operational risk encompasses hazard risk, external events can include natural disasters such as windstorms or earthquakes. Operational risks from external events can include business interruption in addition to loss of property.

Examples of external events that don't always involve natural occurrences are the loss of a key supplier, whether temporarily or permanently, or the loss of a key customer. The organization may be unable to meet production or sales goals until replacements are found.

Similarly, a local utility's failure or inadequacy could cause operational risk. Although insurable hazards cause some utility failures, many result from an electrical-system overload. Such interruptions can cause production delays and other problems. For example, a cyber breach that disrupts a utility's operations is not insured under most standard commercial policies and could severely cripple an organization's output.

Another example of an external event that could pose an organizational risk would be if the publisher of software an organization is dependent upon released a major upgrade. The organization may need to have its employees retrained to take advantage of the upgrades, taking time away from production.

OPERATIONAL RISK INDICATORS

Risk managers can't always rely on historical data to know where risks lurk within an organization's operations. For example, a new warehouse operation would not have a history of workers compensation losses suggesting that it needs an ergonomics program, but if its employees complain of back pain at the end of their shifts, the company may want to pursue one.

Risk management is most effective when issues are identified before losses occur. For example, a bank may require that any incident of a trader trading outside his or her authority level be reported, whether or not the trade results in a loss, as a means of discouraging the practice before a catastrophic loss occurs. This approach requires developing **key risk indicators (KRIs)**.

Key risk indicator (KRI)

A tool used by an organization to measure the uncertainty of meeting a strategic business objective.

What Do You Know?

To be effective, a key risk indicator should be a

a.   Lagging indicator.
b.   Leading indicator.
c.   Loss ratio.

Feedback: The correct answer is *b*. To be effective, a key risk indicator should be a leading indicator.

If risky issues can be identified before they lead to incidents, and before the incidents lead to losses, then those issues can be either removed or managed. To that end, KRIs must be leading, rather than lagging, to be effective. If a bank learns of rogue trading after a billion-dollar loss, the bank may not survive long enough to use this lagging indicator to prevent future occurrences.

Indicators by Risk Class

Although each organization has risk indicators that apply exclusively to its type of business or operations, generic risk indicators can be identified by three operational risk classes: people, processes, and systems. To learn more, see "Risk Indicators by Operational Risk Class."

Risk Indicators by Operational Risk Class

Operational Risk Class	Risk Indicators
People	• Education
	• Experience
	• Staffing levels
	• Employee surveys
	• Customer surveys
	• Compensation and experience benchmarked to industry
	• Incentives such as bonuses
	• Authority levels
	• Management experience
Processes	• Quality scorecards
	• Analysis of errors
	• Areas of increased activity or volume
	• Review of outcomes
	• Internal and external review
	• Identification of areas of highest risk
	• Quality of internal audit procedures
Systems	• Benchmarks against industry standards
	• Internal and external review
	• Analysis to determine stress points and weaknesses
	• Identification of areas of highest risk
	• Testing
	• Monitoring

[DA08721]

The list of KRIs is not stagnant by any means—for example, the continuing development of artificial intelligence (AI) allows banks to monitor communications between its brokers for the subtlest indication that something may not be right. Simply including the phrase "let's take this discussion offline" in an email may raise a red flag in a company's system.[1] Used with other indicators, such as discussion of gambling debts or a nasty divorce, the bank may be able to take action to ensure the broker has the organization's best interest in mind when finalizing any financial deals. Additionally, a bank's computer system can be programmed with red flags to provide KRIs for irregular financial transactions. Unauthorized attempts to access a computer can also provide KRIs of potential hacking or fraud.

Outside of banking, an example of a new KRI may be provided by the use of telematics in the trucking industry—if a truck's sensors indicate a high frequency of hard braking, the driver's employers may want to consider providing the driver with some safety training to not only prolong the life of the brakes, but to protect other drivers on the road.

Exposure Indicators

Exposure indicators are indicators that are integral to an organization's operations, such as a taxi company's risk of loss to auto accidents. Exposure indicators are also referred to as inherent indicators.

Most organizations have data that can identify key exposure indicators—for example, an insurer tracks losses for regulatory and financial reporting purposes as well as for its own information. Details about these losses are readily available from various functions within the organization.

Exposure indicator

A metric used to identify risk inherent to an organization's operations.

Control Indicators

Control indicators usually provide information about management. For example, a chain of pizza delivery restaurants can develop key control indicators regarding customer satisfaction and sales. Indicators such as orders placed, on-time deliveries, and customer complaints can provide risk indicators regarding the management of individual locations. The average time it takes to prepare orders and the accuracy of orders prepared can provide process indicators. Benchmarking between different locations could help identify issues and risks that the chain's home office needs to manage in order to protect the financial health of specific sites.

Apply Your Knowledge

Explain how a risk manager could apply risk management to prevent the progression of an issue into a loss.

Feedback: Issues can lead to incidents, which can progress to losses. Risk management is most effective when these issues are identified and managed before losses occur. While analyzing historical losses can identify root causes, a more successful approach involves analyzing near misses, or incidents, before losses occur and the most successful risk management approach is to identify issues before incidents occur.

Relating Indicators and Outcomes

Risk management professionals may want to evaluate how a control indicator affects outcomes. For example, a temporary staffing organization may want to analyze how the experience of its employees in their fields relates to complaints received from the company's clients. The first level of analysis may be to chart the number of complaints received from clients and the experience level of employees assigned to those clients. To learn more, see "Risk Indicator: Client Complaints Versus Years of Employee Experience."

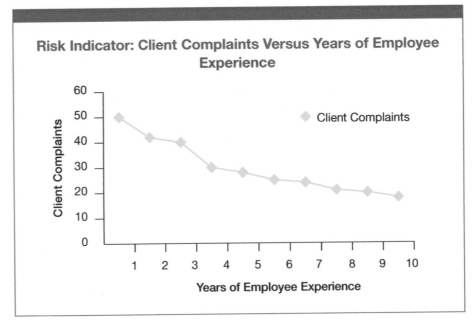

[DA08722]

The staffing company sees a correlation between the experience level of its employees and its client complaints and decides to analyze the trend. To do this, the company's risk manager can use a regression analysis to evaluate the relationship between average employee experience (x) and client complaints (y) over a four-year period.

After confirming this relationship, the staffing company decides to benchmark its employee experience against others in its industry; however, data regarding complaints is not readily available from other companies. The staffing company did find that its employees' average years of experience is higher than the industry benchmark of four years ago, but decreased during the four-year period and is now lower than the benchmark. To learn more, see "Risk Indicator: Employee Experience Versus Industry Benchmark."

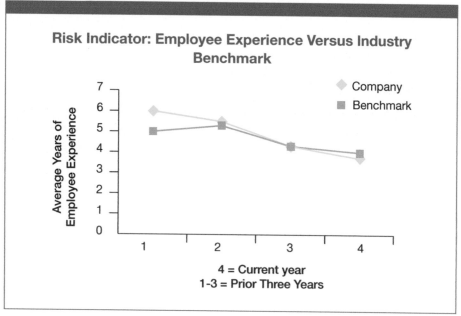

Risk Indicator: Employee Experience Versus Industry Benchmark

[DA08725]

The staffing company has several risk indicators of issues to be managed. It already knew that inexperienced workers tend to have more occupational injuries. But it learned that client complaints appear to be correlated to employee experience. It also learned that the average experience of its employees is decreasing and currently lower than the industry benchmark. Finally, the company learned that the number of client complaints is increasing.

Through these KRIs, the company has identified an issue of decreasing experience level in its employees and can now manage this issue. It can change its advertising and recruitment strategies to attract employees with more experience. It can also consider benchmarking its compensation to the industry to be sure that it is paying experienced employees appropriately. The company can further take steps to conduct basic customer service training for all of its employees to improve client satisfaction.

E'

SELF-ASSESSING OPERATIONAL RISK *B'*

Self-awareness isn't just for people—an organization that is aware of the risks it faces, especially from an internal operational standpoint, is in a better position to control those risks and meet its operational goals.

Risk assurance refers to the level of confidence in the effectiveness of an organization's risk management culture, practices, and procedures. A healthy risk assurance, measured through the use of a control risk self-assessment (CRSA) model and supported by a strong risk monitoring and reporting program, will bolster the confidence of an organization's stakeholders, which, in turn, will help the organization achieve its goals.

For example, an automaker with strong risk assurance may have an easier time hiring and retaining high-caliber employees, achieving its sales goals, and maintaining shareholder confidence even through recalls or less-than-optimal reviews of a new model.

What Do You Know?

True or false: Risk assurance is developed through internal resources because external resources could provide biased information and opinions that don't reflect the strength of an organization's financial status.

Feedback: False. Internal and external resources both have a role to play as an organization builds risk assurance.

Risk Assurance

Internal and external resources both have a role to play as an organization builds risk assurance. Internally, the establishment and use of policies and procedures, safety manuals, disaster recovery plans, and employee training all help manage operational risk. For example, let's consider a nightclub that was destroyed when faulty wiring caused a fire. If it was discovered that the club's management team didn't comply with its own safety manual because it didn't want to spend the money to rewire the building, it's unlikely the club's stakeholders—both the investors and the patrons—would trust that management team again.

Risk assurance can also be fostered through internal auditing procedures, internal controls, and the preparation and review of financial reports. Strategic and business continuity plans are also essential elements of risk assurance. For example, if rumors spread about a chain of department stores being several months behind in paying rent and suppliers, its bankers, business partners, and vendors may begin withdrawing financial or material support.

Externally, third-party audits confirm that financial statements are a true and fair depiction of the organization's financial position. Positive press reports can enhance the organization's reputation and help portray it favorably to the public. Other external methods of building risk assurance include supplier and lender confidence, reports and rankings from legal and regulatory authorities, and customer surveys.

Control Risk Self-Assessment

When conducting a control risk self-assessment (CRSA), all employees (including management) work together to identify and evaluate the organization's risks and their controls. The CRSA complements other risk management techniques an organization may use and is an acceptable method of satisfying the compliance requirements of corporate governance and regulatory bodies.

In short, the CRSA process reviews the effectiveness of the business's internal procedures, systems, and personnel in these ways:

- Categorizes and prioritizes objectives
- Evaluates the risk management process and risk controls currently in place
- Identifies risk controls that may be needed and weaknesses in existing risk controls
- Cultivates action plans
- Ensures the process is used consistently in all areas and at all levels of the organization

CRSAs are conducted through workshops and questionnaires. The primary advantage of a workshop approach is the quick dissemination of information; it allows a real-time, informal exchange between personnel at all levels.

Workshops, however, aren't always practical for an organization. For example, there may be too many employees involved to hold workshops, or employees might not be centrally located. The corporate culture may not invite frank, open communication at all levels (a characteristic that the CRSA may want to address), or management may simply want to avoid the time and expense of workshops. In these instances, questionnaires may be the preferred method of conducting the CRSA.

Questionnaires allow for the collection of comprehensive and detailed data, along with conceptual information. They can show the operational risk roles and responsibilities of everyone within the organization, as well as identify operational risks and compare them with controls already in place. Questionnaires can also encourage respondents to volunteer information. To learn more, see "Hypothetical CRSA Questions."

Many organizations use both workshops and questionnaires at different stages of the process. For example, workshops might be followed up later in the year with a questionnaire to gather additional facts, figures, and impressions about topics discussed during the real-time exchanges.

Hypothetical CRSA Questions

A CRSA does not replace an internal audit; it supplements it. For example, a CRSA questionnaire might ask the following questions, calling for a response that is "yes," "no," or "N/A":

- Question 1: All employees are familiar with the company's internet and cyber policy.
- Question 2: Backup and recovery procedures for all company computers and networks appear adequate.
- Question 3: All employee-owned computers and devices used for company business are documented and approved.

[DA13053]

Risk Management Monitoring and Reporting

To be effective, a risk reporting system must provide a flow of information both up and down the lines of authority. Senior management establishes management policy, which is disseminated downward through different levels of management. Managers then report on compliance through risk response plans, financial reports, and incident reports.

Risk reports should focus on key risk indicators that show whether the organization is meeting its goals and objectives. They should also include trends, comparative performance measures, and compliance with standards using both internal and external sources.

However, something to keep in mind is that an organization can become overwhelmed by the flow of data if it is not managed properly. For instance, while reports from individual departments can contain a great deal of information, they don't necessarily show whether performance achieved the organization's objectives. A report from the Production Department may show that manufacturing goals are being met, but it won't indicate at a glance whether sales targets are being achieved, which is essential information when determining the health of an organization. Individual reports can also take a lot of time to analyze and compare before they can, collectively, portray the organization's condition and direction accurately.

When reporting data, an organization should be aware of the advantages and disadvantages of the different types of data to be collected, and the different methods used to report them. A risk management monitoring and reporting system should use both quantitative and qualitative data.

For example, reports of credit default rates, profit ratios, and equipment utilization rates contain quantitative data that measures how well the organization manages its operational risks. Conversely, a customer satisfaction survey can combine both types, gathering qualitative information in a comments section that might explain quantitative information gathered by the numeric scores provided in response to certain questions.

The manner in which the reports are designed is also key to their effectiveness. A silo reporting approach requires each department to create its own risk reports. However, this approach doesn't factor in how other departments experience—or don't experience—the same risk exposure or perspectives. An integrated risk report collects data from each department and reports on the effects across all departments, providing a much more concise and useful picture. For example, if an organization sought a cyber risk report only from its IT Department and not its Human Resources Department, it would not know about all the risks its employees faced when using their personal devices at home for work purposes.

EMERGING TECHNOLOGY AND OPERATIONAL RISK

Confronting an organization's operational risk means dealing with a wide array of disparate factors, including people, processes, systems, and external events, each with their own individual risks. Fortunately, new technologies continue to emerge and evolve, creating more efficient, less fallible processes that decrease operational risks.

Operational risk is often the by-product of human actions, whether intentional or accidental. The smallest examples of procedural errors, from misfiling information to incorrectly transcribing meeting notes or an eyewitness account, can create liabilities and loss exposures. Fortunately, new technologies, such as blockchain and **robotic process automation (RPA)**, can reduce inconsistencies among data sources, as well as increase overall efficiency throughout an organization and limit strain on employees.

Robotic process automation (RPA)

A program that automates repetitive organizational processes. Most often used for administrative tasks, such as data entry.

What Do You Know?

True or false: RPA and business process management can be complementary in nature, but should remain separate at all times.

Feedback: False. RPA can be a useful part of a business process management plan.

Emerging Technologies, Data Accuracy, and Operational Risk

Emerging technologies related to operational risk have focused heavily on data accuracy and process efficiency, aiming to achieve as much as possible while also being as accurate as possible. Data can be gathered quickly, through sensors, cameras, and similar hardware, and then stored and accessed through technologies such as blockchain and RPA. These new capabilities allow organizations to enhance their customer experience and relieve their workforce of routine tasks by creating a more efficient, accurate process of storing and retrieving data.

Learn more from an expert in the online video.

Blockchain is often discussed alongside smart contracts, with verification of contract completion made with information provided by a trusted third-party source. An example of this is a hardware store that has a standing agreement to purchase a set amount of plywood whenever a hurricane is expected to strike within a certain number of miles. The smart contract would include a source of weather information that is agreed upon by both the store and supplier, such as the National Weather Service (NWS), and an established protocol: such as, that whenever the NWS included the store's geographic area in an approaching storm's "cone of uncertainty," an order for wood would automatically be placed and paid for at the set price.

This process would reduce the operational risk involved with human fallibility, such as an employee at the store forgetting to place an order for the plywood or not paying close attention to weather reports. The supplier would not have to worry about an order being placed incorrectly and resulting in unneeded merchandise.

From an insurer's standpoint, discrete insurance transactions could be handled in the same way as ongoing ones—for example, when a vendor purchases weather insurance for an outside event, such as a county fair. Similarly, the smart contract could be linked to weather data provided by the NWS, and if the amount of rain that falls during the fair exceeds a threshold mentioned in the contract, the vendor would be indemnified according to the contract, and payment could be transferred immediately to the vendor's bank account.

Blockchain can also alleviate operational risks caused by the inaccuracy and inefficiency of current record-keeping practices.

For example, record keeping can be a significant source of operational risk for medical facilities and practices because of legal liability regarding patient privacy and treatment. Both of those risks can be controlled if a patient's records are kept in a verifiable system, such as a blockchain, where a patient can determine who accesses them and where the records will contain the most up-to-date information.

So, if a patient moves from one medical practice to another, that patient could grant the new doctor access to all of his or her information through the blockchain. That way, the patient wouldn't have to spend time filling out repetitive paperwork, and the new office wouldn't have to wait for the previous practice to send the records. Additionally, the patient could close access to the previous practice to maintain privacy and security.

Theoretically, blockchain use could also be expanded to monitor prescription use, collecting information on what prescriptions were provided and when, ensuring that the most recent professional visited has the information necessary to avoid potentially harmful combinations of medications. And in the financial sector, blockchain can provide an agreed-upon source of information regarding benchmark values for trades and investments.

For example, without a transparent verification process for the interest rates charged by international banking firms, the London Interbank Offered Rate (LIBOR) was found in 2012 to have been manipulated for several years. LIBOR has served as the basis for the loan rates banks charge one another, with rates that are based on each bank reporting their own interest rate. Without any outside verification, banks were able to manipulate the rates to their benefit.

Blockchain would work to reduce similar operational risks in the financial sector because the participating banks' rates would need to be verified before being added to the record. There would be no taking their word for it.

Much like with the medical field, blockchain could also help reduce redundant record keeping throughout the financial world. Financial firms that come together in a syndicate to participate in a transaction, such as a loan, could use a blockchain as a verifiable record of the transaction, rather than keeping individual records at each firm. This would help control the operational risk of inaccuracy that is involved whenever an employee is in charge of creating or maintaining records—a risk that is multiplied by the number of organizations that each have a different employee undertaking the same responsibility.

Controlling operational risk through technology can also involve putting older technologies to new uses. For example, in some parts of the world, Uber has begun using a passenger's rating to weed out problematic customers. After receiving a ride from an Uber driver, customers are rated on a scale of one to five stars, with one being the worst and five being the best. If a passenger's rating is consistently below 4, they'll no longer be allowed to use the service. By enacting this policy, Uber is addressing an operational risk that bad customers will discourage good drivers from continuing to offer their services, as well as operational risks that could affect their drivers' safety.[2]

Telematics can also provide a technology-driven solution to some operational risks. Sensors placed in commercial vehicles can notify drivers and fleet mechanics of needed repairs, as well as provide information regarding drivers' safety habits. Office equipment can notify users of needed maintenance in the same way, addressing potential financial risks arising from necessary repairs during off hours or resulting in lost sales because of down time.

Robotic Process Automation and Operational Risk

RPA is a bit of a paradox in that, although it can help control some organizational risks, it can also create others. For example, if a manufacturing company were to automate the task of organizing heavy crates on warehouse shelves rather than relying on employees to lift them, it could help control the risk of worker injuries. However, that same action could create the organizational risk of weakened morale, if employees felt that their job security was threatened. So before any RPA programs are put in place, a company's risk manager should consider all angles.

Learn more from an expert in the online video.

Despite the "robotic" part of its full name, RPA does not always involve robots. While the field of robotics involves several disciplines that work together to create a machine capable of various tasks, RPA is more focused on creating a process to complete one task. For example, a small robot that is designed to vacuum your floor could, conceivably, also be programmed to deliver drinks to your guests at a party. It may not do the new job well, but it could get it done. An RPA, however, would more likely have the simple goal of determining when the robot should begin its vacuuming according to a schedule and telling it to do so.

RPA can be put to use within an office without much notice; examples include a program that automatically verifies the balances of a bank's customers and notifies those who have balances below the required minimums and a program that contacts a dentist's patients when they have upcoming appointments. RPAs such as these not only reduce the organizational risks of low balances going unnoticed or forgotten appointments being missed but they also allow staff members to concentrate on tasks that require more substantive thought and skill. So with assurances from management, the result could be better morale as employees are given more responsibility and less boring tasks, rather than decreased morale stemming from job insecurity.

As helpful as RPA can be in boosting organizational efficiency and controlling some operational risks, to reach its full potential RPA should be used as part of **business process management (BPM)**. BPM looks at an organization's operations from beginning to end. Its goal is to make the organization more efficient and productive, which, as with RPA, involves limiting operational risks where possible.

For example, let's say a bank is looking to introduce a comprehensive BPM plan that will make use of RPA where possible. While the bank may want

Business process management (BPM)

An enterprise-wide approach that looks to optimize business processes, making use of automatization when appropriate.

to control the operational risk of its loan officers being accused of bias in addressing mortgagors who are late with their payments, they would not want to automate that process, either. Doing so could lead to accusations that the bank was cold-hearted and detached from its customers, as well as to foreclosures against customers resulting from data entry errors or miscommunications (for example, a direct withdrawal from the borrower's account not going through). So keeping a human being who is experienced at making judgment calls in charge of that process would be important.

BPM, as an alternative, may suggest providing further training for the bank's lending officers. This training could take place during the time the lending officers would normally contact late-paying borrowers, as this action could be done by an RPA.

SUMMARY

Risk management professionals should help organizations understand and define their operational risk. A system that effectively categorizes an organization's operational risk provides a framework to manage it and may include the Basel II categories of people, process, systems, and external events.

KRIs provide leading information regarding issues that risk management professionals should manage before the issues lead to incidents and then losses. KRIs can be categorized by exposure and control indicators in each operational risk class. Trend analysis and benchmarks assist in determining how KRIs affect outcomes.

A CRSA can help an organization assess its operational risks by building risk assurance through the use of internal and external sources. Workshops, questionnaires, and effective monitoring and reporting of processes, systems, and personnel communicate information up and down the lines of authority so management can respond to threats and opportunities.

Emerging technologies such as blockchain and RPA help control operational risks by providing accurate data and improving the efficiency of processes already in place. Although it could be tempting to rely solely on RPAs, they provide better results when used as part of BPM.

ASSIGNMENT NOTES

1. Laura Noonan, "Banks Use AI to Catch Rogue Traders Before the Act," *Financial Times*, March 25, 2019, www.ft.com/content/be7a5584-2ee7-11e9-80d2-7b637a9e1ba1 (accessed April 4, 2019).

2. Mike Cherney, "Stuck With an Uber Rating Under Four? Better Hit the Bricks," *The Wall Street Journal*, September 5, 2018, www.wsj.com/articles/stuck-with-an-uber-rating-under-four-better-hit-the-bricks-1536141080 (accessed April 8, 2019).

Making Sense of Financial Risk

7

B'

Making Sense of Financial Risk

7

TYPES OF FINANCIAL RISK

During the first half of the 1980s, interest rates and stock dividend yields were historically high. Simple money market funds yielded more than 10 percent, and insurers found good returns from safe, liquid investments. Insurers in a competitive market could endure loss ratios of 105 or 110, covering underwriting losses with investment gains. But when rates began a steep decline around 1985, many insurers struggled to remain profitable. They had not properly managed a key element of market risk.

An organization owning or using a financial instrument is exposed to financial risk—the uncertainty arising from the effect of market forces on a financial asset or liability. A financial instrument is a check, a bond, a share of stock, another document with monetary value, or a binding agreement between parties for payment of money. Risk management professionals need to understand these risks in order to mitigate them.

Market Risk

What Do You Know?

When the United States dollar appreciates against the euro,

a. One dollar buys more euros than it had previously.
b. Swiss banks are forced to hedge currencies to make up the difference.
c. Imports rise because of demand for U.S. dollars.
d. There is no effect on importing companies who use U.S. banks.

Feedback: *a.* When the U.S. dollar appreciates against the euro, one dollar buys more euros than it had previously.

Market risk is the risk that the value of an investment or a portfolio of investments will decrease or increase because of changes in the market for that investment. Associated market risks include these:

- **Interest rate risk**
- **Exchange rate risk**
- Liquidity risk

Interest rate risk

The risk that a security's future value will decline because of changes in interest rates.

Exchange rate risk

Uncertainty about an investment's value because of potential changes in the exchange rate between currencies.

Interest Rate Risk

Interest rate risk involves uncertainty over the movement of interest rates and the effect that has on the value of an investment. Movement in the interest rate could affect the value of an organization's assets or liabilities in either direction.

[handwritten margin note: uncertainty of IR's & effects on investments]

For example, suppose ABC Company invests $1 million in a 10-year government bond that pays 3% interest annually. One year later, newly issued bonds of the same type are yielding 3.5%. The market value of ABC's bond falls because buyers prefer the newly-available higher yielding bonds. Of course, if the new bonds yield only 2.5%, then the market value of ABC's bond increases.

Exchange Rate Risk

Exchange rate risk is a concern to an organization with cash flows denominated in a foreign currency. Changes in the exchange rate can affect the value of an organization's assets and liabilities.

[handwritten margin note: uncertainty of XR of foreign currencies compared to dollar]

For example, a U.S. buyer contracts with an Italian shipbuilder and agrees to make payment in four yearly installments in euros as a ship is being built. The buyer bears risk that the dollar may depreciate in value in relation to the euro. If that happens, it will require more dollars to make the stipulated payment in euros.

Liquidity Risk

Will an organization have enough cash, or assets easily converted to cash, should an immediate need for it arise? That uncertainty is liquidity risk. Typically, the amount of cash needed during a given time period can be reasonably estimated; however, if an unusual event occurs, demand for the organization's cash may increase suddenly and significantly.

[handwritten margin note: uncertainty whether you have enough cash / assets easily liquidatable]

After the readily available cash has been spent, the organization may try to borrow additional funds or sell assets that can be converted to cash with little loss in value. If the organization still can't meet the demands for cash, it may be forced to sell assets that can be sold only in a short time period at a substantial discount. The discount represents a loss in value in the organization's assets, which is also reflected in a reduction in the organization's net worth.

For example, say ABC Company lost its insurance coverage when its policy was nonrenewed because of high claims frequency. The bank issuing ABC's $1 million loan requires that ABC maintain insurance coverage. When the insurer notifies the bank that the coverage has not been renewed, the bank demands that the loan be repaid immediately. ABC is then in a position where it must quickly obtain cash to repay the loan.

Credit Risk

Credit risk (also referred to as **counterparty risk**) relates to the uncertainty about a party who is obligated to pay money per a binding agreement. Will the party actually pay all of the money owed and on time? The party could be, for instance, a customer who bought the organization's products or services on credit. If every customer paid the amount owed on time, there would be no credit risk. However, if a customer defaults on the credit agreement, the income from the sale of the products or services is at risk.

Similarly, if the obligated party received a loan from the organization and then defaulted on the loan agreement, the principal loaned and the interest are both at risk. For example, if an organization discovers that a $50,000 loan is in default and uncollectible due to the deteriorated financial condition of the obligated party, the organization will have to adjust its balance sheet. The asset account for loans made by the organization will have to be reduced by $50,000, and, to maintain balance, the net worth account will also be reduced by the same amount.

Counterparty risk

The risk that the other party to an agreement will default.

Price Risk

Price risk relates to the uncertainty of setting the price of an organization's product correctly. Input price risk or output price risk can lead to loss of revenue. Input price risk is the uncertainty of the price of the resources used to produce an organization's product. An increase in the price of a resource, such as, for example, copper for a wire manufacturer, will lower the manufacturer's margin on wire unless it raises the price of the wire.

Output price risk is the uncertainty regarding the price an organization can charge for its product. A competitor's pricing may force an organization to lower the price for its product to one with a very thin margin for profit. For example, a baker might have to lower the price of his baked goods if several other bakers are located in the same town.

Price risk

The potential for a change in revenue or cost because of an increase or a decrease in the price of a product or an input.

ASSESSING A BALANCE SHEET

Why should a risk management professional care about a mundane topic like accounting? What's the value of the balance sheet in assessing risk?

The balance sheet is a listing of everything that the organization owns and everything that it owes at a particular moment in time. It is a snapshot of the company's financial position as of that date.

Financial analysts, investors, and underwriters evaluate an organization's financial strength by examining its balance sheet. Using information from it, they can quickly assess aspects of an organization's financial health by calculating measures like liquidity ratios and leverage ratios.

Let's get to know the balance sheet.

The Balance Sheet

What Do You Know?

On a balance sheet, what is a term for the value calculated by subtracting liabilities from assets?

a. Owners' equity
b. Book value
c. Surplus
d. All of the above
e. None of the above

Feedback: *d.* All of the above. Owners' equity, book value, and surplus are all terms for the value calculated by subtracting liabilities from assets. Let's learn more.

A balance sheet is a snapshot of a business's financial position at a particular moment in time. Assets, listed on the left-hand side of the balance sheet, are the resources a business owns or uses to operate. Liabilities, listed on the right, are the debts and obligations that represent claims against the business's assets.

The difference between assets and liabilities in a for-profit business is called shareholders' equity (also known as owners' equity, net worth, or book value). Shareholders' equity is shown on the liabilities side of the balance sheet because a business does not own its net worth—it "owes" its net worth to its owners. To learn more, see "TMT Balance Sheet."

The balance sheet gets its name because both sides, assets on one and liabilities plus shareholders' equity on the other, must be the same, or balanced—even if shareholders' equity must be a negative number for balance to occur. Shareholders' equity is calculated in this way:

Assets – Liabilities = Shareholders' equity (owners' equity)

Assets

Assets are the resources an organization owns or uses to operate its business. They are grouped into current assets and noncurrent assets. Current assets can include cash, marketable securities, receivables (accounts and notes), inventories, and prepaid expenses. Noncurrent assets are assets that will be used over a period greater than one year; they are grouped into tangible assets (such as land, buildings, and equipment) and intangible assets. Intangible assets include all assets that cannot be seen or touched, such as leaseholds, patents, copyrights, and trademarks, and they are often categorized as intellectual property.

TMT Balance Sheet

TMT, Inc.
Balance Sheet
For the year ended 12/31/20X1

Assets		Liabilities	
Current Assets:		Current Liabilities:	
Cash and Cash Equivalents	$ 300,000	Accounts Payable	$ 500,000
Short-Term Investments	150,000	Taxes Payable	250,000
Account Receivable	150,000	Total Current Liabilities	$ 750,000
Inventory	1,000,000		
Total Current Assets	$1,600,000	Long-Term Debt	$2,000,000
		Other	650,000
Property and Equipment	$4,400,000		
Long-Term Investments	1,500,000	Total Liabilities	$3,400,000
Goodwill	0		
		Shareholders' Equity	4,100,000
		Total Liabilities and	
Total Assets	$7,500,000	Shareholders' Equity	$7,500,000

[DA06501]

Noncurrent assets, by definition, are used over multiple years. The value of many noncurrent assets, such as machinery, declines over time due to a variety of factors, including usage, wear and tear, and obsolescence.

Depreciation is an accounting term used to describe allocation of a noncurrent tangible asset's value over its useful life. There are many methods of depreciating assets, such as straight-line depreciation or declining balance depreciation. On the balance sheet, the historical cost of a noncurrent asset is reduced by the depreciation amount, leaving the net value of that asset (Historical cost – Accumulated depreciation) on the balance sheet.

Liabilities

Liabilities are the debts and obligations that represent claims against an organization's assets. As with assets, liabilities are categorized as current or noncurrent. Current liabilities can include accounts payable, short-term debt, or the current position of a long-term debt. Noncurrent liabilities are those that will be paid or satisfied more than one year after the balance sheet date, such as long-term notes payable.

Shareholders' Equity

Shareholders' equity (owners' equity) is the net amount of assets after deducting an organization's debts and obligations (liabilities). It includes capital contributed by owners and accumulated earnings retained by the organization (retained earnings) since its inception. Also, for specified assets and liabilities, it includes cumulative changes in value that were not used to calculate cumulative earnings. On the balance sheet of a not-for-profit organization, shareholders' equity is often called "surplus."

If some or all of the assets on the balance sheet are listed at the price paid for them (historical cost) rather than at current fair market value (fair value), net worth would not reflect the market value of the assets. Because historical costs may be significantly higher or lower than fair value, shareholders' equity (net worth) based on historical cost of assets may differ significantly from shareholders' equity (net worth) based on fair values of assets. This same concept applies to liabilities.

Shareholders' equity is negative whenever liabilities exceed assets. A business with negative shareholders' equity may be close to bankruptcy. Let's look next at how we can use balance sheet information to measure financial health.

Liquidity Risk and Liquidity Ratios

Liquidity ratios measure a company's ability to convert assets to cash. For most organizations, liquidity can be measured using working capital, the current ratio, and the acid-test (quick) ratio. The higher the value, the larger the margin of safety the company possesses to cover short-term debts.

[handwritten margin note: measures ability to convert assets to cash]

Working Capital

Working capital is the excess of a company's current assets over its current liabilities:

Working capital = Current assets – Current liabilities

Current assets are cash and those assets that are likely to be converted to cash within one year of the balance sheet date—primarily marketable securities, accounts receivable, and inventory. Current liabilities are obligations that will need to be paid within the same one-year period, including accounts payable; the current portion of loans payable; and accrued expenses, such as wages payable, interest payable, and taxes payable. Although a company may not have enough cash on hand to meet all its obligations for the next year, it expects to collect accounts receivable and sell inventory to provide the required cash.

Current Ratio

Most financially sound companies have positive working capital. However, an analyst must further know whether that working capital will adequately meet the company's upcoming obligations. The current ratio provides this information:

$$\text{Current ratio} = \text{Current assets} \div \text{Current liabilities}$$

When calculating the current ratio, an analyst should be aware that different inventory valuation methods produce different inventory values for the balance sheet and therefore can produce different values for the current ratio. In addition, because the current ratio uses balance sheet data, a company's liquidity and this ratio can be significantly affected by transactions entered into after the balance sheet date, such as taking on additional short-term debt.

Acid-Test (Quick) Ratio

The acid-test ratio is a more conservative measure of liquidity than the current ratio because it includes only cash, marketable securities, and accounts receivable in its numerator. Because of its simplicity, it is also called a quick ratio:

$$\text{Acid-test ratio} = (\text{Cash} + \text{Marketable securities} + \text{Accounts receivable}) \div \text{Current liabilities}$$

Now let's take a look at leverage ratios. To learn more, see "Financial Ratios by Category."

Financial Ratios by Category

Category	GAAP-based measurement	Ratio formula
Liquidity	Current ratio	Current assets ÷ Current liabilities
	Acid-test, or quick, ratio	(Cash + Marketable securities + Accounts receivable) ÷ Current liabilities
Leverage	Debt-to-equity ratio	Long-term debt ÷ Shareholders' equity
	Debt-to-assets ratio	Total liabilities ÷ Total assets

[DA07484]

Leverage Ratios — *measures degree of borrowing $*

Leverage ratios measure the degree to which a company has borrowed money. A company without debt employs no financial leverage and thus has a leverage ratio of zero. Conversely, a company that relies extensively on borrowed funds (for example, to acquire assets) is highly leveraged and would have a correspondingly high leverage ratio.

Interest payments on debt must be paid before any profits can be returned to shareholders in the form of dividends. Debt repayments remain unchanged regardless of profit. If profits increase, more money is available to be paid out in dividends to shareholders. Conversely, if profits decrease, debts still have to be repaid. Therefore, the money remaining to distribute to shareholders decreases. At the extreme level, if the company does not have sufficient funds to repay debt, the shareholders risk losing some or all of their investments.

One of the most common measures of financial leverage in noninsurer financial statement analysis is the debt-to-equity ratio. This ratio relates total liabilities to shareholders' equity. The debt-to-assets ratio, sometimes referred to as the debt ratio, provides another view of how a company has financed its assets.

Debt-to-Equity Ratio

The debt-to-equity ratio is commonly used to assess the relative extent of an organization's debt financing compared with other organizations in the same industry.

$$\text{Debt-to-equity ratio} = \text{Long-term debt} \div \text{Shareholders' equity}$$

In some cases, an analyst may substitute total liabilities for long-term debt—that is, calculate the debt-to-equity ratio by dividing total liabilities by shareholders' equity. As noted in the discussion about current ratio, it is important to know how the ratio is calculated because different calculation approaches can produce significantly different ratios.

Debt-to-Assets Ratio

The debt-to-assets ratio, or debt ratio, is a leverage ratio that shows the extent to which a company's assets are financed by debt. For this ratio, the term "debt" is used in a broad sense to include not only borrowed funds but also other obligations, such as accounts payable.

$$\text{Debt-to-assets ratio} = \text{Total liabilities} \div \text{Total assets}$$

An advantage of this ratio is that it shows how the assets of the company are financed. If the ratio is less than 0.5, then the company is financing most of its assets through the equity contributions of its shareholders. If the ratio is greater than 0.5, then most of the company's assets are financed through debt. Typical debt-to-assets ratios vary by industry. However, a high debt-to-assets ratio indicates that a company is highly leveraged and could be at risk if it is not able to keep up with debt repayments. *E*

SECURITIZATION

While some sources credit the Dutch for the first instances of securitization during the 1700s, a more modern version began in the United States in 1970, when the Government National Mortgage Association (GNMA) began to sell securities that were backed by mortgage loans. There are now many other ways to buy mortgage-backed securities, but those from GNMA remain the only ones backed by the U.S. government.

Organizations seek to generate cash to maintain liquidity, fund current operations, and expand into new markets. Because of the high financial and regulatory stakes, risk management professionals should understand how organizations convert an income-producing asset to a cash asset, particularly when the organization needs additional cash quickly.

Securitization

What Do You Know?

The activity of buying a bundle of mortgage loans and then selling to investors an interest in those income-producing assets is

a.   Prohibited if subprime home loans are involved.

b.   Transacted with a commercial mortgage broker.

c.   Required under statutory accounting as a means to mitigate financial risk.

d.   Performed by an intermediary known as a special purpose vehicle.

Feedback: *d*. The activity of buying a bundle of mortgage loans and then selling to investors an interest in those income-producing assets is performed by an intermediary known as a special purpose vehicle.

Securitization is the process of creating marketable investment **securities** based on a financial transaction's expected cash flows. When an organization uses an intermediary for this purpose, it allows investors to decide whether to invest in a security based solely on the risk presented by the income-producing asset and not the credit risk of the organization who owned the asset before transferring it to the intermediary.

An organization can use securitization to exchange income-producing assets for cash from the purchaser of the security, assuming that a market exists for the asset. This exchange allows the organization to convert the asset to cash on its balance sheet.

For example, a bank can securitize its mortgage loans. Individuals who have received mortgage loans are expected to pay them back. Therefore, the loans are recognized as an asset and are referred to as mortgage receivables on the bank's balance sheet.

Cash, however, is often a more desirable asset because of its versatility. The bank could use cash to make more mortgage loans to individuals. Also, unlike mortgage receivables, cash does not carry credit risk, such as the possibility that the mortgage loan will not be repaid. If the bank wishes to convert the mortgage receivables asset to cash, it could sell it to an intermediary. While a single mortgage could be securitized, the common practice is securitization of a bundle of mortgages.

> **Securities**
>
> Written instruments representing either money or other property, such as stocks and bonds.

[Handwritten margin note: I.e. Bank sells mtg/loans to intermediary. Intermediary buys loans b/c of interest rate profit & Bank sells b/c cash is less risky & more versatile than mortgages]

Special Purpose Vehicle

The intermediary that enables the bank to convert its mortgage receivables asset into a cash asset is referred to as a special purpose vehicle (SPV), a facility established for the purpose of purchasing income-producing assets from an organization, holding title to them, and then using those assets to **collateralize** securities that will be sold to investors.

The SPV securitizes the mortgage receivables by using them as collateral for securities it sells to investors. It then uses the interest and principal repayments on the mortgage receivables to fund the interest and principal repayments to the security investors. The securities carry the risks of the mortgage receivables held by the SPV. These risks include the possibility of default by the mortgagors (the borrowers) and the risk that the mortgagors might cancel their mortgages in order to refinance them at lower interest rates elsewhere.

In essence, securitization transfers the risk inherent in the mortgage receivables from the bank to the security investors.

Income-Producing Assets

When an SPV is involved in a securitization transaction, investors can base decisions solely on the risk presented by the income-producing assets held as collateral by the SPV. If an organization directly securitized its income-producing assets without an SPV, investors would also need to consider the overall credit risk of the organization.

Analyzing overall credit risk is complex because an organization holds many different types of assets and incurs many different types of liabilities. Even expert investors frequently have difficulty accurately analyzing the credit risk of an organization. An SPV reduces this associated credit risk.

Securitization Model

In a basic securitization model, the organization sells income-producing assets to an SPV in exchange for cash. The income-producing assets are no longer owned by the organization but by the SPV to sell to investors.

The investors purchase the securities for cash and receive a return on their investment commensurate with the risk inherent in the income-producing assets that back the securities, free of the organization's credit risk. To learn more, see "Generic Securitization Model."

Regulatory Requirements

Regulators, auditors, and potential investors scrutinize the use of SPVs because they have been used to manipulate organizations' income statements and balance sheets. Therefore, a firm that uses an SPV for securitization must take the utmost care to meet all regulatory requirements and maintain a high level of disclosure regarding the SPV's assets, finances, purpose, and management.

Collateralize

The act of pledging an asset, like real property, to secure a loan or investment by providing recourse in the event of default.

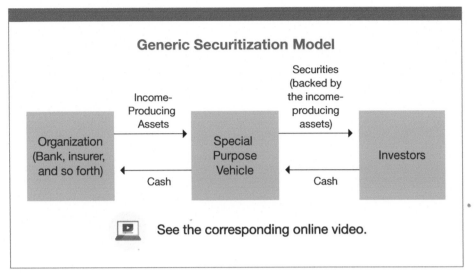

Generic Securitization Model

See the corresponding online video.

[DA02520]

Insurers can participate in a securitization transaction in a number of ways. For example, an insurer can securitize its financed premium receivables by transferring them to an SPV in exchange for cash. The SPV could then use those premium receivables to collateralize securities it sells to investors.

SUMMARY

Financial risk refers to the uncertainty about the future investment returns of a given asset and can be classified as market risk, credit risk, or price risk. Market risk is the risk that the value of an investment or a portfolio of investments will change because of a shift in the value of associated market risk factors. Associated market risks include interest rate risk, exchange rate risk, and liquidity risk. Credit risk relates to the uncertainty about a party who is obligated to pay money per a binding agreement. Price risk includes input price risk or output price risk.

The balance sheet lists the assets and liabilities of an organization. This financial statement provides valuable information to stakeholders regarding the organization's financial condition. Ratio analysis shows the extent to which a company can meet its current financial obligations. Liquidity ratios measure a company's ability to convert assets to cash to satisfy its obligations. Leverage ratios measure the extent to which a company has borrowed money to finance its operations.

Securitization is a means to create a marketable security based on the expected cash flows from a financial asset. Using an SPV as an intermediary allows investors to decide whether to invest in a security based solely on the risk presented by the income-producing asset, without regard for the credit risk of the organization that owned the asset before transferring it to the SPV.

E'

7.13

Optimizing Risk for Strategic Advantage

Educational Objectives	Outline

- ▶ Assess an organization's strategic risk.

- ▶ Apply the strategic management process to an organization.

- ▶ Assess how an organization's risks influence the development and implementation of its strategy.

- ▶ Apply each of the following to an organization's strategic management process:

  - Risk appetite

  - Risk tolerance

  - Risk assessment

  - Risk control

Optimizing Risk for Strategic Advantage

8

BASICS OF STRATEGIC RISK

To fully protect its position in the marketplace and maximize opportunities for growth, an organization needs a holistically informed decision-making process. This requires the organization to identify and analyze strategic risks that can affect—positively or negatively—its long-term performance. Assessing strategic risks effectively can ensure the organization protects its assets and reputation by making strategic decisions that avoid or mitigate the consequences of negative risks and/or improve its financial position by maximizing gains from opportunities.

Put simply, strategic risks are any factors that could affect the business. They include the upside and downside associated not only with a business strategy itself but also with the implementation of a strategy. Strategic risks can be created and affected by external factors such as economic conditions, consumer demand, or government regulations, or by internal factors such as an organization's structure, culture, or processes. Because strategic risks may have far reaching ramifications that can alter the course of an organization's future, illustrating their importance can be an effective tool in convincing decision makers of the value of a holistic risk management program. To learn more, see "How They Did It: TruMark Financial."

It's best for organizations to approach strategic risks with an eye toward both preventing problems and exploiting opportunities. The process of identifying and analyzing strategic risks should also extend beyond what might cause a single strategy to succeed or fail to account for risks that could affect the organization's long-term health. The goal of strategic risk assessment is to accurately determine whether a particular business decision is worth the risk.

People often confuse strategic risk with operational risk, but here's a good way to distinguish the two: With operational risks, the focus is often on making sure that things (whether they are products or processes) are done right; with strategic risks, the focus is on doing the right things and making the right decisions to ensure the organization achieves its strategic goals.

Knowing the factors that can create and affect strategic risks will help risk professionals identify and assess the risks that create the biggest threats to or opportunities for strategic goals.

How They Did It: TruMark Financial

As part of making the ERM business case, I explained how strategic risks could negatively affect an organization. While operational and credit risks could be problematic, they are overshadowed by the potential negative impact of a major strategic risk and the ability of an organization to recover from it.

To obtain sufficient resources for the ERM program, I needed to give the board and executive team compelling examples of strategic risk failures. So, I focused on the experiences of Kodak and Wells Fargo. Kodak failed to consider the digital camera revolution and deliberately ignored their customers' needs. And Wells Fargo is a great example of a failed risk culture because they prioritized profitability over ethical business practices. These examples helped me convince the CEO and the board of the strategic business value of an ERM program.

Kelly Botti (Chief Risk Officer, TruMark Financial), interviewed by Mike Elliott, July 2019, transcript, The Institutes, Malvern, Pa. [DA13151]

What Do You Know?

Does strategic risk intersect with the other risk quadrants (hazard, operational, and financial)?

Feedback: Yes. This section will explore how strategic risks can be created or affected by factors associated with the other risk quadrants.

Strategic Risk Factors

Strategic risks are often associated with external factors that are beyond a single organization's control, such as shifts in consumer demand, changes in regulations, financial crises, inflation, changes in the labor market, competitive pressures, societal shifts, politics, and international trade agreements or restrictions.

However, strategic risks can also arise from internal factors such as business decisions, business policies and processes, hiring practices, resource allocation, culture, and stakeholder pressure.

Strategic risks can even be created or affected by factors associated with the other risk quadrants. For example, safety and fire threats (hazard risks), cybersecurity threats (operational risks), and credit availability and investment performance (financial risks) can affect strategic decisions and the ability to gain market share.

Let's explore how various types of strategic risks might play out in business scenarios:

- Competition and innovation risk—An electronics manufacturer significantly changes the operating system used in its devices (cell phones, tablets, computers, and so on) in an attempt to differentiate its products from the competition. Potential negatives: Customers dislike the new operating system and switch to a competitor. Potential positives: Customers view the new operating system as superior to the competition and increase demand.

- Liquidity and financial risk—A restaurant chain decides to build and open two new locations in the same city using its own capital. Potential negatives: Liquidity risk develops if the restaurants fail and the buildings can't be sold right away. Potential positives: Increased demand for commercial real estate in the area allows the restaurant chain to sell the buildings quickly and profitably.

- Acquisition and economic risk—A large insurance company acquires an innovative software company, thinking that the acquisition will help it analyze claims data to better predict risk and price insurance policies. Potential negatives: The software company is unable to integrate the insurer's data into its systems to improve its predictive or pricing capabilities. Potential positives: The insurer is able to secure more customers (through lower prices) and more profitable customers (through better predictive analytics).

- Marketing risk—A clothing retailer agrees to market and sell a line of clothing from a new, unknown fashion designer. Potential negatives: The clothing designs aren't popular, and the retailer's marketing dollars are wasted. Potential positives: The retailer is able to bring in new customers and additional revenue from the clothing line.

- Foreign economic risk—An automotive manufacturer decides to introduce an expensive sport utility vehicle (SUV) to a new foreign market. Potential negatives: Economic conditions worsen in the foreign market, consumer wages decrease, and demand for the SUV dries up. Potential positives: The manufacturer expands its customer base, so if demand for the SUV dries up on one market, it may be offset by higher demand in other markets.

- Procurement risk—A steel fabricator switches from its long-time supplier of raw materials to a new, up-and-coming supplier that promises lower prices and faster delivery. Potential negatives: The new supplier fails to deliver materials on time, leading to delays in the production process and delivery to end users. Potential positives: The steel fabricator is able to deliver products to end users faster and at a lower cost.

- Regulatory risk—A pharmaceutical company launches a new medication in several foreign markets simultaneously. Potential negatives: Studies show the medication may be unhealthy, leading some foreign governments to ban the medication or some of its ingredients. Potential positives: Increased revenue from the new medication increases the company's ability to sustain losses should this medication or others face future bans in some markets.

[DA13071]

Assessing Strategic Risk

With strategic risk, the goal isn't to eliminate negative risks and/or their consequences; it's to use information about strategic risks to make holistically informed decisions that optimize the risk-reward ratio. This can be difficult because strategic risk is the most intangible and abstract of the four risk quadrants. Therefore, it's more difficult to put a dollar value on a strategic risk than it is a hazard, operational, or financial risk. Still, it's important to attempt to measure the amount of negative risk and/or opportunity associated with a business decision.

The metrics used to quantify strategic risk include these:

- **Economic capital**—The amount of capital required to remain solvent and cover the risk retained by an organization.
- Risk-adjusted return on capital (RAROC)—A measure of the return on investment after accounting for risk. Often used as a measure of profitability, RAROC is calculated by taking the total return on an asset or initiative, subtracting taxes, and dividing it by its economic capital.
- Shareholder value added—A measure of profitability after funding costs are considered. It's often used to measure a corporation's worth to shareholders, and it can be an indicator of management effectiveness.

Economic capital

The amount of capital required by an organization to ensure solvency at a given probability level, such as 99 percent, based on the fair value of its assets minus the fair value of its liabilities.

While these are among the most common metrics, organizations often use a variety of others to quantify, assess, and manage strategic risks.

Two metrics that play a big role in assessing strategic risks are risk appetite and **risk threshold**. Risk appetite represents how much risk the organization wants to take on. It's essentially a target. Meanwhile, risk threshold represents the total range of uncertainty the organization is able to accept.

Risk threshold

The range or amount of risk that is acceptable.

Learn more from an expert in the online video.

Kodak is a prominent example of what can happen when a strategic risk isn't assessed, calculated, and managed effectively. The company's overreliance on film photography products resulted in a failure to innovate. To learn more, see "The Wrong Side of Strategic Risk."

The Wrong Side of Strategic Risk

While The Eastman Kodak Company (Kodak) was dominating the film photography market, the company had a breakthrough: One of its engineers invented the first digital camera. The possibility that digital photography could eat into its film business was now a strategic risk. But despite research indicating that digital camera technology could overtake its film business in the years ahead, Kodak's management believed that consumers would still prefer film over digital photography options. So Kodak's management decided to focus on the film business rather than diversify product offerings to include a more even mix of film and digital products. As a result, companies that focused more on developing and marketing digital photography products caught up with and surpassed Kodak in the photography market. Kodak watched its business shrink as film became less popular, and it eventually filed for bankruptcy protection.

In recent years, automakers have found themselves at an innovation crossroads similar to what Kodak faced. As the technology surrounding electric vehicles (EVs) has improved and the cost of EVs has decreased, consumer demand is increasing. So automakers face a significant strategic risk—sales of EVs could overtake sales of gas-powered vehicles. Automakers must decide whether to invest in innovative EV technology, or bet that gas-powered vehicles will continue to dominate the market.

[DA13072]

STRATEGIC MANAGEMENT

Strategic management is the process of identifying, describing, and continually reviewing business decisions in a way that will propel an organization to perform better. Knowing how to properly implement the strategic management process will help management select strategies that have a high probability of being executed successfully. It will also spur management and employees to plan for both predictable and unforeseeable consequences of business decisions and changes in the business environment so the organization remains positioned to handle adverse circumstances and capitalize on new opportunities.

Strategic management defines the organization's strategies. It establishes and creates a means to evaluate the decisions and actions that ultimately determine how the organization performs.

All business decisions carry some risk, but an effective strategic management process drives an organization to make decisions that have an optimal risk-reward ratio. Strategic management is the responsibility of senior-level executives, who make strategic decisions based on input from the board of directors.

The strategic management process includes five interdependent stages: developing short- and long-term goals, analyzing internal and external environments, formulating strategies, implementing the strategies, and evaluating the strategies. This section will examine each of these stages.

Strategic management

The process of identifying, describing, and continually evaluating the business decisions and strategies of an organization to facilitate better performance and/ or create a competitive advantage.

What Do You Know?

Can you describe Porter's Five Forces Analysis and in which stage of the strategic management process it would be applied?

Feedback: Porter's Five Forces Analysis is a method of evaluating competitive opportunities or threats that may influence the success of an organization. It is used in the second stage of the strategic management process (analyzing internal and external environments). Each of the five forces the analysis evaluates will be explored later in this discussion.

Developing Goals

Before determining specific short- and long-term goals, senior-level executives must establish the organization's **vision statement** and **mission statement**. The vision statement describes what the organization wants to become, and the mission statement describes the process that will achieve that vision; together, they affect all further analysis and strategy.

Once armed with this direction, the executive team must identify the products, services, values, and people that will be used to reach the organization's goals in both the short and long term. This is how employees are shown what success looks like at the organization.

Vision statement

The aspirational description of what an organization will accomplish in the long-term future.

Mission statement

A broad expression of an entity's goals.

Analyzing Environments

Internal and external issues that could positively or negatively affect the organization's ability to achieve its goals must be examined.

Internal analysis focuses on the strengths and weaknesses of a business. Strengths might include a great reputation, expert knowledge, unmatched customer data, valuable patent rights, and large market share. Weaknesses might include high expenses, lack of market penetration, untrained personnel, and outdated information technology systems.

External analysis focuses on outside opportunities and threats to an organization. Opportunities might include increasing customer demand, decreasing prices of supplies, and ongoing technological advancements. Threats might include decreasing customer demand, new government regulations, and increasing competition.

One method of evaluating an organization's internal and external environments is a **SWOT analysis** (strengths, weaknesses, opportunities, and threats). A SWOT analysis enables risk professionals to view an organization's capabilities objectively, to determine how receptive the market would be to products and services, and to evaluate its competitive position within the market. To learn more, see "SWOT Analysis."

SWOT analysis

A method of evaluating the internal and external environments by assessing an organization's internal strengths and weaknesses and its external opportunities and threats.

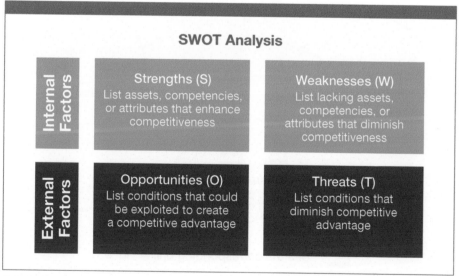

[DA13077]

In a SWOT analysis, strengths can be paired with opportunities to identify areas of competitive advantage, and weaknesses can be paired with threats to identify risks that should be avoided. This analysis helps construct a framework for a high-level strategic plan.

Similarly, a **PESTLE analysis** (political, economic, sociological, technological, legal, and environmental) can be used to analyze an organization's

PESTLE analysis

A framework used in strategic management for the purpose of assessing the external political, economic, sociological, technical, legal, and environmental arenas in which an organization operates.

external environment to identify opportunities and threats—and a SWOT analysis can be used to take a deeper dive into each of the six PESTLE categories.

Porter's Five Forces Analysis is another example of the many methods that risk professionals use to assess success factors. It focuses on five forces within an organization's competitive environment to analyze how successful an organization, product, or service might be. It's often used to identify opportunities or threats within a SWOT. To learn more, see "Porter's Five Forces."

Porter's Five Forces Analysis

A method of evaluating five forces that affect an organization's competitive environment, including the threat of new entrants to the market, the threat of substitute products or services, the bargaining power of customers, the bargaining power of suppliers, and competition among existing firms.

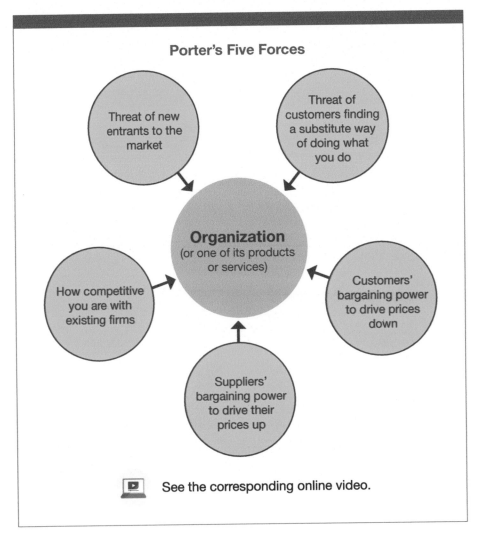

[DA13078]

Formulating Strategies

Based on the organization's goals and analysis of internal and external environments, the executive team develops long-term strategies to improve performance and/or create a competitive advantage.

Factors this team should consider when developing a long-term strategy include changes needed to implement the strategy, cost (including the cost of delaying or diverting resources from other projects to pursue the strategy), overall return on investment, risks involved, and risk appetite. To learn more, see "Questions That Help Develop a Strategic Plan."

Questions That Help Develop a Strategic Plan

When developing a strategy, senior-level executives should address questions like these:

- Is the plan suitable? Executives must consider the strategy's appropriateness for the organization and marketplace, the likelihood that personnel will support the strategy, and changes needed to fully implement the strategic plan.

- Is the plan financially feasible? Resource allocation, cost, and overall impact need to be considered. This includes the cost of time needed to break even and the cost of delaying any other projects to allocate resources to implementation of the proposed strategy.

- Is the plan acceptable? Executives should determine whether the strategy will yield an acceptable overall return on investment in the form of profit, stock price, increased customer satisfaction, or another metric. Anticipated results must also take into account the costs of lost opportunities that may result from diverting resources from other areas to pursue the strategy.

- What risks are associated with the plan? Identifying risks that may present obstacles to success and determining how much risk the organization can accept are also key parts of the decision-making process. Risks include the possibility that the strategy will fail or that it will be more successful than anticipated, resulting in, for example, increased customer demands on the organization.

[DA13079]

The next step in the strategy formulation stage is developing short-term strategies that come together to achieve long-term strategies. Essentially, this step involves formulating the "who," "what," and "when" responsibilities of each department.

Implementing Strategies

Strategy implementation, also called execution, is the process of making strategies work. This stage is more difficult to complete and requires more time than the strategy formulation stage. All parts of an organization play a role in implementation, which involves five steps that are usually carried out by mid-level or department managers:

1. Identify and document the specific processes, tasks, and responsibilities necessary to execute the strategic plan throughout the organization or department
2. Frequently communicate information regarding the strategic plan throughout the organization
3. Assign specific responsibilities, tasks, authority, and accountability throughout the organization or department
4. Allocate adequate resources for successful implementation, such as finances, staff, training, time, equipment, space, data, and technology
5. Make necessary adjustments to remain on track for achievement of goals

Evaluating Strategies

The accomplishment of senior-level goals may be derailed by unexpected circumstances. Strategy evaluation, also called strategic control, involves monitoring progress toward goals and follows these three steps:

1. Establish performance standards and measurements (usually completed during the strategy implementation stage)
2. Compare actual results with established standards
3. Identify and implement corrective actions when goals are not being met

Some organizations apply a balanced scorecard approach to strategy evaluation to measure overall goal attainment based on achievement of specific objectives. As the name implies, a balanced scorecard balances specific goals and actions with both long- and short-term and both financial and nonfinancial goals.

The strategic management process is cyclical. When internal or external circumstances change, or when corrective actions are needed to meet goals, the strategic management process may need to be revisited. For example, a manufacturer implementing a strategy to introduce a new product may rely on a supplier for a specific raw material. If the supplier becomes bankrupt, the manufacturer will have to find a new supplier, likely resulting in temporary delays, higher supply costs, and increased expenses stemming from overtime worked to get back on schedule. This set of circumstances might lead to revisions in cost or delivery expectations.

RISK AND STRATEGY

To maximize performance, executives need to understand how to account for strategic risks as they formulate strategies. If management fails to do so, it will have to deal with risks as they come to fruition—when it may be too late to minimize their consequences or fully capitalize on their opportunities.

When a once-successful company goes out of business, people often ask: Why didn't it change to survive? Often, the answer is that management didn't properly plan for the strategic risks it faced, and by the time the consequences occurred, it was too late—the company was too far behind the competition to catch up, or it no longer had the capital or other resources to make the changes needed to survive.

Strategic risks are a necessary part of doing business. An organization can deal with them either after consequences have occurred (downstream) or before, as the organization develops its business strategies (upstream).

The scenario above illustrates the danger of dealing with strategic risks downstream—they may not be recognized until it's too late (or too expensive) for an organization to do anything about them. It can also lead to significant lost revenue if opportunities aren't fully exploited or other crippling negative consequences if hazard, operational, or financial risks aren't properly mitigated.

Tackling strategic risks upstream by incorporating them into the strategic management process helps prevent negative consequences. It also helps senior executives make business decisions that offer the greatest potential risk-reward trade-off and best help the organization meet its goals.

What Do You Know?

What is the downside of reacting to risks as opposed to planning for them when formulating business strategies?

Feedback: Reacting to risks after they've already come to fruition increases the chances that negative risks will cripple the organization and lowers the chances of fully exploiting opportunities from those risks. This discussion explores this concept in greater detail.

Incorporating Risk Into Strategy

A strong, holistic risk management strategy includes a specific process during strategy formation that accounts for the risks associated with the business decisions that the organization's leaders are considering in order to propel the organization forward.

When a business doesn't consider risks while forming its business strategy, it runs the risk of having to be too reactionary downstream, rather than being able to proactively explore risks and proper treatment options before resources are dedicated elsewhere. Having a plan in place to deal with risks early will significantly lower the chances that negative risks will harm the organization. It also increases the chances that the business will be able to fully exploit opportunities.

Companies such as Toys "R" Us and BlackBerry Limited were large, successful firms that failed or experienced major losses because they mismanaged risks or did not react quickly to them. To learn more, see "Two Giants Fall."

Two Giants Fall

Toys "R" Us once dominated the toy industry, but a failure to properly address strategic risks and change its shopping experience to keep up with competitors and with changes in consumers' shopping behaviors helped push the retailer to file for Chapter 11 bankruptcy. A contributor to its downfall was management's failure to effectively address this question: Why would consumers go to Toys "R" Us just to purchase a toy when they could get it at a big-box store for the same (or a lower) price while they do the rest of their shopping?

When smartphones burst onto the scene, BlackBerry devices were among the most sought-after because of their full keyboards. In fact, consumers were so addicted to them that the company earned the nickname CrackBerry. But when other manufacturers, most notably Apple, began offering touch-screen phones, BlackBerry chose to keep full keyboards on its phones to appease its existing user base. It has since become a case study in what happens when a tech giant fails to innovate. As touch screens became more ubiquitous, sales of BlackBerry phones plummeted. The company eventually stopped making phones altogether. But, to its credit, the company later reinvented itself around opportunities in its software and enterprise services.

[DA13097]

Scenario analysis
An analysis that involves brainstorming the worst conceivable set of events that could befall a system, projecting the consequences of those events, and suggesting ways in which those events could be prevented.

Strategy map
A visual diagram showing the plans an organization develops to meet its strategic objectives.

The first component of incorporating risk into an organization's strategic decisions involves the strategic management process, when an organization analyzes its internal and external environments. It may conduct this analysis using such techniques as a SWOT analysis (strengths, weaknesses, opportunities, and threats) or a PESTLE analysis (political, economic, sociological, technological, legal, and environmental). A SWOT and a PESTLE analysis can be linked together, and each may reveal similar opportunities and threats. For example, both analyses might find that increasing labor costs are an economic threat. The key difference between the two is that a PESTLE analysis focuses solely on external factors that could affect an organization's ability to achieve its goals, while a SWOT analysis focuses on both internal and external factors.

The second component is assessing the risks associated with the strategic plans senior executives are considering to meet organizational goals. Techniques an organization can use to assess risks as they develop strategic plans include a **scenario analysis** and **strategy map**. A scenario analysis can help an organization prepare strategies to deal with multiple future events and make an organization more resilient. It's a means of preparing for different scenarios, not predicting them. A scenario analysis can help an organization create a strategy map, which identifies key objectives that, when achieved together, will result in obtaining a strategic goal. You can think of a strategy map as a visual guide of everything that must be accomplished to achieve a strategic goal.

The third component is determining the organization's risk threshold, risk appetite, key risk indicators (KRIs), and treatment trigger levels for identified risks.

In addition to KRIs, organizations also use **key performance indicators** (KPIs) to inform their strategies. The difference between them is that KPIs measure an organization's progress toward achieving its goals, while KRIs measure risks and volatility that can affect whether those goals can be achieved—KPIs measure what has occurred rather than predicting the future, while KRIs are predictive. KRIs help an organization maintain a level of risk within its defined risk appetite. Thresholds define the boundaries of risk appetite. KRIs indicate when the thresholds are, or are about to be, breached.

Treatment trigger levels indicate when an organization must take corrective action to prevent risk-appetite thresholds from being breached. To learn more, see "Applying Risk to Strategy."

> Key performance indicator (KPI)
>
> A measurement that defines how successfully an organization is progressing toward its long-term goals.

Applying Risk to Strategy

An organization's senior management team could use a scenario analysis to determine whether the risks associated with proposed strategies allow the organization to operate within its risk appetite—and how close those risks may come to breaching the risk-appetite thresholds. From there, management can select the strategies with the highest potential risk-adjusted return and incorporate treatments and trigger levels into those strategies to manage the associated risks.

[DA13098]

Meeting Strategic Goals

The final component is to decide which strategies the organization will use to meet its goals. This includes planning how to avoid, exploit, or manage risks associated with those strategies. For example, if an organization decides to enter a foreign market, risk management should be applied to the strategy to plan for hazard, political, exchange rate, and other risks.

What this does is merge what are often two separate discussions—about broad goals/strategies and risk-treatment prioritization—into the same process so that they aren't each conducted in their own silo. By combining the two, they can be used to influence each other and enable the organization to determine where capital, employees, and other resources should be allocated to produce the best possible returns.

Even when strategic risks are properly integrated into the strategy-formation process, it's important that an organization remain alert to emerging risks when executing a new strategy. For example, if an organization is planning to acquire another company and either that company's financial results or the market in general changes, the organization may want to cancel, pause, or revise its plan.

Companies such as Netflix and The Home Depot are successful firms that made strategic decisions to address risks and opportunities before trouble hit. To learn more, see "Two Giants Jump Out in Front of Risk."

Two Giants Jump Out in Front of Risk

While its DVD-rental subscription service was still highly successful, Netflix shifted its strategy to focus on providing streaming video to exploit the fact that more and more consumers were buying mobile devices with significant broadband and streaming capabilities. This put the company at the forefront of the streaming-video marketplace, and Netflix soon became synonymous with the video-delivery format.

Home-improvement retailer Home Depot, realizing that customers were changing their shopping habits, decided to shift its focus away from opening new stores in favor of updating its online and e-commerce offerings and improving its delivery and in-store pickup infrastructure. The shift has helped the company maintain sales growth without adding retail space and prepare for a future when more home-improvement shopping is done online.

[DA13099]

APPLYING STRATEGIC RISK MANAGEMENT

When properly applied to the overall strategic management process, strategic risk management identifies, assesses, and manages risks that could affect the formulation and execution of organizational strategies. As a result, knowing how to implement strategic risk management is key to making and executing business decisions that maximize benefits for the organization.

Strategic risk management

The process of identifying, assessing, and managing risks that affect an organization's strategic decisions and performance.

Applying **strategic risk management** principles to the overall strategic management process drives senior-level executives to set procedures and resources in place to manage risks to the organization's advantage and make decisions that are in its best interests. For risk professionals, the ability to communicate openly and frankly with executives and decision makers plays an important role in articulating and executing these strategic risk management plans.

The most important strategic risk management principles that managers need to know how to apply include risk appetite, risk tolerance, risk assessment, and risk control—all of which we'll discuss in this section.

What Do You Know?

Can you describe risk tolerance, risk capacity, and risk appetite and their relationships to one another?

Feedback: Risk tolerance, risk capacity, and risk appetite are closely related and often confused with one another. Risk tolerance and risk capacity are often used interchangeably. They represent the same thing: the total amount of risk an organization can accept. Risk appetite, on the other hand, represents the amount of risk the organization is willing to (or wants to) accept.

Risk Appetite

When formulating strategic decisions, an organization's senior executives should identify and articulate risk appetites. Some of the elements and benefits of effective risk-appetite statements include:

- Articulating the activities the firm is willing to engage in and level of risk it's willing to take on
- Providing a framework for formulating strategic and tactical business decisions
- Engaging internal and external stakeholders in a discussion of strategic risk
- Creating a consistent plan for risk decision making
- Promoting a shared understanding of risk
- Limiting excessive risk taking
- Deciding on appropriate capital and resource allocation
- Creating a means to measure, monitor, and adjust strategies to account for risk

Risk appetites can be defined both quantitatively and qualitatively. Quantitative measures may include financial targets, while qualitative measures may include things such as reputation and management/workforce capabilities. To learn more, see "How They Did It: Clorox."

In addition, management can describe an organization's general risk-appetite philosophy as being risk averse or aggressive. These descriptions can guide the actions of the board of directors, executive team, and workforce. Risk averse indicates that the organization isn't willing to risk more than a low percentage of capital or revenue to achieve a goal. An aggressive philosophy indicates just the opposite and tends to be adopted by organizations that must innovate to grow, such as technology product developers.

An organization's risk appetite shouldn't be static; it should shift over time as internal and external factors change.

How They Did It: Clorox

We follow a process to align our risk appetite and strategy. Our strategy is based on metrics, such as growth in sales or in market share. We extract the goals from our strategy, and then determine risk appetite metrics that align with those goals. For example, if our goal is to grow sales by a certain percentage, we develop risk appetite metrics that align with that goal, including an acceptable risk appetite range.

The more specific and quantitative you can get with risk appetite statements, the better, because most everything else we do in ERM is qualitative. Also, this approach is consistent with our cultural quality of using metrics.

Allison Zheng (Program Manager, Clorox) and Laura Cisi (Vice President—Global Risk Management, Clorox), interviewed by Mike Elliott, July 2019, transcript, The Institutes, Malvern, Pa. [DA13150]

Risk Tolerance

Risk tolerance

The amount of risk an organization is able to accept.

An organization's **risk tolerance** is closely related to its risk appetite. Think of risk appetite as the amount of risk the organization wants to accept to achieve a goal—essentially, it's the target amount of risk that the organization wants to take on. Risk tolerance is broader than that; it's the total amount of risk the organization can accept. To learn more, see "Layers of Risk."

Unlike risk appetite, risk tolerance is always stated in quantitative terms. Risk tolerance levels have high-end thresholds, low-end thresholds, or both. A zero-risk tolerance level typically results in risk-based decisions that are very rigid. For example, if an organization has a zero-risk tolerance level for cost overruns on a product development project, it may make achieving a successful product more difficult.

An organization's risk appetite rests between the high-end and low-end risk tolerance thresholds. This area also contains high-end and low-end appetite thresholds as well as treatment trigger levels to indicate when a corrective action must be taken to prevent the risk appetite thresholds from being breached. To learn more, see "Threshold, Appetite, and Treatment."

To achieve a balance of risk, an organization that's taking on a lot of risk in one venture may select lower tolerance thresholds in other areas.

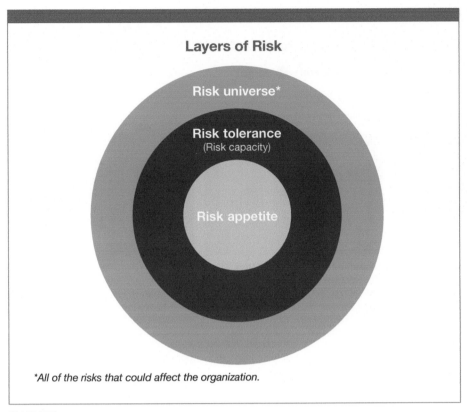

Layers of Risk

All of the risks that could affect the organization.

[DA13100]

Risk Assessment

After senior executives determine the organization's strategic goals, risk tolerance, and risk appetite, they need to determine possible strategies that will achieve the goals and yet fall within the risk tolerance and appetite. This should include a scenario analysis based on current trends as well as an assessment of the risks associated with each scenario.

For example, assume that a strategic goal of a technology company is to develop a new consumer product within two years. If the company's research and development division has been working on both a cutting-edge television and smartphone, it must decide whether to develop one or both of these products. This decision should involve an analysis of previous product launches and various scenarios based on well-documented consumer technology trends and an assessment of the risks and opportunities involved with each. A working group representing all of the relevant organizational stakeholders would then meet to identify and address the risks associated with a particular strategy, plan, or project. To learn more, see "Risk Assessment Process."

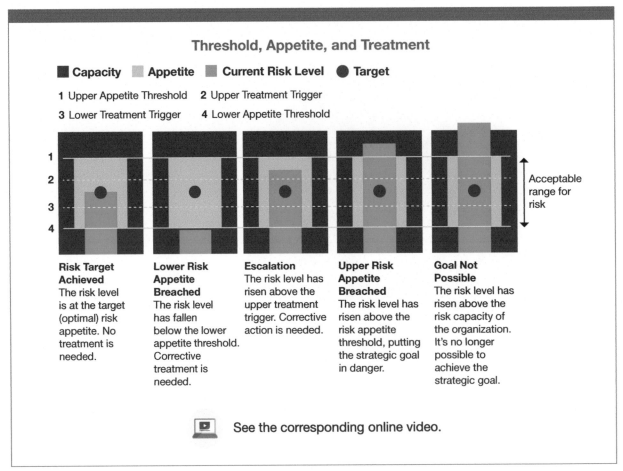

Threshold, Appetite, and Treatment

■ Capacity   ■ Appetite   ■ Current Risk Level   ● Target

1 Upper Appetite Threshold   2 Upper Treatment Trigger
3 Lower Treatment Trigger   4 Lower Appetite Threshold

Acceptable range for risk

Risk Target Achieved
The risk level is at the target (optimal) risk appetite. No treatment is needed.

Lower Risk Appetite Breached
The risk level has fallen below the lower appetite threshold. Corrective treatment is needed.

Escalation
The risk level has risen above the upper treatment trigger. Corrective action is needed.

Upper Risk Appetite Breached
The risk level has risen above the risk appetite threshold, putting the strategic goal in danger.

Goal Not Possible
The risk level has risen above the risk capacity of the organization. It's no longer possible to achieve the strategic goal.

See the corresponding online video.

[DA13101]

Risk Control

After an organization has developed and implemented its strategic plan, it will need processes and procedures in place for controlling risks at various levels and ensuring that risks stay within its risk tolerance and risk appetite. For example, say an organization is considering either developing a new product or acquiring a competitor that manufactures a similar product. It should be able to lean on its control process to direct senior executives to weigh the organization's experience managing the risks with each option and determine whether it previously received a positive return on investment from one or both of them and whether it can achieve positive returns this time.

A control process like this promotes consistency in risk-taking and risk-avoidance activities at all levels. Without controls that direct managers and employees to determine which risks are worth taking and how to balance risk levels through smart decision making and effective risk treatments, an organization could find itself assuming too much risk or unacceptable types of risks.

Specific control measures can be developed for different kinds of risk. For example, an organization may adopt control measures to address expenses or capital allocation. Then, if a manufacturing unit within the organization faces

Risk Assessment Process

Here's an approach that can help an organization assess strategic risks:

- List risks that could affect (positively or negatively) a proposed decision or activity.
- Use a risk map to assess the likelihood and potential consequences for each risk.
- Identify the five highest-priority risks.

Answer these questions for each of those five risks:

- What is the risk tolerance and appetite?
- What are we doing currently to treat the risk?
- Is what we're doing keeping the risk at an acceptable level?
- What else can we do to keep the risk at an acceptable level?
- Do we move forward with the decision or activity?

[DA13102]

cost overruns to complete a large order on time, the control process will give the unit's managers a way to weigh the level of risk involved with exceeding the production budget against the costs of delaying delivery. It'll also provide the tolerance levels for cost overruns. In other words, managers will be in a better position to make decisions to help the organization meet its goals.

Control measures are typically designed around a framework structured to facilitate understanding, communication, and appropriate action. Control measures should be implemented at all levels of the organization and include reporting systems structured to allow senior management to determine whether goals are being met. To learn more, see "What a Control Process Looks Like."

What a Control Process Looks Like

Hydro One, a power distribution company based in Ontario, Canada, held risk workshops that were attended by the risk management group and managers from each business unit. The business unit managers had to identify and manage key risks associated with the organization's strategic objectives.

The purpose of the workshops was to determine how capital resources would be allocated. Funding for a specific project would be based on the risks identified by each unit's managers and the proposed risk treatments. For example, to receive funds to replace power transmission lines, the risks associated with the existing lines had to be identified and assessed. Another example: A request to replace a computer system would be based on a comparison of the risks associated with keeping the old system versus installing the new one. Capital allocations were prioritized based on which risks were given a higher rating.

[DA13103]

SUMMARY

An organization needs to make holistically informed decisions to protect its long-term health. This requires them to identify and assess strategic risks, which include the upside and downside associated not only with a business strategy itself but also with the implementation of a strategy. Strategic risks can be created or affected by external factors such as economic conditions, consumer demand, or the regulatory environment. They can also be created or affected by internal factors such as an organization's structure, culture, or processes. The goal is to use strategic risk information to make business decisions that optimize the risk-reward ratio. Some of the metrics used to assess and quantify strategic risk include economic capital, risk-adjusted return on capital (RAROC), and shareholder value added.

Through the strategic management process, an organization identifies, defines, and continually evaluates business decisions. The process is the responsibility of senior-level executives. It includes five stages: developing short- and long-term goals, analyzing internal and external environments, formulating strategies, implementing the strategies, and evaluating the strategies.

Incorporating strategic risks into the process of formulating business strategies allows senior executives to make decisions that will provide the greatest benefits to the organization. Applying these risks to strategic decisions involves analyzing internal and external environments; assessing the risks associated with the strategies management is considering; determining the risk threshold, risk appetite, key risk indicators, and treatment trigger levels of known risks; and picking the strategies that will be used to meet goals.

Properly applying strategic risk management principles to the overall strategic management process will help senior-level executives make and implement business decisions that maximize an organization's performance. These strategic risk principles include risk appetite, risk tolerance, risk assessment, and risk control.

Breaking Down Risk Modeling

9

▶ Apply probability analysis to estimate the likelihood and consequences of an event.

▶ Apply various metrics to estimate the volatility of risk outcomes.

▶ Apply the concepts of value at risk and earnings at risk to measure financial risk.

▶ Apply trend analysis to forecast an organization's gains and losses.

▶ Compare decision tree analysis and event tree analysis in terms of the methods they use to evaluate event consequences.

Breaking Down Risk Modeling

9

PROBABILITY ANALYSIS

Risk professionals need to be able to estimate the likelihood that a loss will occur and the consequences if it does. Without that information, it's nearly impossible to determine the best course of action to take regarding that risk. To do so, you should understand how to create and use a probability analysis and probability distribution.

The probability of an event is the likelihood that it will happen (or the frequency with which it will happen) over a specific period of time, assuming that the environment remains stable. Typically, events also have a range of consequences (severities), each with its own probability of occurring. Risk professionals can use a **probability analysis** to predict the likelihood of an event and a **probability distribution** to show all of the possible outcomes of an event next to the likelihood of those outcomes.

This section will also explore other probability concepts risk professionals need to be familiar with, including theoretical probabilities, empirical probabilities, and the law of large numbers.

What Do You Know?

In addition to predicting the likelihood of an event or its consequences, can you come up with any other benefits of a probability analysis or distribution?

Feedback: Some of the additional benefits include prioritizing loss exposures (by likelihood or potential severity), predicting and estimating both the positive and negative consequences of risk, and evaluating and prioritizing risk management decisions.

Probability analysis

A technique for forecasting events, such as accidental and business losses, on the assumption that they are governed by an unchanging probability distribution.

Probability distribution

A presentation (table, chart, or graph) of probability estimates of a particular set of circumstances and of the probability of each possible outcome.

Probability

Any probability can be expressed as a fraction, percentage, or decimal. For example, the probability that a coin will land with its heads side facing up can be expressed as 1/2, 50 percent, or 0.50. The probability of an impossible event is zero, and the probability of a certain event is 100 percent or 1.0. Therefore, the probabilities of all events that are neither totally impossible nor absolutely certain are greater than zero but less than 100 percent (or 1.0).

Theoretical and Empirical Probabilities

Probabilities can be developed from either theoretical data distributions or historical data. **Theoretical probability** is unchanging. It's associated with events such as coin tosses or dice throws. For example, from a description of a regular coin or die, a person who has never seen either can calculate the probability of flipping a heads or rolling a four.

Empirical probability is associated with historical data. An example is the probability that a male will die at age sixty-eight. This is an empirical probability because it's estimated by studying the loss experience of men. These probabilities may change as new data is discovered or the environment that produces those events changes.

Empirical probabilities are only estimates. To be accurate, the samples under study must be sufficiently large and representative. In contrast, theoretical probabilities are constant as long as the physical conditions that generate them (such as how many sides a die has) remain unchanged.

Although it may be preferable to use theoretical probabilities because of their unchanging nature, they are not applicable or available in most of the situations that risk professionals are likely to analyze, such as fires or workers compensation claims. As a result, empirical probabilities are often used for risk management applications.

Law of Large Numbers

Empirical probability analysis is particularly effective for projecting the likelihood and consequences of losses or gains in organizations that have both a substantial volume of historical data (experience) and fairly stable operations so that loss and gain patterns will presumably continue unchanged. Such organizations may view past experience as an accurate sample of all possible losses or gains the organization might sustain in the future.

The larger the sample of past losses an organization can use in the analysis, the more accurate the projections will be. This illustrates the **law of large numbers**, which also applies to gains and other outcomes.

However, the law of large numbers is only relevant and accurate when forecasting future events that meet all these criteria:

- They occurred in the past under substantially identical conditions and resulted from unchanging forces.
- They can be expected to occur in the future under the same unchanging conditions.
- They have been and will continue to be both independent of one another and sufficiently numerous.

Theoretical probability

Probability that is based on theoretical principles rather than on actual experience.

Empirical probability (a posteriori probability)

A probability measure that is based on actual experience through historical data or from the observation of facts.

Law of large numbers

A mathematical principle stating that as the number of similar but independent exposure units increases, the relative accuracy of predictions about future outcomes (losses) also increases.

Probability Distributions

Although risk managers occasionally analyze loss exposures using theoretical distributions, most of the work they do involves empirical probability distributions. A properly constructed probability distribution always contains outcomes that are both mutually exclusive and collectively exhaustive.

For a deeper dive, let's look at the hypothetical probability distribution of the number of hurricanes making landfall in Florida during hurricane season. To learn more, see "Probability of Hurricane Landfall."

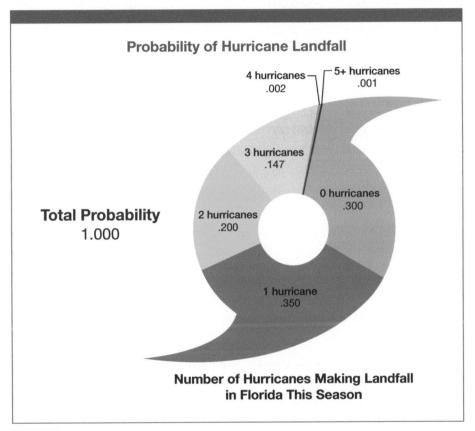

Probability of Hurricane Landfall

4 hurricanes
.002

5+ hurricanes
.001

3 hurricanes
.147

0 hurricanes
.300

Total Probability
1.000

2 hurricanes
.200

1 hurricane
.350

**Number of Hurricanes Making Landfall
in Florida This Season**

[DA02573]

The exhibit shows every possible outcome (Florida will be hit by either zero, one, two, three, four, or five or more hurricanes), so the outcomes are mutually exclusive. In addition, the sum of the outcomes is 1.0, so they are collectively exhaustive.

For certain types of probability distributions, like those dealing with an investment's possible gains or losses, an infinite number of outcomes may be possible. So to provide a mutually exclusive, collectively exhaustive list of outcomes, a distribution's categories (bins) must be designed so that all outcomes can be included. One method is to divide the bins into equal, standard sizes. The probability distribution then predicts the likelihood that the outcome will land within one of the bins. To learn more, see "Probability of Investment Gains or Losses."

Probability of Investment Gains or Losses

Size Category of Gains/Losses	Probability (Percentage of Total Gains/Losses)
–$50,000 – –$40,001	1
–$40,000 – –$30,001	2
–$30,000 – –$20,001	7
–$20,000 – –$10,001	16
–$10,000 – –$ 1	20
$ 0 – $10,000	22
$10,001 – $20,000	18
$20,001 – $30,000	10
$30,001 – $40,000	3
$40,001 – $50,000	1

[DA08726]

The exhibit on investment gains and losses shows an empirical probability distribution with bins of $10,000 each. (Note that the probabilities in the second column total 100 percent.)

Probability distributions come in two forms: discrete probability distributions and continuous probability distributions. Discrete probability distributions (such as the hurricane exhibit) have a finite number of possible outcomes, whereas continuous probability distributions (such as the investment exhibit) have an infinite number of possible outcomes.

Discrete probability distributions are usually displayed in a table that lists all possible outcomes and the probability of each. These distributions are typically used to analyze how often something will occur; that is, they are shown as frequency distributions. The number of hurricanes making landfall in Florida is an example of a frequency distribution.

There are multiple ways to represent a continuous probability distribution. To learn more, see "Continuous Probability Distributions."

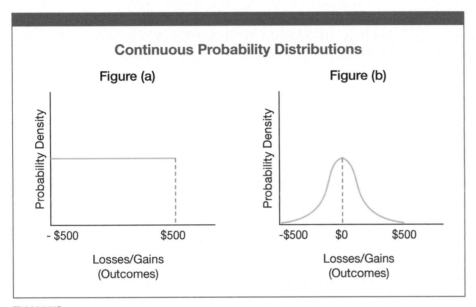

[DA08715]

The "Continuous Probability Distributions" exhibit illustrates two representations of continuous probability distributions. The possible outcomes are presented on the horizontal axes, and the likelihood of those outcomes is shown on the vertical axes—specifically represented by the height of the line or curve above the outcomes. The outcomes in a continuous probability distribution are called probability density functions. Continuous probability distributions are typically used for the consequences of an event—they depict the value of the loss or gain rather than the number of outcomes.

Figure (a) in the "Continuous Probability Distributions" exhibit, which has a flat line above the interval −$500 to $500, illustrates that all the outcomes between −$500 to $500 are equally likely. Figure (b), which has a curve that starts at near-zero probability and −$500 and increases until it reaches a peak at $0 before declining to near-zero probability again at $500, illustrates that the high losses (−$500) and high gains ($500) are very unlikely and that losses and gains around $0 are much more likely.

By definition, continuous probability distributions have an infinite number of possible outcomes. So by dividing the continuous distribution into a finite number of bins, a risk manager can calculate the probability that an outcome will fall within a certain range.

For example, in a discrete frequency distribution, the probability that no fires will occur in a high-rise office building may be 0.50. The probability that one fire will occur might be 0.35, and the chances of having two or more fires could be 0.15. If a fire occurs, the damage may cost between $0 and $100 million, which is a continuous probability distribution. Assigning a probability to the likelihood of having a loss amount of $35,456.32 would be nearly impossible. However, if the severity distribution is divided into a finite number of bins ($0–$1,000,000, $1,000,001–$2,000,000, and so on), a probability can be assigned to each bin.

ESTIMATING VOLATILITY

Although many organizations are subject to the same or similar risks, some experience far greater consequences (good and bad) than others, and some experience no consequences at all. The reason for this is volatility in the internal and external factors that affect businesses. And while this volatility can vary significantly among industries and organizations, its effects can be predicted by those with a strong understanding of various risk management metrics.

Volatility is the degree of variation a subject, such as a risk, may have. Risk managers can use probability distributions to reveal and assess the volatility of risks. The characteristics of the results of these distributions can be analyzed using various metrics to determine how volatile a subject is and to improve outcomes. These metrics include expected value, standard deviation, coefficient of variation, and normal distribution.

Let's explore each of these metrics and how they can be used to assess volatility.

What Do You Know?

True or false: The less volatility a subject has, the riskier it is.

Feedback: False. A subject that has higher volatility is riskier and more likely to need to be monitored or managed. This is why it's important to be able to accurately determine volatility.

Expected Value (or Mean)

The expected value is the weighted average of values. Weights are given to each value based on its theoretical probability (likelihood of occurrence).

Expected value is also referred to as the mean. It essentially amounts to the most obvious return that one can expect from the action being taken.

Phrased another way, if a probability experiment were repeated numerous times, the expected value is the average of all the results. For example, if a risk manager wants to predict the number of workers compensation claims that will be filed in the next twelve months, he or she could add up the total number of workers compensation claims filed over the past five years and then divide the total by five. To learn more, see "Determining Expected Value of a Risk."

Determining Expected Value of a Risk

Let's look at how you'd calculate the expected value of taking a risk, such as entering a raffle.

You are considering purchasing a ticket to enter a raffle for a $25,000 car. To determine whether you should enter the raffle, you decide to calculate the expected value of your gain from purchasing a ticket. Each ticket costs $100, and 2,000 tickets will be sold.

Here's how you'd calculate your expected gain:

The most you could gain after spending $100 on a ticket is $24,900. The most you could lose is $100.

First, you multiply your potential gain of $24,900 by your probability of winning, which is 0.0005 (1 ÷ 2,000). This equals $12.45.

Next, you multiply your potential loss of –$100 by your probability of losing, which is 0.9995 (1,999 ÷ 2,000). This equals –$99.95.

Finally, you add the two values together ($12.45 + –$99.95). This equals –$87.50, which is your expected value.

You could then compare this expected value to the expected values of other raffles to determine which raffle has the best expected value (and is likely the one most worth entering).

 See the corresponding online video.

[DA13031]

Standard Deviation

Risk managers often use standard deviation during the analysis of loss exposures to determine the possible spread of potential results. The greater the standard deviation between the values in the distribution, the more volatile they are. The higher the volatility, the more subject to change and the less predictable losses will be. To learn more, see "Formula for Standard Deviation."

Formula for Standard Deviation

These are the steps for calculating standard deviation:
1. Find the mean of the values in the distribution.
2. Subtract the mean from each individual value, and square the results.
3. Find the mean of those squared results.
4. Find the square root of that mean.

[DA13032]

Let's say an organization is considering acquiring one of two different businesses (Business X and Business Y), but it wants to compare their profitability before deciding which one it should acquire.

Over the past five years, Business X has turned a gross profit of $600,000, $470,000, $170,000, $430,000, and $300,000. The mean of these values is $394,000, and the standard deviation is $147,000.

Business Y, on the other hand, has turned a profit, over the past five years, of $550,000, $375,000, $200,000, $400,000, and $600,000. The mean of these values is $425,000, and the standard deviation is $141,000.

What do these results tell a risk manager? Business Y's average gross profit is not only higher but also less volatile.

Coefficient of Variation

Coefficient of variation is another way to measure the spread of results. It measures variation from a mean by dividing the standard deviation of a distribution by its mean. Coefficient of variation is often used to compare results from two different sets of data (such as surveys or tests) to learn which one has more variation.

To illustrate, let's say a risk manager wants to compare the wage volatility between the Marketing Department and the Sales Department of a large organization. The Marketing Department has forty employees, and the mean weekly wage is $900 with a standard deviation of $50. The Sales Department has sixty-five employees, and the mean weekly wage is $750 with a standard deviation of $20. Using the formula for coefficient of variation (the distribution's standard deviation divided by the mean), the Marketing Department has a higher coefficient of variation (5.5 percent), and, thus, higher volatility.

Normal Distribution

A normal distribution is a probability distribution that helps forecast volatility around a central, or an expected, value. When data is distributed evenly around a central data point and forms a bell curve, it is considered a normal distribution. To learn more, see "Different Data Distributions."

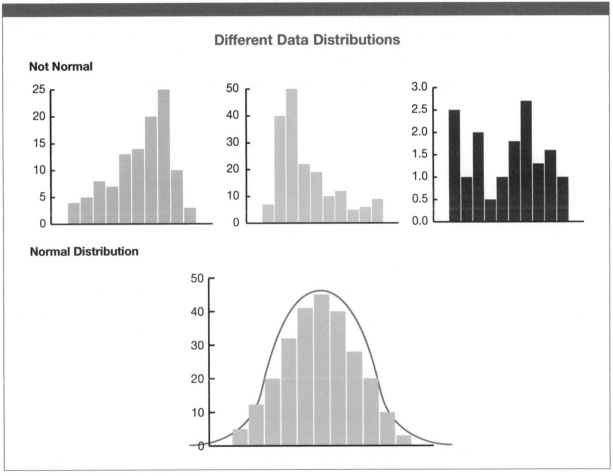

[DA13033]

A normal distribution graph will show the percentage of outcomes that fall within a given number of standard deviations above or below the mean. The spread typically looks like this:

- 68 percent of the values are within two standard deviations of the mean (one above and one below).

- 95 percent of the values are within four standard deviations of the mean (two above and two below).

- 99 percent of the values are within six standard deviations of the mean (three above and three below).

Practical Application

Freedom Widget, Inc., has a large woodworking shop that produces a lot of combustible dust—which is a major fire hazard. So its risk manager uses a normal distribution to determine how often to replace its industrial dust collection systems.

Based on historical data from the systems' manufacturer, the mean number of operating hours a dust collection system can be expected to last is 8,000, with a standard deviation of 2,000. To learn more, see "Freedom Widget's Normal Distribution: Machinery Output."

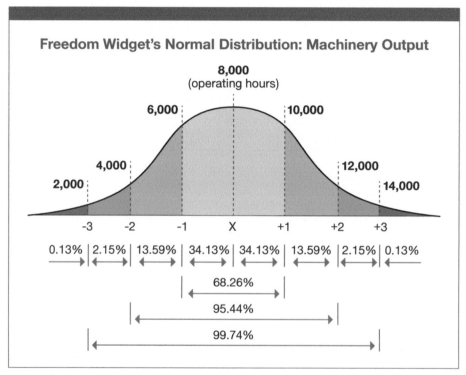

[DA13034]

The risk manager wants to be 95 percent certain the woodworking shop replaces its dust collection systems before they fail and create a fire hazard. So, the risk manager recommends replacing the systems after 4,000 operating hours, which is two standard deviations from their mean life expectancy.

VALUE AT RISK AND EARNINGS AT RISK

To thoroughly evaluate financial risk, a risk manager needs to be able to analyze the full range of potential financial outcomes of an action or investment.

To help with this analysis, risk managers can use various measurement techniques to determine the probability of particular financial outcomes.

Measurement techniques such as value at risk (VaR) and **earnings at risk (EaR)** can be used to determine the likelihood of different financial outcomes and help risk management professionals measure and control risk exposures.

Earnings at risk (EaR)
A technique to assess earnings volatility by measuring the likelihood that earnings will be below a specific dollar amount over a specific period of time.

What Do You Know?

True or false: VaR and EaR are measurement techniques that only financial institutions can use.

Feedback: False. While VaR and EaR are primarily associated with financial institutions, both measurement techniques are also beneficial for nonfinancial organizations of all varieties that need to evaluate the financial risks associated with business decisions.

VaR is typically used to determine the probability of loss on an investment portfolio over a certain, usually short, time period. EaR is mainly used by financial institutions to determine the amount by which the net income (or earnings) of an investment may shift as a result of changes in market conditions, such as interest rates going up or down. Nonfinancial organizations, however, can also use both VaR and EaR to assess financial risks.

Value at Risk

VaR measures the probability of incurring a loss in value that exceeds a threshold level. It is typically characterized by measuring over a short time period and a low probability. For example, let's say an organization sets a VaR loss threshold level of $300,000. A one-day, 5 percent VaR of $300,000 means there is a 5 percent probability of losing $300,000 or more over the next day.

VaR provides these three benefits as a risk measure:

- Quantifies the potential loss associated with an investment decision
- Articulates complex positions (typically involving multiple investments) as a single figure
- Expresses loss in easy-to-understand monetary terms

However, VaR has a limitation: It doesn't accurately measure the extent to which a loss may exceed the VaR threshold. This limitation can be addressed with **conditional value at risk (CVaR)**.

CVaR provides the same benefits as VaR but with the added benefit of helping to analyze the extremely large losses that may occur, usually with very low

Conditional value at risk (CVaR)
A technique to quantify the likelihood of losing a specific dollar amount that exceeds the VaR threshold.

probabilities, in the tail of a probability distribution. To learn more, see "VaR Distribution for Period of One Day."

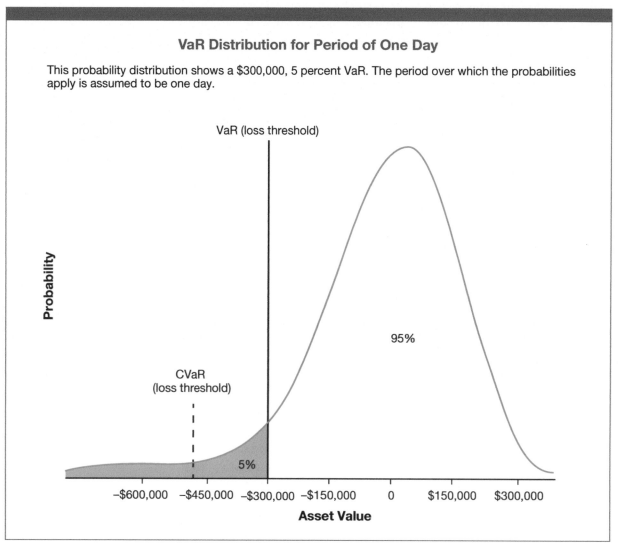

VaR Distribution for Period of One Day

This probability distribution shows a $300,000, 5 percent VaR. The period over which the probabilities apply is assumed to be one day.

[DA10431]

CVaR is particularly important in fat-tailed distributions, for which the extremely large losses have higher probabilities than with most other probability distributions. For example, hurricane risk has a fat-tailed distribution.

Earnings at Risk

Determining EaR entails modeling the influence of factors such as changes in interest rates; sales; production costs; and the prices of products, commodities, and components used in production. Models are developed using a **Monte Carlo simulation**, and the results are presented as a probability distribution curve or a histogram of individual probabilities.

The EaR threshold is the low end of projected earnings within a specific confidence, such as 95 percent. The probability that an organization's earnings will be greater than the EaR threshold is represented by the area under the distribution curve to the right of the EaR threshold. The area under the curve to the left of the EaR threshold represents the probability that earnings will be below the EaR threshold. For example, if earnings at risk are $100,000 with 95 percent confidence, then earnings are projected to be $100,000 or greater 95 percent of the time and less than $100,000 5 percent of the time. To learn more, see "EaR Distribution for Period of One Year."

Monte Carlo simulation

A computerized statistical model that simulates the effects of various types of uncertainty.

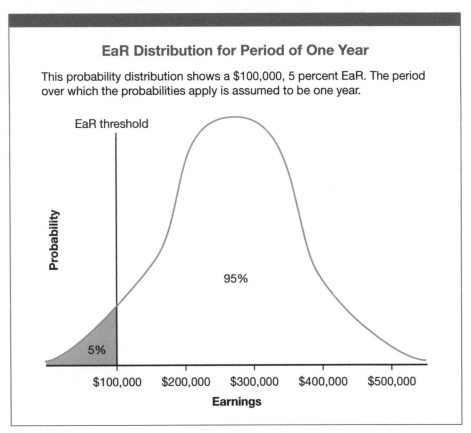

EaR Distribution for Period of One Year

This probability distribution shows a $100,000, 5 percent EaR. The period over which the probabilities apply is assumed to be one year.

[DA10432]

EaR is helpful in comparing the likely effects of different risk management strategies on earnings. However, one drawback is that the calculations can be complex.

TREND ANALYSIS

Risk management professionals use trend analysis techniques to forecast an organization's gains and losses. Such forecasts help managers make cost-effective risk management decisions.

Organizations use **trend analysis** techniques to identify predictable patterns of change in dynamic environments and, from those patterns, develop forecasts. **Regression analysis** is one of those techniques, and it can increase the accuracy of forecasting by examining relationships between the variables that affect trends. For example, changes in hazard loss frequency might correlate with changes in some other variable, such as production output, in such a way that loss frequency can be predicted using production output data.

Organizations must develop sound forecasts of their gains and losses associated with risk exposures. To develop these forecasts, risk management professionals examine data on past gains and losses and subject that data to probability analysis and/or trend analysis to project the expected value of future gains and losses. Resulting projections help managers determine the costs and benefits of business decisions and choose the ones with the greatest benefits over costs.

Trend analysis is commonly used to adjust forecasted future dollar amounts of gains or losses using an anticipated inflation rate. For example, projected inflationary trends would increase the cost of future physical damage losses; therefore, inflation must be considered in estimates of property losses.

Trend analysis

An analysis that identifies patterns in past data and then projects these patterns into the future.

Regression analysis

A statistical technique that is used to estimate relationships between variables.

What Do You Know?

If your organization had two injuries in one year, then four injuries the next year, and then seven injuries the year after that, what would be an effective way to project how many injuries would occur in the fourth year? Would it be beneficial to find the mean number of injuries and use it to project future injuries?

Feedback: The mean number of injuries (4.3) would not help project future injuries in this case because injuries are clearly on the rise, and finding the mean doesn't account for that trend. Instead, a better technique would be to use a linear regression analysis, which we discuss in this section.

Linear regression analysis

A form of regression analysis that assumes that the change in the dependent variable is constant for each unit of change in the independent variable.

Regression Analysis

Many risks vary predictably in relation to another variable, so they can be forecast using a regression analysis. In a regression analysis, the variable being forecast is the dependent variable. The variable that determines the value of the dependent variable is the independent variable. **Linear regression**

analysis deals with a constant rate of change. For example, if the independent variable is time that is measured in years, then a linear regression analysis assumes that the change in the dependent variable is the same from year to year. In this case, the regression line is straight (linear), not curved. To learn more, see "Charting a Linear Regression Line."

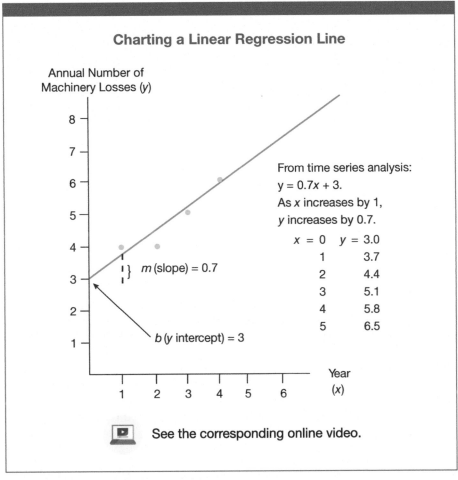

Charting a Linear Regression Line

Annual Number of Machinery Losses (y)

From time series analysis:
y = 0.7x + 3.
As x increases by 1,
y increases by 0.7.

x = 0	y = 3.0
1	3.7
2	4.4
3	5.1
4	5.8
5	6.5

m (slope) = 0.7

b (y intercept) = 3

Year (x)

See the corresponding online video.

[DA12710]

The exhibit plots annual machinery losses over time on a graph. The dependent variable (annual number of losses) is charted on the vertical (y) axis; the independent variable (year) is charted on the horizontal (x) axis. The data points show that 4, 4, 5, and 6 losses occurred, respectively, in Year 1 through Year 4. The goal of regression analysis is to find the equation for the line that best fits these four data points and to project this line forward to forecast the number of future losses.

The first steps in calculating a linear regression line are to plot the data points, find the slope (m) of the line, find the y intercept (b), and sketch the line. The mathematical equations for finding the slope of the line and the y intercept using multiple data points are beyond the scope of this discussion, but they can be determined using a computer program or calculator.

The slope of the line (m) is the amount by which y increases or decreases with a one-unit increase along the x axis. In this example, m equals 0.7. The y intercept (b) is the point at which the line crosses the y axis (the value of y when x equals zero). In this example, b equals 3.

The y intercept and slope determine a line. A line slanting upward from left to right has positive slope; a line slanting downward has negative slope. This is the equation of a line:

$$y = mx + b,$$

where

y is the dependent variable

x is the independent variable

b is the y-intercept

m is the slope of the line

Two aspects of interpreting linear regression lines always need to be considered. First, a line tends to become less accurate the farther away it gets from the actual data values used. For example, this linear trend line may work to forecast losses in Year 5 or Year 6, but it probably wouldn't be accurate for forecasting losses in Year 25 or Year 26.

Second, for any past year, the dependent variable's value calculated by the linear regression line isn't likely to exactly equal the historical value for that past year. Any regression line represents the best fit of a line to actual historical data for all past years. For any given year, the projected trend value will probably differ from the actual outcome.

Alternative Regression Analysis Example

An alternative possibility that a risk management professional could assume is that the annual number of machinery losses is affected by a variable other than the passage of time, such as the volume of items processed. This variable (such as volume of output) could then be substituted for time as the independent variable to project the number of future machinery losses.

Let's say a risk manager wants to use a firm's annual output (in 100,000-ton units) to project the annual number of machinery losses. He or she compiles data that shows the number of machinery losses sustained and the tons of output (in hundreds of thousands, to convert it to units of 100,000) in each year from Year 1 to Year 4. To learn more, see "Relationship of Losses to Output."

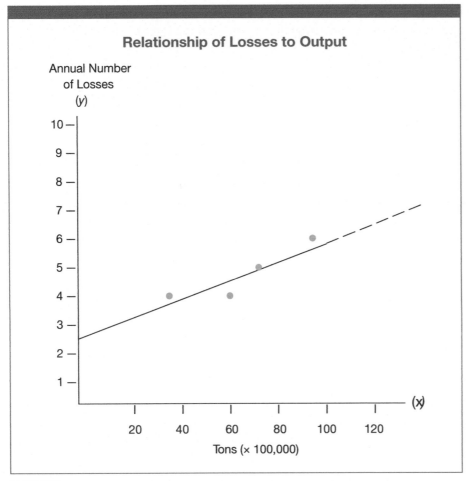

Relationship of Losses to Output

Annual Number
of Losses
(y)

Tons (× 100,000)

(x)

[DA02080]

The exhibit plots machinery losses in relation to the firm's annual output. The data points show that 4 losses occurred in Year 1 when output was 35 (x 100,000); 4 losses occurred in Year 2 when output was 60; 5 losses occurred in Year 3 when output was 72; and 6 losses occurred in Year 4 when output was 95.

The solid portion of the linear regression line approximates the trend of the historical data. The dashed extension of the regression line projects annual numbers of machinery losses for levels of output (in units of 100,000) beyond the range of this particular historical data.

In this example, the indicated value for b is 2.46 machinery losses. The indicated value for m is 0.035, implying that with each 100,000-ton increase in output, 0.035 additional machinery losses can be expected.

In some cases, a risk manager may need to apply a curvilinear regression line. This technique is used to measure a relationship between the independent and dependent variables that changes at an accelerating or decelerating rate rather than at a constant rate. Forecasts should be accepted only if the underlying assumptions are valid. Therefore, knowing these assumptions and recognizing the potential limitations in these forecasting techniques are important.

ANALYZING EVENT CONSEQUENCES

Organizations use decision tree analysis and event tree analysis to predict the likelihood and severity of consequences or gains arising from decisions and events. This helps managers make decisions that will best propel an organization toward its strategic goals, as well as manage its risks.

Decision tree analysis examines the consequences, including costs and gains, of decisions. A risk management professional may use decision tree analysis to compare different decisions and select the one most likely to help the organization obtain a strategic goal.

Event tree analysis examines all possible consequences of an accidental event, their probabilities, and existing measures to prevent or control them. A risk manager may use this approach to examine the effectiveness of systems, risk treatment, or risk control measures and to identify, recommend, and justify expenditures of money, time, or resources for improvements.

What Do You Know?

If you wanted to analyze the potential consequences and probabilities of different items or components in a system failing, would you use a decision tree or event tree analysis?

Feedback: Event tree analysis would be used to assess the consequences and probabilities associated with the failure of an item, component, or process. But let's explore what makes both decision tree and event tree analysis valuable.

Decision Tree Analysis

An organization might use a decision tree in selecting the best course of action from multiple options or to manage risks associated with a project. By analyzing various options and the events that may affect them, decision makers can reduce the uncertainty involved in decision making.

Decision trees can provide both qualitative and quantitative analysis. Qualitatively, they can help generate scenarios, progressions, and consequences that could potentially result from a decision. Quantitatively, they can estimate probabilities and frequencies of various scenarios resulting from a decision.

Constructing a decision tree begins with identifying the decision under consideration—for example, whether to develop a product. From that point, various sequences of events (pathways) are charted for each potential decision. Each pathway then leads to an outcome. For a quantitative analysis, probabilities are assigned to each pathway, and expected values (costs or gains) of each pathway can be estimated for the outcome. The probabilities of each pathway and the value of its outcome can be compared to determine the pathway that produces the highest expected value.

Decision tree analysis offers the advantages of visual portrayal of event sequences and outcomes and a means to calculate the best pathway through a problem. To learn more, see "Decision Tree Analysis."

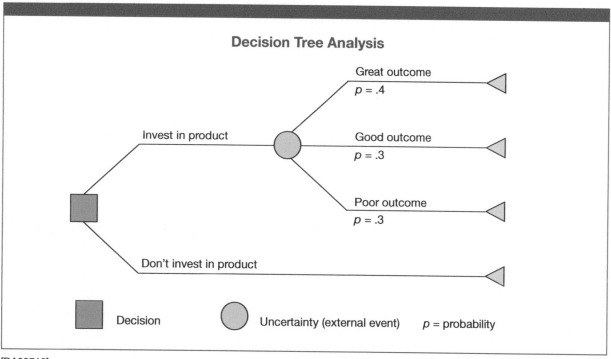

[DA08712]

Event Tree Analysis

Event trees are similar to decision trees in their portrayal and analysis of various pathways and their outcomes. However, event trees analyze the consequences of accidental events rather than decisions.

Like a decision tree, an event tree can provide both qualitative and quantitative analysis. Qualitatively, it can help generate scenarios, progressions, and consequences that could potentially result from an accidental event. Quantitatively, it can estimate probabilities and frequencies of various scenarios and outcomes and help organizations determine the effectiveness of or need for controls and safeguards. Event trees are often used to determine the need for and to examine the effectiveness of risk treatment methods.

The first step in building an event tree is identifying the first accidental event related to a product or process that could result in unwanted consequences. It's typically the first significant unwanted departure from a normal series of events. The various progressions of events that could follow the accidental event are then identified, along with any barriers to those consequences (such as alarm or detection systems, emergency procedures, or other loss control measures). The progression of events that are identified could be based on factors such as human responses, interaction with other systems, weather, or the performance or failure of barriers to consequences.

The analysis ends in a list of potential consequences of the initial event. To learn more, see "Event Tree Analysis."

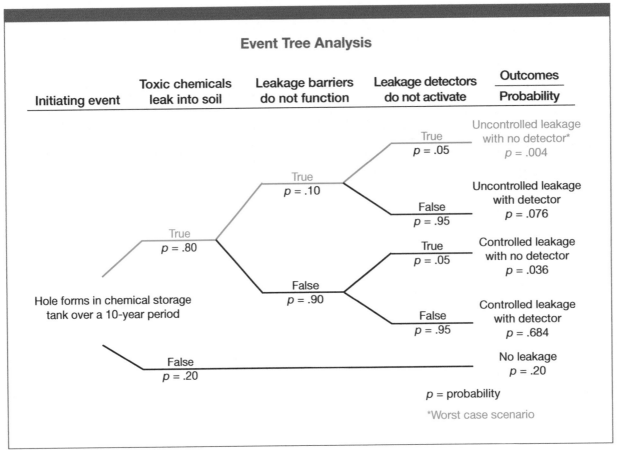

[DA08713]

In the event tree diagram shown, barriers are listed along the top in the sequence in which they would be activated should the designated accidental event occur. In each pathway, every barrier has the potential to either function or fail; therefore, the pathway splits in two, and an estimated probability—determined by experts or other analysis—is assigned to each pathway.

For each pathway in the diagram, the end probability represents the likelihood that every event in the pathway will occur. This probability is calculated by multiplying together the probability of each event in the pathway that occurs after the initial accidental event (for example, in the worst case scenario $.80 \times .10 \times .05 = .004$). The sum of all probabilities at the end of the diagram should equal 1 (for example, $.004 + .076 + .036 + .684 + .20 = 1$).

Like a decision tree, an event tree creates a visual portrayal of event sequences and outcomes. Specifically, it illustrates the potential effectiveness of control systems following accidental events and accounts for timing, other contributing factors, and domino effects. But one of the limitations of event tree analysis is that it typically provides only two options—success or failure—and thereby fails to reflect the complexity of some processes or products (for example, some components or barriers may not fail completely).

SUMMARY

The probability of an event is the likelihood that it will happen over a period of time, assuming that the environment remains relatively unchanged. A probability analysis predicts the likelihood of an event, and a probability distribution shows all of the possible outcomes of an event next to the likelihood of those outcomes. A properly constructed probability distribution always contains outcomes that are both mutually exclusive and collectively exhaustive. All probability distributions can be classified as either discrete or continuous. Theoretical probabilities are based on principals rather than actual experience. Empirical probabilities, meanwhile, are based on actual experience and become more accurate as the sample size increases, illustrating the law of large numbers.

Various metrics can be used to estimate the volatility of a subject (such as a risk) and improve outcomes. Expected value (or mean) is the weighted average of values and the most obvious return one can expect from an action. Standard deviation and coefficient of variation are different ways to measure the spread of results. A normal distribution is a probability distribution that helps forecast volatility around a central, or an expected, value.

VaR and EaR are measurement techniques used to evaluate financial risk. VaR is typically used to determine the probability of loss on an investment portfolio over a certain time period. EaR is used by financial institutions to determine the amount by which the net income (or earnings) of an organization may shift as a result of changes in market conditions. However, both VaR and EaR can be used by nonfinancial organizations.

Trend analysis is used to develop sound forecasts of an organization's gains and losses associated with risk exposures based on predictable patterns of change. Regression analysis can increase the accuracy of an organization's forecasts by examining the relationship between variables that affect trends.

Organizations use decision tree analysis to compare the consequences, costs, and gains of alternative decisions and to select the most effective strategy to achieve a goal. Event tree analysis is used to examine all possible consequences of an accidental event and the effectiveness of existing measures to prevent or control those consequences.

Diving Into Data

10

Educational Objectives	Outline

▶ Categorize the various characteristics and sources of big data available for risk management applications.

▶ Summarize traditional data analysis techniques and their application to risk management.

▶ Summarize modern data analysis techniques and their application to risk management.

▶ Explain how data-driven decision making applies to risk management.

Diving Into Data

10

BIG DATA FOR RISK MANAGEMENT

Big data and risk management are business partners, in a sense. But data stripped of its context—even at high volume—won't necessarily help you answer critical questions or make faster, better risk management decisions. You have to also be able to trust the data being used to make those decisions. Part of developing that trust lies in understanding the sources of the myriad streams of data that flow into and out of your organization and the distinguishing features of the types of information those sources offer.

Learn more from an expert in the online video.

Before we examine the ways that big data can be categorized for analysis, let's first look at five characteristics that make data big:

- Volume—Businesses have access to an enormous amount of data. Organizations collect data from a variety of sources, including business transactions, social media, sensors. In the past, storing current volumes of data would've been a problem— but today's cloud storage technologies have minimized that issue.

- Variety—Big data comes in all types of formats, from structured, numeric, transactional data and social media.

- Velocity—The speed at which data grows and becomes available to a business is unprecedented. Velocity includes the growing rate of change in the types of data and the need to deal with it in a timely manner. Technology, such as radio-frequency identification (RFID) tags, sensors, and smart metering are helping companies deal with torrents of data in near-real time.

- Veracity—This refers to the completeness and accuracy of the data. Unstructured data, by definition, can be uncertain and imprecise. Structured, transactional, and master data may also have flaws because of inadequate edits or user error.

- Value—Big data has great potential to add business value (certainly for risk management), but it must be obtained and analyzed with techniques that provide meaningful results.

What Do You Know?

Although big data by itself is helpful, imposing standards on it can increase its usefulness. Can you identify the role a data governance program would play in regard to big data?

Feedback: Data governance programs establish standards and oversee the management of an organization's data assets. Big data is a valuable resource, but to be useful it needs to meet certain standards of quality. It also must be protected from being abused.

Internal and External Data

As the volume and types of data continue to grow, organizations make choices about capturing and storing that data. Some businesses implement a data governance program to establish standards and oversee the management of their data assets. But risk assessment is not limited to analysis of internal data captured and processed by various departments; it also encompasses external data, such as surveys, industry reports, federal and state regulations, and economic news (stock markets and interest rates, for example).

If data is reusable or needed for ongoing analysis, processes are put in place to capture and store the data in proprietary databases. Risk managers and other executives look for outside sources of data that may supplement their own internal data. Integrating and analyzing internal and external data is a fundamental task for those charged with risk management.

Internal Data

Data captured and stored by organizations, categorized as internal data, includes master data identifying customers, vendors, and prospects; accounting records (sales and purchases, for example); Human Resources records (payroll, vacations, benefits); and employee/customer correspondence (emails, contracts, and so on). Internal data also includes files specific to the type of business. Manufacturers deal with inventory and process controls. Banks maintain customer financial records. Software companies have feature enhancement logs and project tracking records.

Risk managers rely on internal data to monitor various risk factors. They watch cash flow and other financial data to improve investment opportunities or mitigate payable/receivable imbalances. Sales and inventory records may alert manufacturing teams to potential problems meeting product demand.

Risk managers have access to all the internal data an organization owns but may be limited by the sheer volume and/or lack of techniques to compile and analyze it. That's where data analytics can be helpful. For example, exploratory data analysis (EDA) is a category of graphical and statistical techniques used to explore the structure of a dataset and identify data deviations. Data errors are often uncovered by investigating the validity of any deviations.

External Data

External data belongs to an entity other than the organization that would like to acquire and use it. Open data is one type of external data, and anyone can freely use it, as there are no existing legal restrictions on access or usage. Wikipedia is a well-known source of open data. Similarly, public data generally refers to open government records.

Sometimes there's a fine line between internal and external data. For example, external data may become stored as internal data, depending on how it's to be used. If it's for trend analysis over various periods of time, it may need to be maintained chronologically and updated regularly. An organization may not be able to rely on its availability from the external source when it's needed. However, if it's simply a one-time data resource to plug into a spreadsheet, then it is referred to as external data.

Although the usage or application of the data is the primary concern of risk management, whether it's identified as internal or external is not totally unimportant. Where the data comes from can make a big difference. For example, internal data is more reliable (for safety analysis) and carries greater risk around privacy issues (than external data).

One example of overlapping internal/external data is the use of vehicle telematics technology. Transportation companies use fleet telematics to monitor a wealth of data about both the vehicle and its operator, captured over cellular connections. Data collected can provide clues for a broad range of improvements, from increasing fuel efficiency and optimizing routes to reducing collisions and saving lives. Transportation companies are investing heavily in telematics to protect their human and physical assets. Vehicle data is more likely internal data, while the driver's driving habits should probably be categorized as external data.

Regulatory information is another typical type of external data. All companies have risk concerns related to compliance with safety, environmental, or privacy issues. Risk managers must stay abreast of external changes in regulations and discussions about pending legislation, for example.

Privacy issues constitute legal and regulatory concerns when personal information is obtained from public sources, including social media. For example, companies might access credit files or public records of a prospective employee, and in such instances they need to be diligent about informing and, in most cases, gaining consent from a job applicant. The same caution is necessary for banks that must obtain and use credit ratings for both personal and commercial loan applications.

Other sources of external data include published statistical data related to demographics, industry trends, survey results, and other subjects. **Economic data**, such as interest rates, asset prices, and exchange rates, is a commonly

Economic data

Data regarding interest rates, asset prices, exchange rates, the Consumer Price Index, and other information about the global, the national, or a regional economy.

used type of third-party data. Consumer Price Index and other information about global, national, or regional economies is also valuable risk analysis data.

Structured and Unstructured Data

The format of data is described as structured or unstructured. Traditional internal master and transactional data is structured; that is, organized into specific fields in databases. The structure allows for easily linking files to each other. For example, a risk manager could create an analytical report through a query of two files: a customers' purchases and payments transaction file and a customer master file for demographics. Likewise, one report linking data from different databases can be used to analyze cash flow risk factors.

Telematics provides an example of structured external data. A database contains formatted fields for information that transportation companies receive from telematics, such as distance traveled, location, engine temperature, distance from other vehicles or objects, and road conditions.

Unstructured data is not organized into defined fields and is not consistent in format. Prospect notes are an example of internal unstructured data. Although the notes may be contained in a customer relationship management (CRM) database, they're not likely to be categorized or consistent from one sales rep to another. Unstructured external data includes information from the internet, such as social media sites.

Data analytics is used for both structured and unstructured data, but it's especially useful for the latter. Information that's not uniformly formatted or may need contextual interpretation is more difficult to analyze. Risk managers have to use various techniques to gather, categorize, and analyze unstructured data. Two graphs about interest rates, for example, may have different contexts: one may represent historic trends, while the other is related to home mortgages.

Structured data is instrumental in what is known as business intelligence (BI) because it's quantifiable. It's formatted in a database, making it easier to search and analyze. Too often, however, business leaders default to snapshots of structured data to make decisions, which can be shortsighted. A strong BI plan also relies on unstructured data for additional insights. Here's a risk management example from a software business of how structured and unstructured data is categorized. To learn more, see "Big Data Categories and Examples."

Big Data Categories and Examples

	Structured	Unstructured
External	Telematics Financial data Labor statistics	Social media News reports Internet videos
Internal	Policy information Claims history Customer data	Adjuster notes Customer voice records Surveillance videos

[DA11944]

Apply Your Knowledge

Which one of the following is an example of structured external data?

a. Customer data

b. Telematics data

c. Social media

d. Adjuster notes

Feedback: Telematics data is an example of structured external data. The information involved in telematics is easily placed in a database with formatted fields, while the other sources of data can be too varied for easy categorization.

TRADITIONAL DATA ANALYSIS

Businesses have long relied on data analysis techniques to evaluate and improve their risk management decisions. Risk management professionals measure all kinds of data—financial data to improve the bottom line, production data to bolster efficiency, customer feedback data to meet or exceed service standards—and use countless other sources of information to increase the certainty associated with their forecasts. Analytical techniques are therefore vital tools for solving the business problems you'll confront as a risk management professional.

Data analysis is typically used to determine one of these types of outcomes:

- A nonnumerical category to which data belongs—For example, a food-products manufacturer may want to identify product categories that would compete with a potential new product.

- A numerical answer—A retail chain uses existing data to measure day and hour customer traffic by store.

- A probability score based on historical data—A manufacturer may want to determine the probability that a safety solution will reduce the frequency of worker accidents.

- A prediction of future results based on current and past data—Revenue predictions for a new product or new market, for example, based on previous similar product sales.

Analysis has become more valuable as well as more complicated. Technological advancements and access to unprecedented volumes and types of data have paved the way for new and improved analysis options. Organizations and their risk management teams routinely use predictive analytics to reduce risks, optimize operations, and increase revenue.

Common data analysis techniques include these:

- Exploratory data analysis
- **Classification trees**
- Regression analysis
- **Cluster analysis**

Exploratory Data Analysis

Classification tree

A supervised learning technique that uses a structure similar to a tree to segment data according to known attributes to determine the value of a categorical target variable.

Cluster analysis

A model that determines previously unknown groupings of data.

Exploratory data analysis can be used before developing and testing a predictive model to produce a basic understanding of the data on which the model will be based. This is important because a model's predictive ability is only as strong as the data it's built on. The better understood the data, the better the model.

The techniques used for exploratory data analysis are relatively simple. They involve charts and graphs that show data patterns and correlations among data.

For example, a scatter plot (and its close relative, a bubble plot) is a two-dimensional plot of point values that represent the relationship (or correlation) between two attributes. A correlation matrix is another type of exploratory data analysis technique.

Say a risk management professional identifies a few attributes to test driver safety. By building a correlation matrix of selected attributes, the graph may indicate that certain combinations of attributes such as variable shifts, age, and overtime, correlate strongly with driver accidents. That, in turn, can lead to revisions in shift assignments and overtime and, subsequently, fewer accidents. To learn more, see "Bubble Plot: Average Accident Frequency and Severity by Driver Age."

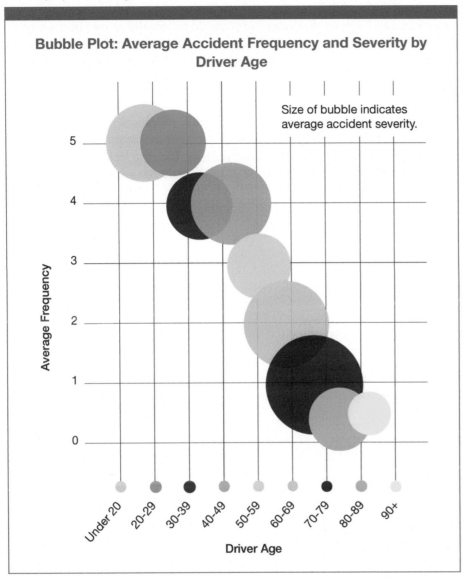

[DA12022]

Classification Trees

To solve business problems using data analysis, the data used must usually have certain relevant characteristics. For example, to determine whether an employee is likely to be able to return to work after an accident, a risk management professional might use such attributes as type of occupation, age, qualifications for retraining, and available positions with lighter physical requirements.

In this example, a classification tree (also known as a decision tree) could be used to segment workers compensation data. The tree would contain nodes, arrows, and leaf nodes. The leaf nodes of the tree indicate the values of the target variable. Each worker's attributes would follow the arrows of the tree through leaf nodes that segment the data by attribute to an ultimate leaf node labeled "Return to work" or "No return to work." It is important to understand that these classifications are not necessarily what the actual outcomes will be.

Decision trees are helpful, not only because they graphically depict what you're thinking but also because making a decision tree requires a systematic, documented thought process. Gerber Products, Inc., the well-known baby products company, used decision tree analysis to decide whether to continue using the plastic known as polyvinyl chloride, or PVC. The situation involved a number of organizations, including Greenpeace, the United States Consumer Product Safety Commission, the toy and plastics industries, and the general public.[1]

Regression Analysis

Regression analysis is a statistical technique used to estimate relationships between variables. Two types of regression analysis are linear regression and a generalized linear model.

Linear regression is used to predict the numerical value of a target variable based on values of explanatory variables.

For example, a risk manager at a software company wants to build a model to predict impending sales (the target variable). The model will look at the relationship between the number of prospects a sales representative is involved with and what sales stage the prospect is at. Training data and holdout data (other data not used as part of the training data) with known values of the individual attributes are used to develop and test the model. Because the target variable is numerical, the analyst or risk management professional uses linear regression as the algorithm. He or she develops this algorithm using a method that minimizes errors, represented by the differences between the actual target-variable values in the data and those forecast by the model.

The second type of regression analysis is a generalized linear model (GLM), a statistical technique that increases the flexibility of a linear model by linking it with a nonlinear function. Also used for more complex data classification, GLM should not be confused with a general linear model, which is a broad group of different types of linear models.

Apply Your Knowledge

Adelaide is a risk manager for a nationwide chain of pizza shops. Before launching a new promotion for its pizzas, management wants to analyze the financial risks by testing the promotion in a few limited markets. Explain how Adelaide could use regression analysis to predict sales for the test promotion.

Feedback: Adelaide would treat the potential number of pizzas sold as the target variable. The model would look at the relationship between normal and forecasted pizza sales in each market. Training data and holdout data (other data not used as part of the training data) with known values of the individual attributes would be used to develop and test the model. Because the target variable is numerical, Adelaide would use linear regression as the algorithm. She would try to develop that algorithm using a method that minimizes errors, which would be represented by differences between the actual number of pizzas sold during the test promotion and the number forecasted by the model.

Cluster Analysis

Sometimes, risk management professionals want more information but do not know the precise nature of that information. For example, to determine whether there is a relationship between the time lag in reporting employee injury claims and the size of those claims, data analytics techniques that use known variables would not be effective. Cluster analysis can be used to search data for previously unknown information or relationships.

There are different methods of cluster analysis that segment data according to similarities in various attributes. And to provide more granular information, several iterations of cluster analysis can be applied to further subdivide clusters. So if an organization identifies segments of customers according to age, it may want to identify characteristics of, for example, millennial customers in an effort to gain insight into applicable products and effective marketing approaches for that group.

Cluster analysis is not so much a typical statistical test as a collection of algorithms that put data into groups or clusters according to well-defined similarity rules. It's commonly used when a risk management professional has a general problem to solve but does not know the variables a predictive model must analyze to do so.

For example, every Information Technology (IT) Department must occasionally refresh its server(s) and storage hardware, but there are no hard and fast rules about when to do so. Decisions may be driven by the availability of new technologies, changing workload requirements, new applications, or simply because the organization can save money and improve application performance by updating its equipment. Deciding how and when to get maximum value out of new IT servers and storage is both a challenge and opportunity facing risk management professionals and IT teams. Too soon and you waste money; too late and you waste opportunity.

Decision makers must answer critical processing and storage questions to achieve IT modernization and transformation. The only real way to answer them is by grouping and analyzing real data from the current IT environment and workload.

A data analyst would develop a model to analyze various datasets, such as capacity, performance, reliability, and application and operating system environments. The results may show, for example, a clustering of processing bottlenecks around certain applications. The analyst could then apply the information gained through cluster analysis to develop a predictive model.

MODERN DATA ANALYSIS

Our lives are filled with patterns and connections. Examining them can reveal a lot about what we do and who we are. That information, in turn, can be used to predict what risks need to be accounted for in the future.

Data mining

The process of extracting hidden patterns from data that is used in a wide range of applications for research and fraud detection.

Risk managers have always known that they need to acquire information continually and refine their ability to interpret it in more meaningful ways. **Data mining** techniques, which are constantly evolving and improving, provide incredible amounts of data, but once an organization amasses data, it must know what to do with it, how to glean insights from it, and then how to transform that awareness into constructive outcomes.

Text Mining

Every organization possesses an abundance of data, much of it text—whether on paper or stored in computers and other electronic devices. Text mining turns text into numbers that are then used in mathematical equations or models.

The first step of the text mining process is to retrieve and prepare the text. Usually, this data is considered unstructured. What that means is that is the data has no basic, universal organization that makes it easy to put in a matrix format. For example, although an email may contain fairly standard information, such as a date, time, sender, recipient, and subject, the actual content of each email usually differs in some way (as opposed to a collection of financial documents, which may follow the same format). Other examples of unstructured text-based data include letters or reports, PowerPoint presentations, books, social media posts, and medical records. To learn more, see "Examples of Unstructured Data."

By its nature, unstructured data is very difficult to analyze. Therefore, during the second step of the text mining process, the unstructured data needs to be converted into structured data before a modeling algorithm can analyze it. Structured data stores information in a precise, consistent format that can be searched much more easily. Examples of structured text-based data include names, street addresses, and genders.

Examples of Unstructured Data

Human-Produced	Machine-Produced
Email, spreadsheets, and text documents	Satellite imagery, such as weather data and land forms
Websites and social media posts	Scientific data, such as seismic imagery and atmospheric data
Text messages, instant messages, and phone recordings	Digital surveillance, such as photos and videos
Digital photos, audio files, and video files	Sensor data, such as that from traffic and oceanographic equipment

[DA13035]

During the third step, different techniques are used to create a data mining model to help the organization achieve its goals. These techniques involve identifying previously undetected groups of data, finding the most similar instances of data, and predefining certain attributes as target variables.

One use of text mining by risk managers might be to evaluate notes taken by an organization's safety officer in connection with workplace injuries to help identify past and future occurrences of fraud. The model would track certain key words or phrases in employee reports that are known elements of fraudulent workers' compensation claims (for example, prescription, back, Monday morning) and report them to the organization for additional scrutiny.

The fourth step in the text mining model is to evaluate its effectiveness in multiple areas. Obviously, no single approach to collecting and examining data will give an organization all the answers it seeks, and a text mining model's predictions are not always correct. For example, an organization could mine text to rate written customer feedback as positive, negative, or neutral, but context would not be taken into account. The adjective "bad," though generally used to indicate negative feelings, occasionally will be used as slang in a complimentary manner. Text mining alone might not be able to make such a distinction when the word is used in customer feedback, resulting in positive feedback being classified as negative.

Apply Your Knowledge

Jessica is a risk manager at an advertising agency facing a morale problem. This issue has caused some employees to get lazy in their work, with effects ranging widely from poor production to physical harm caused by poor posture while working. Jessica sent an essay-based survey to the agency's employees and is now trying to mine the data for the factors that the employees consider to be the most prevalent problems. Explain what her main concern regarding the collected data should be.

Feedback: Jessica's main concern, at least at the start of her analysis, should be that the data she's collecting is unstructured. If her survey had consisted of multiple-choice questions, it would be easier to model an algorithm to analyze it, but because each essay will most likely have its own format and flow, she will need to convert all the information she's collected into a structured format first.

Neural Networks

Neural networks, another modern data analysis technique risk managers should be familiar with, are a form of artificial intelligence (AI) that enable a computer to learn as it accumulates more data. A neural network's analysis is also referred to as deep learning.

Neural networks comprise three layers: input, hidden, and output. The input layer collects the data to be analyzed, and the output layer offers the results of the analysis. The hidden layer is where all the work takes place.

During the input phase, relevant information is entered into the model and assigned an importance level. In the hidden phase, the network executes the mathematical processes it was programmed to perform. The organization reviews the results and compares them with the outcomes it had anticipated. From there, the organization can determine how accurate the model is based on the gap between anticipations and actual results.

The network can then learn from any inaccuracies in its calculations by reversing the process—in other words, entering information that shows what end result is desired and running the process backwards. Alternately running the forward and backward processes numerous times (sometimes hundreds of times) allows the network to teach itself how to arrive at the desired result.

One use of neural networks in risk management is to compare the risks of proposed and current projects with historical results. Data regarding both successful and failed past projects is entered into the network. Then it takes data relating to the proposed or current project so that the network can perform its predictions about the probability of success. Information about the current project can also be analyzed to predict the probability of success at each stage of the project. Of course, the factors that caused previous successes or failures must be understood to choose appropriate input data.

One drawback of neural networks is that they can be overtrained. This occurs when a network reviews data in so much detail that it is unable to operate in a larger framework with other types of data. Another drawback is that the processes undertaken by the network during the hidden phase may be too incomprehensible to be evaluated thoroughly enough.

Social Network Analysis

In today's society, the phrase "social network" brings to mind Facebook, LinkedIn, Instagram, and other forms of electronic media that connect people. However, by definition, a social network encompasses a broader scope of connections.

In the context of social network analysis, a social network is a group of individuals who share relationships and the flow of information. The network can consist of humans or websites, computers, animals, organizations, countries, etc., which are referred to as nodes. Each link between two nodes represents their relationship.

Social network analysis measures and charts the relationships between the nodes in a network, along with the flow of communication between them. The effectiveness of the analysis is based on quantifying the relationships between the nodes. To learn more, see "Centrality Measures."

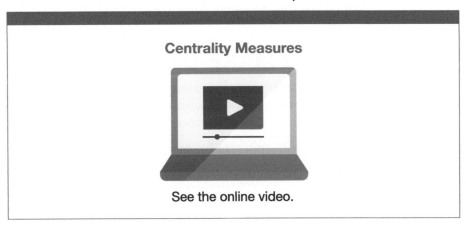

Centrality Measures

See the online video.

[DA13076]

The efficiency of the flow between social network connections can be determined through these **centrality measures:**[2]

- Degree—A measure of the connections each node has. For example, degree would measure the number of external webpages the organization's webpage links to or the number of Facebook friends one of its sales associates has.

- Closeness—The measure of the average distance, or path length, between a particular node and the other nodes in a network. For example, John and Anne both find out that a company policy is changing. Because Anne has a higher closeness to the company's other employees than does John, as measured through the company's email traffic, it is reasonable to assume that Anne will spread the news to more people more quickly through email than will John.

- Betweenness—The measure of how many times a particular node is part of the shortest path between two other nodes in a network. If a scholarly

Centrality measure

In a social network context, the quantification of a node's relationship to other nodes in the same network.

article is posted online and most of its readers click on one of its cited references, read the graduate thesis it cites, and then connect with the thesis's authors, the article has a high degree of betweenness because it connects two groups of people: the authors of the thesis and the readers of the scholarly article.

Another function of social network analysis is to determine trends and make predictions. For example, if an organization began experiencing shipment delays from a linked group of suppliers, its risk manager might want to investigate the reasons for those delays and consider forming relationships with new suppliers.

Learn more from an expert in the online video.

USING DATA TO MAKE DECISIONS

Using data to drive decisions is not exactly a new concept. What is relatively new, however, is the inordinate growth of available data and the advanced technology and methodologies available to process and examine that data.

Data-driven decision making describes the organizational process of gathering and analyzing relevant and verifiable data and then evaluating the results to guide business strategies. Companies have been broadening the definition to encompass improved and expanded types of data, new methods of analysis, and more valuable results. Risk managers who use data-driven decision making have more sophisticated tools and greater knowledge to help their organizations reduce losses, avoid extensive risks, and make better decisions.

What Do You Know?

When a risk manager sets out to solve a specific problem, such as lowering the frequency of workplace injuries, he or she should follow a specific decision-making process. One general process involves five particular steps. How many of the steps can you name?

Feedback: The process for data-driven decisions usually involves these five steps:

- Defining the risk management problem
- Gathering quality data
- Analyzing and modeling the problem

- Determining insights by identifying trends, relationships, behavior, and events
- Making decisions

Data Science and Data-Driven Decision Making

The use of big data and **data science** for decision making is becoming more commonplace. Risk managers have access to a wealth of existing data and are still learning how to tap into all the data and find the talent to process and extrapolate from that data. There's also a rapidly growing quantity of external data available from various sources, such as the Internet at large and the Internet of Things (IoT).

Data-driven decision making can be applied across a risk manager's organization to solve a variety of business problems, avoid future potential problems, or identify opportunities and competitive advantages. Risk management sometimes involves trying to solve an existing problem, such as an assembly line bottleneck that is causing production delays. Other times it involves looking at potential outcomes of a decision. That is, what are the risks or opportunities involved in a particular decision, like opening a branch office? Data-driven decision making offers two basic approaches to solving a problem or deciding a future outcome: descriptive and predictive.

The Descriptive Approach

The descriptive approach is usually a one-time solution that a risk manager uses to solve a specific problem. Data science is used to provide data that will help solve the problem. Once a resolution to the problem is reached, the particular data-driven model that was used is, at least theoretically, no longer needed. However, if there is a case where the same or a similar problem occurs, the risk manager could perhaps use that model as a template to create a new model.

For example, suppose a specialty food manufacturer's sales to a supermarket chain are declining. Management may ask the risk manager to lead an examination into this specific problem to determine the causes and possible corrections.

The risk management team might work with marketing to gather sales data for each store in the identified chain. They would want to see historical data over the past two or three years. Additional data that may be valuable are the demographics of the area where each store is located. A survey could be used to gather additional information from the store managers about product choices and placement of the manufacturer's product(s) in the stores. Now the risk management team can compare sales trends by area and season to

Data science

An interdisciplinary field involving the design and use of techniques to process very large amounts of data from a variety of sources and to provide knowledge based on the data.

determine whether the decline is isolated to certain area(s) of the country or occurs at particular times of the year. The team can factor in individual survey results for additional analysis.

The risk manager would use the results of the analysis to determine whether the problem exists across all stores in the chain or is isolated to specific stores. Using data-driven decision making, executives can decide whether they should visit specific stores to conduct an on-site investigation and remediation. If the problem exists across the entire chain, a renegotiation of pricing may be appropriate. Because this is an isolated problem, the descriptive model would not be used again. The risk management team could, however, use the framework in the future for a similar analysis.

The Predictive Approach

A predictive approach to data analytics is a method that can be used repeatedly to provide information for data-driven decision making by humans, computers, or both. Predictive modeling involves the use of data, statistical algorithms, and machine learning techniques to identify the likelihood of future outcomes based on historical data.

For example, predictive modeling is often used in online advertising and marketing. Predicting responses to a coupon offer or sales from a pay-per-click advertising campaign can be replicated periodically as a marketing strategy.

In another example, transportation companies use modern telematics—technological devices installed in vehicles to collect, report on, and control all kinds of information. Transportation companies monitor the data received about both the vehicle and its operator, which can provide clues for a broad range of improvements, from increasing fuel efficiency and optimizing routes to reducing collisions and saving lives.

Both of these examples are predictive models that may be useful as repeatable, analytical, data-driven techniques for risk management decision making.

A Model for Data-Driven Decision Making in Risk Management

Following an ordered process in decision making will help ensure the best results. The process for data-driven decisions involves these five steps:

- Defining the risk management problem
- Gathering quality data
- Analyzing and modeling (descriptive or predictive)
- Determining insights: trends, relationships, behavior, events
- Making decisions

The first step in any problem-solving scenario is to know the problem you're trying to solve. As noted in the discussion about descriptive and predictive approaches, risk managers may either try to solve a specific problem or to evaluate risk/reward outcomes. The "problem" in the latter scenario is weighing the risks and possible results of a contemplated action. For example, what are the opportunities and risks involved in a company acquiring a competitor or complementary business? Likewise, a manufacturer that is considering expanding to a new chain of specialty retail stores would also consider the potential risks and rewards.

Suppose a software company that provides a software-as-a-service (SaaS) product is receiving an unusual number of support calls regarding a specific function of their product. The company's risk manager is asked to determine why this is occurring and to develop a solution for the problem. The risk manager should use the descriptive approach because the problem requires a one-time analysis.

Because the company tracks support calls by program function, it can see that the number of calls about a particular function is consistently twice that of any other function area of the software. Thus, the problem is clearly defined—the first step in data-driven decision making.

The next step—gathering quality data—begins with the call data logs. The risk manager will also want to gather data about how the identified function has been programmed and how the program could be changed to function differently.

A report of the call data logs will show the risk analysis team what is happening with the software function. For example, is the function producing an error condition that the user cannot resolve or is the user simply unable to enter the type of data he or she wants in order to receive the desired output? Analyzing the data to find patterns in the reasons users are calling will help the risk management team hone in on a solution. Suppose the software has a process to integrate data from an external source, but the process won't proceed if data is missing from a certain field—there may be different programming options that would solve the problem, depending on what the field represents. Determining why the data is missing and whether the process should run absent the missing data will help the risk management team identify a resolution.

Because there are different approaches to how to make the software function, the team may call on a sampling of customers, via a verbal or written survey, to determine a preference. The data analytics team could then meet with the programming staff to discuss programmatic cost and time estimates to make the necessary changes.

The risk manager can then make several decisions—the last step in the data-driven decision-making process—that would be supported by this data. He or she can determine the best programming option based on customer input. With cost and time estimates, the company can then communicate to customers when a resolution will be available. During the decision-making process, the risk management team can consult with the support team to establish a protocol for communicating with customers who call about the problem.

Apply Your Knowledge

When it comes to finding a data-driven solution to these situations, which would be best suited for a descriptive approach and which would be best suited for a predictive approach:

a.   A construction company is looking to lower accident frequency when equipment is being driven to work sites.

b.   A retailer is concerned about rising theft losses.

c.   An automotive retailer is looking for a more reliable supplier for a particular product.

d.   A bank is considering offering a new small business loan program.

Feedback: Situations *a.* and *d.* would require a predictive data-driven approach because both are examples of outcomes of business strategy decisions that may need to be repeated. Situations *b.* and *c.* are specific problems calling for one-time descriptive approaches to data-driven problem resolution.

SUMMARY

Various characteristics and sources distinguish big data from traditional data. These characteristics include not only the amount of data but also its accuracy, whether it is structured or unstructured, its velocity, and the value it adds to an insurer's business decisions. Sources include an insurer's own internal data and external data, both structured and unstructured. By applying data science techniques to big data, insurers can increase their access to useful information to guide business decisions and strategies.

Traditional data analysis techniques remain crucial to solving business problems, but they also form the foundation of newer methods. These techniques include exploratory data analysis, classification trees, various types of statistical regression models, and cluster analysis.

Modern data analysis techniques such as text mining, neural networks, and social network analysis evaluate and attempt to replicate human communication and thinking in order to predict human behavior. Scientists delve deeper into the workings of the human brain, which allows them to refine computer processing and machine learning. In turn, these developing technologies provide risk managers with an expanding supply of resources they can use to better serve their customer.

To gain competitive advantage and operate more effectively, risk managers must be able to properly frame business problems and questions, and then use data science techniques to perform analysis that will improve results. Descriptive, data-driven approaches are used to resolve particular problems. Predictive approaches are used when a risk management team must look forward to evaluate the level of risk and opportunity involved in a business strategy decision that will be repeated.

ASSIGNMENT NOTES

1. Jay Buckley and Thomas J. Dudley, DBA, "How Gerber Used a Decision Tree in Strategic Decision-Making," 1999, https://gbr.pepperdine.edu/2010/08/how-gerber-used-a-decision-tree-in-strategic-decision-making/ (accessed February 5, 2019).

2. Bart Baesens, Analytics in a Big Data World (Hoboken, N.J.: John Wiley & Sons, Inc., 2014), p. 121.

Building Consensus 11

Building Consensus

11

FUNDAMENTALS OF EFFECTIVE COMMUNICATION

Establishing and practicing effective communication habits is integral to business success. Good communication plays an important role in team effectiveness, employee engagement, client relationships, profitability, and risk management. Those who invest time and energy into developing strong communication practices rapidly build trust among executives, decision makers, team members, and subordinates, leading to fewer mistakes.

Effective workplace communication increases productivity, reduces confusion, mitigates conflict, and improves morale. The communication process involves speaking, analytical, and organizational skills, which need to be studied and practiced. Good communicators actively work at becoming good listeners. They also foster two-way dialogue both up and down the chain of command and among internal and external stakeholders.

What Do You Know?

When disagreeing or identifying difficulties with a co-worker, subordinate, or person outside the organization, is it better to use an "I" message or a "you" message?

Feedback: When disagreeing or identifying difficulties with someone, it's best to send "I" messages. However, people tend to do the opposite in such situations, instead stating their dissatisfaction through "you" messages. For example, when talking with a subordinate who is underperforming, a manager may want to say something like, "Rebecca, you're not doing a good job managing your clients." While this may be accurate, the more constructive and less-deflating way to deliver the same criticism is by sending an "I" message, such as, "Rebecca, I think there is room for improvement in the way you manage your clients."

The Communication Process

Before speaking with a group or individual, it's important to step back and establish a plan that ensures the most clear and productive communication process. Here are some ways to do this:

- Set a clear communication objective. Prior to the conversation, ask yourself, What do you want the other person(s) to do as a result of this message? Take a specific action? File it away for future reference? Having an objective in mind will help you best present your message.

- Analyze your audience. What's the person or group's knowledge of the subject or background of the situation? How much detail or background do you need to give? How is this person or group likely to react? What is the clearest way to deliver my message? Don't try to impress others with complex sentences or jargon. Using so-called big words and complex phrases does not make you sound smarter or more professional. This is a misconception. Instead, it's more likely to muddle your message and damage your credibility.

- Decide when and where to talk. The length and importance of your message should be the determining factors. For example, important conversations shouldn't be held on the spur of the moment; they should be given a set time and place where the discussion won't be interrupted.

- Pay attention to your body language. Your posture, tone of voice, and movements play a key role in connecting with your audience and conveying confidence. Look up from your notes and establish eye contact for a few seconds at a time with those you're speaking to (but don't stare). Maintain an open posture by not slouching or crossing your arms. Try to smile as much as possible when the conversation isn't negative in nature. Practice power poses such as puffing out your chest and planting your hands on the table.

- Ask for feedback. To determine whether your message has been understood, request feedback. Asking questions such as, "Do you see any problems with this?" or "How do you think this will work out?" can indicate whether your message was received as intended. However, one thing to avoid is asking people to repeat your message back to you. Doing so can imply that you doubt their ability to understand.

Identifying problems or disagreeing with internal or external stakeholders may require even more analysis and planning to avoid, or at least minimize, conflict. To learn more, see "Delivering Difficult Messages."

Active Listening

Few people are born good listeners. And despite the widely accepted belief that listening is a critical part of effective communication, many people neglect their listening skills, thinking they are good enough already. But if you're not practicing active listening, chances are your listening skills are

---

Delivering Difficult Messages

At times, you will have to deliver messages that recipients won't want to hear. These messages bring with them a high potential for conflict.

But there are ways to minimize or even prevent defensive reactions. For starters, don't blame the other person. Instead, make it clear that you object to a specific kind of behavior, action, or (if you are a manager) performance level or that you disagree with a specific position or decision. For example, don't say, "You messed this up." Instead, say, "I don't like how this turned out."

It's also important to avoid broad generalizations. Avoid words such as "always," "never," and "all." Instead, state specifically what you disagree with. For example, don't say, "You're always late to work." Instead, say, "I noticed you were late two days this week."

Lastly, it's good practice to avoid sounding hostile while trying to be assertive. It's OK to show conviction about how you feel and confidence in your perceptions. Hostility, however, implies that the other person is to blame and increases conflict. "You" messages, judgmental phrases, generalizations, a loud and angry tone of voice, and unwavering eye contact all express hostility and blame.

[DA13118]

hindering your ability to communicate effectively. Most people become good listeners only by working at it.

Active listeners set aside their judgments and, instead, attempt to empathize with the speaker's concerns. They adopt a conscious process of eliciting information, perceptions, and feelings. Active listening does more than generate information; it contributes to the development of trust and a good working relationship.

But before we address what it takes to be a good active listener, it's important to understand what gets in the way of this endeavor:

- Listening is often seen as a passive activity in which the listener simply keeps quiet and allows others to talk. But the contrary is true. Being a good listener requires skill and a conscious effort.

- Listening is seen by some as a weakness. Assertiveness is often viewed as a positive trait. Society tends to gravitate toward leaders who take fast, decisive action and speak forcefully.

- Silence can make people uncomfortable. Many find silence so distressing that they jump to interrupt silence with their own ideas. These ideas can steer the conversation in a new direction instead of helping the speaker pursue his or her line of thought.

- People want to be heard. Some people think they won't have a chance to comment on a point if the speaker moves on to another point, so they interrupt conversations to interject their thoughts.

- People formulate what they will say next. While doing this, they may tune out the speaker, thereby engaging in intermittent listening.
- The message is resisted. People tend to listen poorly to messages they disagree with. Careful listening carries an element of personal risk: being open to a message can make someone vulnerable to it. We may hear ideas or feelings that threaten us. We may hear things that call for us to change our perceptions or plans. Being a good listener requires recognizing your own feelings and reactions and, in turn, controlling the expression of them.

Becoming an effective listener requires mastering the techniques of active listening, which encourage the expression of ideas and feelings. Active listening consists of three elements: attention, suspension of judgment, and response.

Attention

Most people admit to having a short attention span. We're easily distracted by the sights and sounds around us and by our own thoughts. Active listening demands a concentrated effort to pay complete attention to what the other person is saying.

One helpful technique is to pay frequent attention to the nonverbal signals given by the listener. In effect, you pause periodically to scan for messages conveyed through body language and facial expressions. Another technique is to mirror the posture and gestures of the speaker, when appropriate. For example, when he or she leans forward, you should lean forward.

Suspension of Judgment

You must withhold judgments, especially good/bad and right/wrong ones about the message or speaker, during the presentation. Any hint of disapproval can give the person reason to hesitate sharing with you.

While withholding judgment can help facilitate active listening in just about any situation, it's particularly important when the speaker is a member of your unit. Any indication (even nonverbal) that you disapprove of what's being presented will likely interfere with the statements, if not the thinking, of the presenter and others listening to the presentation.

Response

Active listening requires giving appropriate responses. The overall guideline is to avoid introducing a new idea.

With active listening, you want the speaker to maintain control of the conversation. You can achieve this by paraphrasing the speaker's comments and checking your understanding of them. You should not interject a thought that steers the discussion in another direction. Pushing the conversation in a new direction isn't likely to help the speaker reveal ideas and feelings that lie beneath the surface, which is a goal of active listening. To learn more, see "The Paraphrase Response."

The Paraphrase Response

How can you practice active listening in your day-to-day communication with others? Active listening often employs three steps: (1) listening to a message, (2) paraphrasing, or restating in your own words the message you received, and (3) "feeding" the paraphrased message back to the speaker for confirmation. For example, you might say, "What I hear you saying is ____. Is this correct?"

Communication experts agree that active listening is one of the best ways to listen because it requires you to process in your own mind what the speaker is saying (to paraphrase it) and check your understanding of what was said by repeating to the speaker what you heard.

Although active listening speeds up understanding, it actually slows down communication. The advantages, however, far outweigh this drawback.

[DA13119]

Two-Way Communication

Part of becoming an effective communicator requires making sure stakeholders feel comfortable coming to you with information and ideas. They must feel comfortable not only receiving messages, but also initiating them.

Individuals at all levels of an organization should feel like they can communicate with subordinates (down the chain of command) as well as with supervisors and managers (up the chain). Supervisors need to listen to and gain feedback from their employees, not just their superiors.

Managers and supervisors can cultivate two-way communication by maintaining an open-door policy, encouraging the expression of feelings as well as facts, asking employees for their opinions, rewarding employees for reporting problems, following up with employees on the problems they report, and providing timely answers to employee questions.

Learn more from an expert in the online video.

Send "I" Messages

Managers and supervisors should also practice using "I" messages instead of "you" messages when they disagree with an employee or identify problems with an employee's work. When we are upset, we tend to state our dissatisfaction in "you" messages, which imply that the other person is to blame for how we feel. For example, "Sebastian, you are making too many mistakes in your reports." This type of finger-pointing actually obstructs two-way communication because it can deflate the recipient's confidence, making the person reluctant to engage in a discussion.

Using an "I" message, on the other hand, opens the door for a conversation about the issue. For example, "I believe there are some problems with these reports that need to be corrected." This is a much more constructive way to deliver the same criticism, and it invites the recipient to inquire about the specific problems.

Support Diverse Groups

While working with a diverse group of people has its advantages (such as being able to attack business issues from multiple perspectives), diversity can stifle communication at times. Having different backgrounds, skill sets, perspectives, communication styles, and experiences can sometimes impede collaboration. And if difficulties arise, certain members of the group may take charge and push their ideas, possibly intimidating those who are more reserved.

In these situations, nondirective techniques can be used to encourage people to open up, speak freely, and express their ideas. As the name indicates, nondirective techniques don't direct the flow of the conversation. Instead, they convey support for the speaker. These techniques include posing open-ended questions, asking for clarification, reflecting on the input of others, and empathizing.

COMMUNICATING AND COLLABORATING ABOUT RISK

Without sufficient communication and collaboration, no journey through the risk management process can be considered complete. A risk professional needs to win the cooperation of all stakeholders, and a key element of doing that is ensuring that all parties are properly informed at every stage of the process. Additionally, constant communication with internal and external experts can help risk professionals identify and understand the full spectrum of emerging risks and opportunities the organization faces.

Every step in the risk management process, from scanning the environment to monitoring and reviewing the chosen risk management strategies, is dependent on communicating and collaborating with internal and external stakeholders. This holistic approach that results is referred to as enterprise risk management (ERM).

What Do You Know?

A risk management professional may be best suited to manage an organization's risk—but not necessarily to identify all the risks it faces. In what ways might a manufacturing company's production manager provide valuable input for a risk manager?

Feedback: Being more familiar with the production process, a production manager would probably have more detailed insight than a risk manager into risks such as machine breakdown and supply chain interruptions. A production manager may also be able to provide insight into risks related to product quality, worker safety, and production goals.

Scan the Environment

Scanning the environment cannot be completed without seeking input from experts within and outside the risk professional's organization. Internally, communications should focus on the organization's objectives and how they could be affected by possible risks. Internal communication can also help define the organization's risk appetite, which in turn determines how to handle certain risks.

For example, let's say that a manufacturing corporation needs a specific part to produce its lawn mowers. If the corporation has a high risk appetite, it might be willing to sign an exclusive agreement with one supplier at a very low price, knowing that a disruption in the supply chain could affect its production capabilities. If it has a lower risk appetite, the low price may not be worth the risk of having the supply chain disrupted, so the corporation may opt to sign a non-exclusive agreement and arrange to purchase the needed parts from another supplier as well.

Without having a conversation to determine risk appetite, the risk professional won't be able to effectively treat the organization's risks. And to start these conversations, the risk professional needs to be able to identify who in the organization has the ability and expertise to provide insights. For example, the organization's Human Resources Department would be crucial to managing personnel risk, while a warehouse manager should be able to provide insight into inventory risks.

Talking with external sources helps reveal potential risks an organization might not otherwise be aware of, such as legislation regarding a particular industry or regulations that may affect operations. Environmental considerations, such as protected lands and waterways or changing weather patterns, can also give rise to specific risks that may have to be managed, so it may be worth contacting external scientists and ecological organizations.

Identify Risks

Because the purpose of risk identification is to determine the cause, likelihood, and potential consequences of any identified risks, risk professionals often seek advice and insights from various experts. For example, it'd be easy enough for a risk professional at the manufacturing company we mentioned earlier to determine that an interruption in the supply of lawn-mower parts would hinder the company's production, but the production manager might be the only person able to outline the acquisition process, outline the production budget, and explain why a particular supplier's product is better than another's. In turn, each of those factors will play a role in how seriously the risk is treated. If there are three suppliers of the part who offer it at similar costs and qualities, the associated risk would be relatively small. If there is only one provider, the risk would be more serious.

Internal control

A system or process that an organization uses to achieve its operational goals, internal and external financial reporting goals, or legal and regulatory compliance goals.

An organization's internal audit function and its associated **internal controls** can often provide information regarding risks that aren't obvious. It may, for example, find that employees are creating a risk by not adhering to certain processes.

A risk professional should also seek insight and advice from external experts. They can help determine, for example, risks regarding construction of a new headquarters and the environmental impact it may have on the surrounding area. Another example might be a risk professional who works for an agricultural company: he or she should consult with a climatologist to ensure that the company is protected against weather risks.

At this stage, the risk management professional needs to listen carefully. When presented with an issue that is of concern to the subject-matter experts, asking open-ended questions can help reveal important information. For example, if a production manager expressed concern that a new machine has a lower output than the machine it replaced, further prompting could reveal that employee training for the new machine has been inadequate. This human resource risk would likely not have been revealed if the risk professional had simply listened and not asked open-ended questions.

Analyze Risks

Risk analysis can be straightforward or complex. For example, the lawn-mower manufacturer may not have a problem analyzing the risk posed by the failure of a single machine in its production line. But what if a days-long power outage took all its production machines offline? What if that caused the manufacturer to miss a major shipping deadline, hurting the company's reputation for reliability? And an even more complex analysis would be required if demand for the motors the manufacturer sells dropped after a competitor introduced a more environmentally friendly model.

Data analysts often collaborate with risk professionals to help them understand certain complex risks. By analyzing patterns in big data, these analysts can identify trends and predict possible outcomes that can help the organization avoid the related risks. They may be able to explain a trend of falling sales or rising employee injuries, providing an opportunity to adjust the company's offerings or production procedures to correct those trends. To return to the lawn-mower manufacturer, if an outside research firm found that new homeowners are less likely to use gas-powered lawn mowers, the manufacturer's risk professional must consider the risks that will emerge if the company doesn't produce motors with alternative sources of power.

Learn more from an expert in the online video.

Even if the risk professional is acquainted with the organization's risk appetite, he or she also needs to take into account the specialized knowledge of outside experts to identify the organization's key risks. It's one thing for a risk professional to recommend a high deductible for the organization's property or casualty coverage, but another to ignore a structural engineer's concerns regarding the stability of a warehouse's ceiling supports when doing so.

Consulting with outside experts also enhances stakeholders' confidence in the process. For example, discussing potential environmental risks with a climatologist before building a new manufacturing plant along a shoreline can give an organization's board of directors confidence in the depth of analysis the risk professional has undertaken.

Treat Risks

When determining how risks should be treated, whether by avoiding them, modifying their likelihood or impact, or transferring them, risk professionals should take advantage of the organization's internal expertise. For example, if the organization decides to mitigate the risk of injury in the production line, it should ask its production manager about machines that might provide safer working conditions.

After deciding which course of action to take, it is just as important to communicate the decision up the organization's chain of command. The decision has to be supported by the available data, which should be summarized as clearly and concisely as possible. The executive-level decision makers should be given the ability to explain to others why the decision was made without being weighed down by minutiae.

This phase requires the risk professional to carefully balance his or her own expertise and that of the subject-matter experts. In our example of the lawn-mower manufacturer, if the production manager insists that certain machines need to be replaced but the head of the Accounting Department insists that the company does not have enough money available to do so, the risk manager may decide that its more prudent to simply avoid the breakdown risk by outsourcing production rather than purchasing new machinery. This solution respects both the experience of the production manager and of the accountants, creating the best result for the organization as a whole.

Monitor and Review

Given that the advice and consultation of internal and external experts has been crucial to risk management up to this point, it may be obvious that continued consultation is crucial to the continued monitoring and review of the chosen risk treatment solutions. To learn more, see "How They Did It: Clorox."

How They Did It: Clorox

How do you monitor the effectiveness of your ERM program?

Clorox: We present to the Board twice a year on the progress of our ERM program, which helps ensure that we are consistently delivering value and operating an effective program.

Allison Zheng (Program Manager, The Clorox Company), interviewed by Mike Elliott, April 2019, transcript, The Institutes, Malvern, Pa. [DA13137]

Additionally, with the help of data analysts and internal audit, information can be gathered to monitor the continued effectiveness of risk treatments that have been put into place. Once documented, it can be shared with internal stakeholders to demonstrate the program's effectiveness or to support suggested alterations.

Apply Your Knowledge

Filip is the risk manager at a software firm. After a meeting with the company's Human Resources director, he realized that a high turnover rate among the company's programmers could be affecting the speed and quality of production, which, in turn, could affect the company's profits. In developing a plan to address these human resource and financial risks, he collaborated with members of the Human Resources team and several managers in charge of the programming teams. Together, they came up with a plan to reduce programmer burnout and raise morale in the hopes of retaining the company's talent base. In what stage of the risk management process would Filip inform the company's executive-level decision makers of this plan, and what approach should he take?

Feedback: Once a course of action is decided upon during the risk treatment stage of the risk management process, Filip should communicate the decision up the software firm's chain of command. The analysis that led to the decision should be summarized as clearly and concisely as possible. The executive-level decision makers should be given the ability to explain why the decision was made without being weighed down by overly specific details.

FUNDAMENTALS OF EFFECTIVE COLLABORATION

Organizations are composed of individuals with specialized knowledge and skills in different areas, but those specialists are all tasked with coming together to achieve the same organizational goals. As a result, the ability to foster collaboration is in high demand in today's organizations. Becoming an effective collaborator will help you engage internal and external stakeholders across all levels of an organization and get them to work as a team toward common goals.

Collaboration occurs when individuals, departments, or teams from different areas work together to accomplish a shared organizational task or goal. This could be anything from improving the customer experience, creating a new product, protecting customer data, and beyond. Collaboration typically requires regular communication and information sharing, and the members of the collaborative team must monitor its progress.

What Do You Know?

Some may consider collaboration, cooperation, and coordination to be essentially the same thing, but this is a mistake. Each has its own district meaning, and it's important to be able to clearly define them so that there's no misunderstanding when someone is asked to collaborate, coordinate, or cooperate with an internal or external stakeholder. Can you explain the difference between the three?

Feedback: Collaboration is the act of working together to achieve a shared objective. Cooperation is the act of working together to achieve individual objectives instead of a shared objective. For example, two individuals may cooperate with each other by sharing information and resources, but those individuals might not be using those things to accomplish the same objective. And coordination is the act of improving efficiency and reducing redundancy by some combination of arranging, assigning, organizing, or scheduling activities.

Collaboration has become critical in today's business environment because business functions and departments are becoming more interconnected. Departments that may have once been siloed (think marketing and sales) are now dependent on each other for success. A failure or success in one area would likely affect another. As a result, different business units and their managers are now tasked with understanding each other's vulnerabilities and opportunities and with working as a team to achieve overarching organizational goals. This often means dovetailing the work of one unit with that of others. It may even mean giving up control to other people or sacrificing a bit of efficiency or convenience in one area to help another.

We'll explore three keys to effective collaboration in this section: gaining a holistic perspective, motivating workers, and contributing toward a common goal. To learn more, see "The Importance of Collaboration in Risk Management."

The Importance of Collaboration in Risk Management

Holistic risk management requires the entire organization to be on the same page when it comes to managing risks—i.e., risk management needs to be a collaborative effort. Cyber risk provides a good example of why collaboration is needed.

Virtually every business unit faces some cyber risk, and the risk arising from any one unit could also affect other units or the organization as a whole. For example, someone in Human Resources (HR) could click on a malicious link in an email and infect a company server with malware. That malware could then compromise financial or customer information or shut down critical systems required for production. Managing this risk requires collaboration between HR and Information Technology (IT), two departments that historically haven't worked much with each other. IT would need to train HR (along with other business units) to spot malicious emails and prevent cyber losses in general.

[DA13116]

Gain a Holistic Perspective

The first step to fostering collaboration with internal and external stakeholders is developing a broad perspective of the organization and its interactions with stakeholders. In particular, it requires understanding what demands are placed on them from their managers and what their work environments look like. Collaboration requires knowing about the work performed by other units in the organization and external stakeholders. Although you don't have to become an expert on the work every stakeholder performs, you do need to know enough about how the different work processes interact to create a plan for collaborating effectively.

Develop a thorough understanding of each unit's role and how it supports or depends on other units and stakeholders—go beyond knowing what others do to developing a mastery of the points at which everyone's workflows connect.

Gaining a holistic perspective requires ongoing two-way communication with other business units and stakeholders. Develop a conviction for establishing and maintaining good communications and relations with those stakeholders. In addition, cultivate a sensitivity to lapses in effective communication. When key stakeholders fail to communicate with each other, reestablish the connection.

Learn more from an expert in the online video.

Motivate Workers

An essential part of getting people to collaborate is motivating them to work with others. These are some effective techniques for motivating supervisors, employees, customers, and other third parties to collaborate to achieve a shared goal:

- Get to know as much as possible about the other stakeholders. What do they want, need, value, and hope to achieve in their careers? Try to put yourself in their shoes to understand their point of view, and make a conscious effort to avoid making assumptions about others. When people know that you're open to their point of view, it makes them more inclined to work with you.

- Seek stakeholder input when making decisions. Being consulted is in itself a motivator. This kind of participation, particularly when the group is diverse, also stretches the team's thinking and improves decision making. Plus, seeking input from everyone fosters greater acceptance of decisions.

- Examine how collaborators want to be rewarded. For example, do they want money, praise, or promotions? Link the rewards they want with the work that needs to be done. Cite what must be done, and provide rewards immediately after success is achieved. Give credit where credit is due.

- Seek feedback on yourself from peers, managers, and subordinates. People want to team up with others who are accountable and amenable to criticism.

- When revising job duties, try to enrich individuals' work rather than merely expand it.

- Request (and, if necessary, fight for) equipment, staff, and other resources needed to support stakeholders.

- Help team members see the big picture. Help team members understand how their work contributes to the achievement of a shared goal.

- Explain how collaboration will affect them individually. This is far more motivating than hearing solely how it will affect the organization.

While these actions can effectively motivate workers, other tactics can prove equally detrimental to this cause. To learn more, see "Motivation Killers."

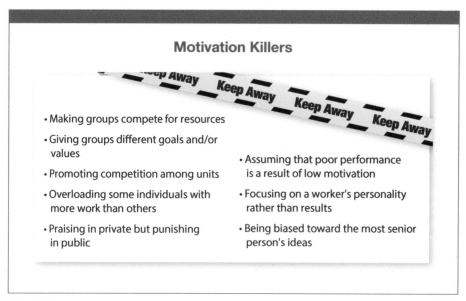

Motivation Killers

- Making groups compete for resources
- Giving groups different goals and/or values
- Promoting competition among units
- Overloading some individuals with more work than others
- Praising in private but punishing in public
- Assuming that poor performance is a result of low motivation
- Focusing on a worker's personality rather than results
- Being biased toward the most senior person's ideas

[DA13117]

Contribute Toward a Common Goal

The key aspect of collaboration is that it requires an active commitment from every group member to achieve a single goal shared by the entire group; it's not about achieving individual goals. This doesn't mean that individual goals can't be accomplished along the way, but for true collaboration to take place, the entire group needs to be moving toward the same finish line.

Ensuring that stakeholders don't veer off course requires the constant attention of group leaders, and it starts by putting the desired project results at the forefront. Make sure that everyone knows what group success looks like. Next, establish clear definitions and agreements on the roles each stakeholder will play on the way to the finish line and how performance will be measured. Don't move forward until all stakeholders have agreed on the methods that will be used to complete projects or tasks.

As work begins, group members should be on the lookout for obstacles that can get in the way of the goal. When problems arise, the group should address them together. This aspect of teamwork is essential at all times.

If someone begins to stray from the group in pursuit of an individual goal or reward, it can jeopardize the project. Think of a team in a tug of war. Everyone needs to be pulling in the same direction for the team to win. If one person lets go of the rope, the team will likely fail.

Keeping everyone pulling in the same direction requires recognizing and rewarding teamwork. Professional basketball, hockey, and soccer teams accomplish this by tracking assists in addition to goals. On the other hand, organizations that focus primarily on rewarding employees for individual performances typically have less success fostering collaboration. It's OK to reward great individual performances, but it's critical to reward teamwork. One way to do both would be to tie a percentage of an employee's annual bonus to how well he or she collaborates with others.

COLLABORATING WITH EXPERTS ABOUT RISK

Just about everything changes over time, and the risks an organization faces are no exception. New technology, new competitors, and new environmental factors will all work to confound risk professionals over time.

Unfortunately, not everyone can be expected to maintain an expertise in every risk that presents itself, so collaboration with internal and external experts will play a major role in updating and enhancing an organization's risk management approach. As such, there are two key tasks a risk professional needs to excel at when working with subject-matter experts:

- Asking the right questions of the right people
- Understanding the answers

What Do You Know?

Why is it important for a risk professional to have a basic, working understanding of a topic before consulting with a subject-matter expert?

Feedback: By having a basic understanding of a topic before speaking with a subject-matter expert, a risk professional will be able to ask follow-up questions and translate the concerns identified by the expert into more basic language to be shared with internal stakeholders.

Asking the Right Questions of the Right People

Collaboration takes cooperation a step beyond communication; instead of just informing stakeholders about the risk management plans, risk professionals work with stakeholders and experts to make sure that the plan is aligned with company goals and uses all available information to be as efficient as possible. To learn more, see "How They Did It: TruMark Financial."

How They Did It: TruMark Financial

First and foremost, this new era of risk management requires risk leaders to have a high degree of emotional intelligence and the ability to build relationships. When partnering with our business line leaders, we focus on solutions rather than implement controls before they are appropriate.

I am passionate about design thinking, which I try to apply in my work with our department and across our business lines so that I can facilitate conversations without using the word "no." We allow our business lines the freedom to think broadly, and the role of our ERM team is to find the right controls, processes, and reporting techniques to help us grow safely. There's a time and a place for risk controls to be introduced, and it's not during the ideation process. That's my risk philosophy, and I feel very passionate about it because risk professionals should focus on collaboration rather than control when working with colleagues.

Kelly Botti (Chief Risk Officer, TruMark Financial), interviewed by Mike Elliott, July 2019, transcript, The Institutes, Malvern, Pa. [DA13147]

Before conducting research by asking questions of experts, a risk professional needs to research what kinds of questions should be asked and of whom. For an organization to put information to use, it must have the necessary skills and resources to gather, manage, and understand the data. It's common for the risk professional to take on this role. When soliciting input from external subject-matter experts, risk professionals should research the applicable field to get a working understanding of the topics to be discussed. For example, if a risk manager is concerned about the potential for water levels near the construction site of a new warehouse to rise over time, he or she will want to perform some basic research into climate change and the local waterways or coastline before speaking with a climatologist. This will enable the risk professional to ask appropriate follow-up questions and translate the concerns identified by the expert into more basic language to be shared with internal stakeholders.

Internal subject-matter experts, meanwhile, can provide valuable information regarding the organization's goals and main concerns. For example, if a new warehouse is being constructed near a coastline vulnerable to rising waters but is intended to be used for only ten years, the owners might not be concerned with climatologists' findings.

Understanding the Answers

Beyond understanding the answers to his or her questions, a risk professional must understand how the answers relate to the objectives and concerns of the organization. For example, a climatologist might be able to provide a multitude of information about temperature change, expected increases in precipitation, and rising water levels, but it's up to the risk professional to decide which of those factors will affect the organization. If the new warehouse will be built on land that is several feet above sea level, the risk of rising waters affecting operations may not be severe enough to warrant action. (It may still need to be considered in the grand scheme, however, if a key supplier is located in south Florida or near New Orleans.)

The risk professional will need to lay out all of the potential risks cited by the subject-matter experts, identify those that are most likely to affect the organization, assess their potential severity, and recommend a treatment technique, such as avoidance, transfer, or reduction. In this effort, predictive modeling can help triage potential risks for treatment.

These tools also help identify both the risks and the treatments that should be discussed with stakeholders throughout the organization. For example, if rainfall is expected to increase in volume and severity, the organization's facilities manager should be brought into discussions on the matter so that the facility's water-drainage equipment, including rain gutters and sump pumps, are properly maintained and able to meet the organization's needs. If severe weather is likely to affect key suppliers, the risk professional should collaborate with the organization's production manager to ensure that there is a plan to meet the organization's supply needs if primary vendors are unable to.

Some risks and treatments will need to be communicated to the board, but it's up to the risk professional to determine which ones meet that criteria. This, of course, will depend on the organization's risk appetite and tolerance levels; the board of a large organization with thousands of employees and several office locations probably won't want to be bothered with the details of each building's water-drainage system. However, that may not be the case for a small, cost-conscious organization with only a few dozen employees and one location.

Apply Your Knowledge

Explain why it is important for communication and collaboration to continue after the risk professional has gotten answers to his or her questions from the subject-matter experts.

Feedback: After having his or her questions answered by subject-matter experts, the risk professional will need to lay out all the potential risks, identify those that are most likely to affect the organization, assess their potential severity, and make treatment recommendations. Continued communication with internal subject-matter experts will ensure ongoing cooperation in effectively treating the identified risks.

DELIVERING YOUR MESSAGE

In business, being a willing and open communicator has little value unless you can also convey messages clearly. Learning how to get internal and external stakeholders to grasp your point of view and knowing how to create persuasive messages will help you gain buy-in from decision makers and forge team collaboration.

Getting your point across can be more challenging than expected. Just because you say something to someone or deliver a message from the front of a room doesn't mean clear communication has taken place. It's your responsibility to make sure your message is understood by your audience.

Becoming a clear, engaging, and convincing communicator requires developing and practicing several skills, such as mastering nonverbal messages, leading effective meetings, using modes of persuasion, and overcoming common problems that create communication breakdowns.

What Do You Know?

Can you name the three modes of persuasion?

Feedback: The three modes of persuasion are ethos, logos, and pathos. Greek words coined by Aristotle, they are considered the three artistic proofs for convincing people. Ethos means "character" and refers to the need to establish the speaker's credibility. Logos means "reason" and refers to the need to support a message, claim, or argument with evidence. Pathos means "emotion" and refers to the need to make an emotional appeal to the audience. This section will detail these modes of persuasion.

Convey the Right Nonverbal Message

How you say something is often as important as what you say, so you need to complement verbal messages with appropriate, effective nonverbal messages. People send nonverbal messages through tone of voice, level of eye contact, and body language.

Tone of voice can affect another person's perception of your words more than the words themselves. For example, if you sound assertive and confident, the other person will think your message is more credible than if you're hesitant.

If, however, your tone is perceived as hostile or critical, the other person may think you're attacking him or her, which could lead the person to withdraw or adopt a similarly antagonistic tone.

For best results, watch how others react to you, and adjust your tone of voice to promote engagement and credibility.

Similarly, eye contact can support or detract from the credibility of your message. Looking down or avoiding eye contact when making a request conveys a lack of confidence and assertiveness. However, staring at someone for a prolonged period can convey hostility. When you're uncertain about appropriate eye contact, shift your vision from the other person's eyes to between the eyes, or to the nose or lower face, and then back again to the eyes.

Your body language—for example, the way you sit, stand, or move your hands—can involuntarily send the wrong message about how you feel about another person. Standing and leaning over people can convey hostility, even if unintentionally. But sitting up and leaning slightly toward your audience can convey confidence in your message and interest in those around you. To learn more, see "Ways to Use Body Language."

Ways to Use Body Language

See the online video.

[DA13158]

Lead Effective Meetings

Effective meetings don't happen by chance. They are carefully planned.

To ensure an effective meeting, you must define specific objectives. Then you can decide who to invite to the meeting. A plan for meeting your objectives should exist at the end of the meeting. Prior to the meeting, double check your knowledge of the material and anticipate questions.

Using visual aids can make your message more effective and interesting. People tend to learn more from presentations that are accompanied by visuals, which can be powerful tools for emphasizing key points or simplifying complex ones. However, if you're going to use slides, make sure they aren't packed with content. They should only contain a few notes or graphics that help audience members remember key points and follow along.

Three additional keys to effective meetings are a strong opening, succinct supporting material, and a powerful conclusion.

Grab listeners with a strong opener. Start with an attention-grabbing fact. For example, "Thank you all for being here today. I want to start by throwing out a number: 10 million dollars. That's how much money we stand to lose if this project isn't a success."

Next, you have to make your claims believable with supporting evidence. Try to avoid drowning the audience in data. Instead, when you make a point, present just enough facts and figures to make it believable.

Finally, end with a bang. This should be your call to action, strengthened by messaging about how audience members (and the organization in general) will benefit accordingly.

You'll also want to avoid several common pitfalls that can ruin a meeting and your message. To learn more, see "Meeting Killers."

Meeting Killers

Here are many of the most common problems with meetings, along with suggestions on how to avoid or minimize them:

- No stated purpose. An objective needs to be stated in writing before the meeting.
- No agenda. An agenda should be circulated among attendees prior to the meeting.
- Wrong people attending. Only those who can offer valuable input regarding the objective should attend.
- Bad timing. Meetings must be held at convenient times. Interest will decrease if, for example, a meeting runs into lunchtime.
- Lateness. Meetings should start and end on time. Attendees become irritated and inattentive if meetings start late or run long.
- Wandering. Stick to the agenda, and try to minimize interruptions.
- Lack of conclusion. Make sure participants know what needs to happen next, and follow up on the results.

[DA13133]

Apply the Modes of Persuasion

Sometimes you have to go beyond making sure your audience understands your message to being persuasive. Aristotle's three modes of persuasion, ethos, logos, and pathos, can prove helpful in this regard.

Ethos, or "character," refers to the need to establish credibility. For your message to be understood, you must first convince your audience that you're worth listening to. Address why others should take you seriously. Have you been in their position before? Have you successfully dealt with similar issues in the past? Look for ways to use your past as a means of persuasion. Use stories and examples rather than a resume.

Logos, or "reason," refers to the need to support your message, claim, or argument with evidence. Point to historical data, statistics, or other authority figures to back up your position. Before determining what types of evidence to bring to the table, ask yourself what materials would best suit your audience.

Pathos, or "emotion," refers to the need to make an emotional appeal to your audience. Emotions move people. Stir up people's emotions and they're more likely to remember what was said or take action. A surprising or relatable story, image, video, or piece of information that drums up a sense of anger, fear, optimism, or happiness can persuade people to see things your way.

Resolve Common Problems

Now let's take a look at how to tackle two of the most common problems that create confusion and communication breakdowns: hidden agendas and status differences.

Hidden Agendas

A hidden agenda is a concern that affects a person's behavior but isn't openly stated by the person. Sometimes hidden agendas reveal themselves when a person's comments seem to be off track.

Hidden agendas can be detrimental to the communication process because people who employ them may attempt to steer conversations down paths that benefit them—without informing others of their intent. This can lead to a dismissal of your message. To learn more, see "Hidden Agendas."

You should attempt to bring hidden agendas into the open. If you suspect that a person's comments are the result of a hidden agenda, ask questions or state your observations and ask for the person's reaction. If you think that a meeting will be impeded by hidden agendas, consider starting the meeting by asking participants to state their concerns or feelings about the subject and meeting objective.

Status Differences

Differences in the informal status and formal rank of participants often hamper communication. People hesitate to contradict people with greater knowledge, standing, or experience. This can lead to a lack of engagement from those who disagree with someone's message but are reluctant to speak up.

Hidden Agendas

Picture, for a second, that your organization just purchased new equipment for your department, and you're holding a meeting to explain when the new equipment will be installed and how it'll be brought online. You want to keep the discussion focused on those two items, but Arlene passionately states that she thinks the new equipment is unnecessary. She keeps interrupting your presentation to argue that there was nothing wrong with the current equipment.

The problem is, Arlene has a hidden agenda that she isn't revealing: Having used the existing equipment for more than decade, she's afraid she won't be able to learn how to use the new equipment. She fears she might lose her job as a result.

Having to address Arlene's comments is preventing you from delivering your message.

[DA13134]

One way to avoid this is by asking for ideas from lower-level persons before turning to those of higher standing. You could also ask higher-ranking individuals to concentrate only on certain aspects of the topic.

Learn more from an expert in the online video.

SUMMARY

Effective communication habits are essential to business success. Good communication increases productivity, reduces confusion, mitigates conflict, and improves morale. The communication process includes speaking, analytical, and organizational skills. In addition to helping the listener obtain information, active listening develops trust and positive relationships. Good communicators foster two-way communication by sending "I" messages and supporting diversity through nondirective techniques.

Every step in the risk management process presents professionals with an opportunity to communicate and collaborate with internal and external stakeholders. Consulting with outside experts can also enhance stakeholders' confidence in the process.

Collaboration occurs when people or business units work together to achieve a single, shared goal. As business functions become more interconnected, collaboration becomes more critical. The first step to fostering collaboration is gaining a holistic perspective of the organization and stakeholders' interactions with it. Supervisors, employees, customers, and other third parties have to be properly motivated to collaborate with each other. Group leaders must remain focused on preventing stakeholders from straying from the common goal.

Collaboration with internal and external experts plays a major role in updating and enhancing an organization's risk management approach. There are two key tasks at which a risk professional needs to excel when working with subject-matter experts:

- Asking the right questions of the right people
- Understanding the answers

For effective communication, you must clearly deliver messages to those working with you. But this isn't always easy. It requires skills such as conveying the right nonverbal messages; leading effective meetings; applying ethos, logos, and pathos; and overcoming hidden agendas and status differences.

Index

Page numbers in boldface refer to pages where the word or phrase is defined.